AWAKENING FROM THE AMERICAN DREAM

AWAKENING FROM THE AMERICAN DREAM

The Social and Political Limits to Growth

Rufus E. Miles Jr.

Universe Books
New York

Published in the United States of America in 1976
by Universe Books
381 Park Avenue South, New York, N.Y. 10016

© 1976 by Rufus E. Miles, Jr.
Second printing, January 1977

Library of Congress Catalog Card Number: 76-34516

Cloth edition: ISBN 0-87663-274-6
Paperback edition: ISBN 0-87663-940-6

Printed in the United States of America

To Nelle
and Bobbi and Mary and Joe
and Jessica and Molly

CONTENTS

	Preface	ix
	Introduction	1
I.	Recession, Depression, or the End of a Two-Century Boom?	7
II.	The Fortuity of American Affluence	21
III.	The Closing of the Second Frontier	45
IV.	The Internal Vulnerabilities of Modern Technological Society	62
V.	The Chasm Between Rights and Responsibilities	76
VI.	The Centrifugal Social Effects of Energy	89
VII.	The Energy Trap: The Search for a Way Out	104
VIII.	The Ethics and Politics of Nuclear and Solar Energy	121
IX.	Human Procreation: A "Right" Without Social Responsibility	136
X.	The Ethics and Politics of Food	152
XI.	The Political Limits to Human Interdependence	170
XII.	The Limits to the Political Management of Nature	191
XIII.	An Upheaval in Religion, Ethics, and Ideology	208
XIV.	A Profound Turning Point	223
	Reference Notes	237
	Index	244

Preface

This book is a work of disturbing cogitation. It did not start out to be what it ended up by being. Nor is the author quite the same person after putting his ideas through a systematic examination as to what seems possible and feasible within the context of what we know about human behavior. Important as may be an optimistic and idealistic view of human possibilities, an excessive degree of faith in the innate goodness of humankind is often the prelude to discouragement and cynicism. A careful assessment of those basic forces most likely to be dominant in shaping the future seems requisite to self-preparation for the world of tomorrow. If such an assessment should run contrary to parts of one's cherished beliefs, it is much easier to dismiss it than to re-examine the soundness of the belief. I ask only for an open mind on the part of the reader, knowing from experience how hard that is to achieve. The more it is achieved, though, the more evident it will become that much of our traditional ideologies—both liberal and conservative—demand reconsideration and reformulation.

For contributions to my thinking, I am indebted to more people than I can acknowledge. Though their names do not appear, I thank them. For helpful criticism of my manuscript, I am deeply in the debt of Junius J. Bleiman, Lester R. Brown, Lynton K. Caldwell, Lester V. Chandler, Rowland Egger, Tomas Frejka, Gerald Garvey, Robert Gilpin, M. King Hubbert, and Robert W. van de Velde. And to Alan Gelperin I am most grateful for a helpful bit of research. For any errors that remain, I accept full responsibility. To Scott McVay, I owe a very special word of thanks for his enthusiastic support of my project. I am also much in the debt of William Watts for wise counsel and Barbara Grindle for her competent typing of my manuscript. And for its editing, I owe much to the skill and pencil of Arnold Dolin. Most of all, I am forever grateful to my patient and loving wife for her support and assistance in more ways than can be mentioned.

All arrogance will reap a harvest rich in tears,
God holds men to a heavy reckoning
For overweening pride.

—Aeschylus

Introduction

The confident belief in unending economic and social progress as a natural condition of free men has been almost a secular religion in America. The seeds of this blend of thought and faith sprouted during the Enlightenment and were fertilized by the new scientific spirit, but only the reality of a living, growing example of such a magnetic concept could convince skeptics that it might be true. That example began with the formation of the United States of America and lasted for nearly two centuries, a more than respectable period as historians count the survival of political experiments. But many thoughtful Americans have begun to wonder whether there is anything natural about the idea of continuous progress. The economic and social development of the United States over the last two centuries might better be characterized as extraordinary, fortuitous, and nonsustainable.

Increasingly, during the 1970s, Americans have shown skepticism about the inevitability and even the desirability of continuing physical growth, supposedly the touchstone of what is left of the free-enterprise system. The adverse side-effects of the American high-consumption, high-waste economy began to trouble a significant and articulate segment of the American public in the late 1960s. Then, in 1972, a report (prepared by Donella and Dennis Meadows, Jørgen Randers, and William W. Behrens III), for the Club of Rome's Project on the Predicament of Mankind, *The Limits to Growth*, captured the attention and imagination of an enormous audience. (Hundreds of thousands of copies were sold in the United States, and nearly two million abroad.) The book's sensational doomsday warning seemed to strike a responsive chord—almost untouched by any previous work—in the strong intuitive feelings of many thoughtful citizens that the end of the era of dependable economic growth and high-energy affluence might be nearer than supposed by economic analysts and forecasters.

1

Perhaps this corroboration by computer technology explains the book's extraordinary acceptance. For its computer printouts indicated that it was impossible for exponential growth to continue at past rates for very much longer. In the "World Model Standard Run," four of the five principal variables—resources, food per capita, industrial output per capita, and pollution—showed crash curves early in the 21st century, and the crash of the fifth—population—was to come shortly thereafter, in mid-century. Such a doomsday scenario—if recent trends continued—was promptly pooh-poohed by most economists, many of whom felt that various adjustments— substitute and recycled materials, new energy sources, better systems of pollution control, improved agricultural production, and the like—would prevent any such debacles as those projected by the authors. The controversy was joined: The discussion stimulated by the book generated other books and a host of articles, and the dialogue concerning the limits to growth seems likely to go on in varying forms for at least the rest of this century.

Although my book was conceived and begun before *The Limits to Growth* was published, it now becomes part of this debate about how much longer the growth trends of the past can be sustained—or would be healthy even if they could be sustained. My perspective is very different from that of *The Limits to Growth*, though. It springs from the conviction that the most significant limits to growth are buried deep within the human psyche and are not yet susceptible of quantification and computerization. They are limits set by the already overstrained capacity of human beings to conceive, design, manage, support, and adapt to extremely complex systems of human interdependence. In short, it is the political limits that are likely to constrain the continuity of physical growth well ahead of all other factors. The United States and other members of the world community are now pressing against their political limits and will find it increasingly difficult to take actions that would be required to assure continuing growth. Affluence, my analysis concludes, may already have reached its zenith and if it has not, that point is probably much nearer than the Club of Rome study indicated.

In a sense, the slowdown that has already occurred and will continue in varying degree far into the future is a fortunate development for the next two generations. The crash curves projected in *The Limits to Growth* for the first half of the 21st century were precipitous because of the expected rapid buildup before the collapse. Recent rates of growth were assumed to continue for several decades until they created unsustainable conditions; excessive physical growth, it was conjectured, would thus create the preconditions for catastrophic declines. If physical growth slows down and comes to an end well before the end of this century, as I project, then the crash curves need not come about. Such a slowdown was advocated by the authors of *The Limits to Growth*. In any event, the lurching that will occur as we round the sharpest turn in recorded history at a reckless speed is bound to produce severe strains.

It is a basic premise of this analysis that the only way we can speculate usefully about the most probable course of the future is to try to understand those dynamics of the past which have been especially influential in shaping the present. Only after attempting to understand the behavior of the forces that have shaped modern civilization is it useful to try to establish tentative hypotheses about how those forces are likely to behave in the future. A major part of this book, therefore, is devoted to that purpose.

It is obviously impossible to analyze all of the significant determinants of the present and future. One can only select those that, from one's perspective, seem to be the most basic and decisive. Influences that are not addressed here are far more numerous than those that are, and some will no doubt turn out to be more important than this set of conjectures anticipates. Nevertheless, if we are to prepare ourselves psychologically for what lies ahead, it seems desirable to seek to comprehend what appear now to be the most basic forces affecting our lives. It is to that purpose that this book is devoted.

The analyses in this book proceed from the assumption that there will be no nuclear holocaust foreclosing a future for mankind in the 21st century—none too solid an assumption. Whether humankind will be able to avoid self-annihilation is chancy. Our greatest hope lies in a generational change of political and military leaders the world over, ushering onto the international stage a group that should be more disillusioned about the benefits of war in relation to its costs than any of its predecessors. For only a new generation of leaders, uncommitted to anachronistic diplomatic and military strategies of the pre-nuclear age, can have any chance of breaking out of that mental prison.

The sequence of chapters in the book deserves explanation. The theory I am seeking to formulate resembles a seamless web rather than a mathematical theorem: All the strands of evidence and logic are connected to all others, and it is difficult or impossible to proceed in the style of a linear argument from start to finish. It is necessary to describe one quadrant of the web and then another, and finally the pattern of the entire web emerges.

The first three chapters deal with the origins and future prospects of American affluence—the intention being to probe beneath the customary assumptions about why the United States is so wealthy a country and to speculate about the economic future of American society in the decades immediately ahead. The next two chapters identify and discuss several serious vulnerabilities of American society, arising from its social dynamics, which are now sufficiently great to undermine the durability of social structures. Three chapters analyzing what energy has been doing to our society and where it is leading us are followed by two chapters concerned with the dynamics of population and food, both within American society and, more important, in the Third World; energy and population are viewed here as probably the two most fundamental and important determinants of the future. Finally, a group of four chapters seeks to bring together the threads from all four sectors of the web. They examine the political limits to economic growth, the ecological hazards of the "one world" ideal, and the environmental and ethical implications of continuing on the road of further physical growth, especially if it means shifting from a massive addiction to petroleum to an even more massive addiction to nuclear energy.

Although the book ends without a road map for Americans moving into their third century, it sees us at the most important crossroads in our two-hundred-year journey—one, in fact, faced by all of Western civilization. What Americans need for the future is a changed set of values and a new sense of direction. The compass we have been following has gone awry.

The experience of living in a civilization that suddenly loses momentum and begins to veer off course may be perceived in different ways. Some will surely be extremely depressed if the theories set forth in this analytical and conjectural essay should turn out to have some validity. The curtain will seem to be coming down on a golden era, and nothing they can visualize will ever be so interesting and exciting. To others—the "true believers" in the

American dream of unlimited economic growth and progress—
doubts about the correctness of our course are inadmissible. We
need only to maintain the faith, in their view, and redouble our
efforts to put the economy back on the growth track from which it has
been derailed. To still others, even though it may take patience that
rivals that of Job, the very idea of participating in a thoughtful search
for a different destiny for Americans can be a deeply satisfying and
self-renewing adventure.

I. Recession, Depression, or the End of a Two-Century Boom?

On March 4, 1933, when Americans were desperately grasping for help to sustain faith in their economic system, the newly inaugurated President, Franklin Roosevelt, rallied them with his memorable words, "The only thing we have to fear is fear itself." Just over a hundred days later, Walter Lippmann wrote: "At the end of February, we were a congeries of disorderly, panic-stricken mobs and factions. In the hundred days from March to June we became again an organized nation, confident of our power to provide for our own security and control our own destiny." Lippmann did not overstate the contrast or exaggerate the resilience of the American people. The Great Depression was the worst in the nation's history, but the faith of Americans in the essential continuity of progress had deep roots. Not even in the worst of times could the Socialists or the Communists shake the belief of most Americans in the basic soundness of their economic and political system. The vast majority of people wanted changes made, and they got them in the form of the New Deal, but they wanted progress, not revolution.

Four decades later, Americans found themselves in a very different mood. The twin gods of growth and progress, which had earlier usurped the place of the Biblical God for vast numbers of self-confident, upwardly mobile members of the production system, were not performing their duties properly. The two-centuries-old faith in the capacity of the gods or the system to continue to improve the human condition was in deep trouble. That the economic downturn of the mid-1970s might be no mere recession or depression but

an augury of the approaching end of the era of physical growth*
became a gnawing suspicion among an increasing number of people.

Even before there were any serious signs of recession, significant
numbers of Americans had begun to show deep concern about the
effects of rapid and seemingly endless physical growth upon the
quality of their surroundings and their lives. In their view,
undiminished growth within a finite environment was not benign but
malignant, just as it is in biological organisms, so they decided to do
something about it. The environmental movement sprang into being
with broad public support. It is surprising to realize that Earth Day, a
kind of first birthday for the ecological awakening of the American
people, occurred as recently as April 22, 1970. Concern for the
environment turned out to be considerably more than the passing fad
that many people predicted it would be. To the dismay of businessmen and economists, an increasingly vocal minority began to lay the
blame for the deterioration of the environment not only on the
conspicuous pollutors but at the doorstep of physical growth itself.

Almost overnight, the members of the environmental movement
manned the barricades to prevent or retard at least those forms of
growth that seemed to threaten the country's precious and precarious
natural heritage. Several states turned their welcome signs to the
wall, hoping to fend off new industry, boxy subdivisions, and even
tourists, whose presence palled when they settled down and over-
loaded the demand for public services. Antipathy to environmental
pollution and the other tangible negative results of physical growth
moved from the talk stage to the arena of action, with public protests
and legal suits against numerous forms of new construction, from
prefabricated suburbs to oil refineries and nuclear power plants. And
such protests became very effective in impeding expansion plans of
some of the nation's largest corporations, who were not used to
having their will thwarted. Nothing comparable to this had ever

---

*The term "physical growth" is used throughout to mean what it implies: growth in
the number of people and the goods and energy they consume, and in the numbers and
size of their structures, roads, vehicles, capital equipment, and the like. A rough but
useful indicator of the rate of physical growth of Western societies is the rate of
increase in the consumption of energy. Physical growth has been the most important
component of economic growth, but the Gross National Product might continue to rise
even if physical growth did not, by a further shift away from the production of goods
toward the exchange of services.

happened before; the god of growth was losing his magic power. What we were witnessing seemed to be the beginning of a profound shift in human attitude toward physical growth.

It is important to note that there are two differing concepts of growth: the compound-interest curve, or exponential curve, used by economists, and the biological-growth curve. An examination of their contrasting forms and their implications should serve as an aid to understanding what is happening to our society.

THE EXPONENTIAL CURVE

The compound-interest, or exponential, curve (see Fig. 1) is a steeply rising curve that points in the general direction of infinity. It doubles at periodic intervals: At a 7 percent annual increase, it doubles every decade; at 3.5 percent, it doubles five times a century. In his *Treatise on Money* (1930), John Maynard Keynes vividly illustrated the power of compound interest by describing what happened to the booty brought back by Sir Francis Drake in the Golden Hind after he had intercepted the Spanish galleons and deprived them of their treasure.

[This booty] may fairly be considered the fountain and origin of British Foreign Investment. Elizabeth paid off out of the proceeds the whole of her foreign debt and invested a part of the balance (about £42,000) in the Levant Company; largely out of the profits of the Levant Company there was formed the East India Company, the profits of which during the seventeenth and eighteenth centuries were the main foundation of England's foreign connections; and so on. In view of this, the following calculation may amuse the curious. At the present time (in round figures) our foreign investments probably yield us about 6.5 percent net after allowing for losses, of which we reinvest abroad about half—say 3.25 percent. If this is, on the average, a fair sample of what has been going on since 1580, the £42,000 invested by Elizabeth out of Drake's booty in 1580 would have accumulated by 1930 to approximately the actual aggregate of our present foreign investments, namely £4,200,000,000—or, say, 100,000 times greater than the original investment.

The calculation offers more than amusement to the curious, and it

MODELS OF GROWTH

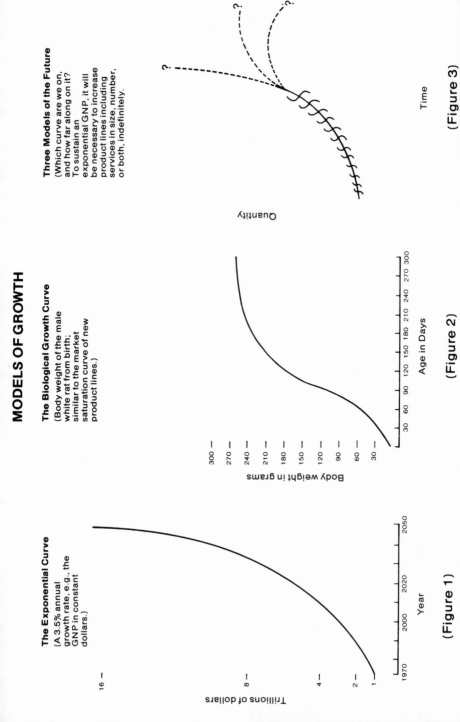

The Exponential Curve

(A 3.5% annual growth rate, e.g., the GNP in constant dollars.)

Trillions of dollars

1970 2000 2020 2050
Year

(Figure 1)

The Biological Growth Curve

(Body weight of the male white rat from birth; similar to the market saturation curve of new product lines.)

Body weight in grams

30 60 90 120 150 180 210 240 270 300
Age in Days

(Figure 2)

Three Models of the Future

(Which curve are we on, and how far along on it? To sustain an exponential GNP, it will be necessary to increase product lines including services in size, number, or both, indefinitely.)

Quantity

Time

(Figure 3)

certainly gives pause to anyone who contemplates its meaning for the future. If even such a modest rate of doubling as that produced by a 3.25 percent growth rate can result in an increment 100,000 times greater than the original investment in three and a half centuries, one must wonder how much longer this kind of growth can go on without running up against the finitude of the earth. Very dramatic increases—as a proportion of original size—can occur without great difficulty when the starting base is small, but when it becomes very large, additional doublings may range between the extremely difficult and the impossible. We are assuming, of course, that money values reflect real wealth; theoretically, there would be no limit to the growth in the foreign investments or the real wealth of a nation if it were to occur on paper through inflation.

Anyone who believes that exponential growth can go on forever is either a madman or an economist, according to the distinguished economist Kenneth Boulding. In their more philosophical moments, all but the maddest economists must surely know that physical growth cannot go on forever, but they have steadily resisted facing the question of when the exponential curve would have to reflex itself and change to something more closely resembling the biological-growth curve.

THE BIOLOGICAL-GROWTH CURVE
The word "growth" derived, naturally, from observation of the course of development of plants and animals—that is, it is a biological not an economic concept. Curiously, however, the word never fully captured the concept, and therein lies a common misunderstanding of the nature of growth. The growth cycle from the birth of an organism to its maturity is not a steady increase, but a rapid increase in the early part of cell division, followed by *controlled slowdown* in cell multiplication until maturity is reached. At that stage, the rate of formation of new cells is approximately offset by the death of old cells. The organism remains in this state of rough balance in size, or it increases very slowly until the organism is no longer able to sustain itself and dies.

The curve that represents the increase in the number of cells from birth to full maturity of a rat, for example, is often referred to as the "S," or logistic, curve. It looks like an "S" in which the top and the bottom tails have been pulled in opposite directions (see Fig. 2).

What the mechanism is for controlling the rate of slowdown in cell division, scientists do not understand. But nature clearly has some remarkable contrivance for telling cells that they should not reproduce too rampantly, and for telling them that when they reach a certain number, they should stop increasing. If scientists knew the secret of that mechanism, they would probably be able to conquer cancer, which manifests itself by the uncontrolled growth of cells. That aspect of the biological pattern of growth that is associated with increase in the size and weight of the organism—roughly measuring its number of cells—we normally call growth; that aspect of the pattern which involves the miracle of controlled slowdown in the rate of increase, ultimately reaching the stage of no increase at all, has no generally accepted word to convey the concept, but "maturation" comes closest to capturing the vital idea. The very lack of an accepted term to express this extraordinarily important distinction has deep psychological significance. One associates growth with youth and vigor and the end of growth with aging and death.

The use of the same word—growth—to mean continuing increase (its use in the world of business and economics) and to mean a gradually declining rate of increase until maturity is reached and all increase stops (the usage in respect to biological organisms) illuminates a major deficiency of thought and language of which we are generally unaware.

THE ASSUMED LINK BETWEEN THE TWO CURVES

Conceptually, many businessmen and market analysts think in terms of the biological-growth curve in respect to specific products, or even industries, but usually without consciousness of the analogy. When a new product is put on the market, if it catches the public fancy and is well advertised, its sales may increase at a very rapid rate in the period of its enthusiastic acceptance, then gradually slow down as the number of prospective buyers who do not own the product declines. The manufacturers then seek to enlarge the market by persuading buyers they need two or three of the product—as with autos, TVs, and radios. When the market begins to approach saturation, the next step is to make the owners dissatisfied with the product because it is out of date. Contrived obsolescence and the design of new models at frequent intervals have been the answer to that problem. Intuitively, businessmen spend their lives trying to push up the ceiling on the biological-growth curve, as applied to their business, by changing the nature of the products or their packaging at such intervals that market saturation is never really reached. If they are imaginative, they are able to impose one growth curve (including its slowdown) on top of another, often deluding themselves that the process can go on indefinitely. Thus the biological growth curve is converted into something resembling an exponential curve (see Fig. 3).

That, in fact, is how the macro-economists have assumed the economy as a whole can sustain its growth for decades to come. As one product, or one industry, tapers off in market demand, another, or perhaps two others, will take its place. The public appetite for goods and services is viewed as unlimited, and, until the energy crisis, it had been assumed that the capacity of the production system to meet this steadily rising demand would continue to increase at very much the same rate as it had in recent decades. Capital formation through savings and investment would also continue at past rates, and economic growth through the balance of the century was expected to continue unabated, with a slow but steady increase in the proportion of the GNP devoted to services as compared to the production and distribution of goods.

It should be noted—and this will be discussed further in Chapter III—that the schematic integration of the growth curves applicable to individual products, studied by micro-economists, and the exponential curve of continuous growth that is the concern of macro-economists, show rather clearly that the upward momentum of the exponential curve can be sustained only by *larger and larger* new-product additions (including services) and substitutes for those that have reached the leveling-off stage. Where are these to come from? What new and larger products are on the drawing boards that will meet such a requirement for sustaining economic growth? They are not yet in evidence.

When pressed, most economists agree that physical growth (as roughly measured by the consumption of energy) within a highly developed society like that of the United States cannot go on for very many more doublings, especially not at the rates of increase prevalent in the 1950s and 1960s. They assert that the quality of life can continue to improve, however, and the GNP can continue to rise through a shift toward more and better services and away from growth in the production of goods. The key question is, What factors are likely to be decisive in bringing about a slowdown and eventually an end to physical growth, and when will they become effective? This is one of the central questions I want to deal with, not for the purpose of establishing a predictive schedule, but so we may try to comprehend whether or not we may be a good deal closer to the upper limits of physical growth than we had heretofore supposed.

THE END OF THE ACCELERATIVE THRUST

One need not be a statistician to begin to wonder whether it is not time, or past time, for the exponential curve of economic growth, so long as it depends primarily on physical growth, to reflex itself and level off toward zero growth, turning into something resembling the biological-growth curve, or, alternatively, to turn back on itself and begin to decline. Some will be alarmed at the latter possibility, but reduction from economic obesity, if handled intelligently, need be no more threatening than its physical counterpart in the case of an excessively fat person.

Effective opposition by the environmentalists to various manifestations of physical growth is but one among a number of signs of slowdown. Less conspicuous has been the general deceleration of technology. All through the 1960s, one of the most commonly repeated bits of new wisdom—to the point of becoming a cliché—was that we were living in a world of accelerating change. That was the promise of numerous articles and books, including Alvin Toffler's best-selling *Future Shock*: Science and technology were said to be changing our world at an ever faster pace; the question then became how we should adjust to this radically different world. But suddenly, the "accelerative thrust" Toffler wrote about began to lose its power.

The major indicators of acceleration set forth by Toffler have shown a marked decelerative shift during the first half of the 1970s. Acceleration in the speed of human transportation—his first indicator of technological speedup—was halted by Congressional defeat of the SST;* and despite the startling triumphs of the moon landings,

*Although the British and French went ahead with the development of the Concorde, the adverse environmental impact and the high costs involved—to little purpose—make it unlikely that the SST project will be resumed in the United States.

Americans quickly became blasé about extraterrestrial exploration. Since we can already get anywhere on earth faster than our bodies can adjust to the time change, and we have seen how lonely and beautiful is our multicolored planet floating upon the black ocean of space, we seem to have decided that faster transportation—either around the earth or away from it—would not be worth the heavy drain on our resources.

The rate of growth of published scientific papers—another of Toffler's indicators of acceleration—has stopped following the exponential curve and is now actually declining. Support for scientists, and consequently for scientific papers, has fallen off significantly since the late 1960s.

Toffler's third indicator—the decreasing length of time it takes for a major new invention to come into common use—seems also to have been reversed. Producers must now put their new products through more rigorous and lengthy testing for safety, efficacy, and non-pollution than formerly. Moreover, there seem to be fewer and fewer inventions that represent real technological breakthroughs.

A fourth measure of the accelerative thrust—one not discussed by Toffler—might be the rate of generation of electric power, which at a steeply rising exponential curve of 7 percent annually had been doubling each decade. The electrical energy boom came to a rather abrupt slowdown coincidentally with, but not by any means entirely because of, the quadrupling of the price of oil by the Arab oil-exporting nations, when the annual rate of increase in the production of electric power dropped to 1.5 percent in 1973.

Has the accelerative thrust come to a temporary or a permanent halt? The more fully one examines the dynamics of the situation, the more tenuous becomes the hope that real growth rates of 3-4 percent per year for the national economy can be sustained over the long term.

WORLDWIDE SHORTAGES AND INFLATION

By the end of 1973, worldwide inflation had become rampant, and economists could not agree on what to do about it. They had based their optimism of the 1960s on the assumption that the era of plenty would continue indefinitely; suddenly, that appeared to be a false hope. Here are a few of the shortages that compounded one another and contributed to the inflationary spiral:

• In 1970, almost unnoticed, the world fish catch peaked, after a long-continuing increase that had deluded many people into believing that the food of the oceans was almost unlimited. Since then, it has declined each year. Small nations like Peru and Iceland, whose economies and nutritional levels depend on the success of their fishermen, extended their claims to territorial fishing waters and thereby ran into intense hostility from competitors from other nations. The possibility of overfishing the oceans, and a consequent rapid decline in this key source of high-protein food, began to emerge as an unnerving prospect in a world with some 75-80 million more people to feed each year.

• Americans suddenly became acutely aware of a world grain shortage in 1972, when huge Russian purchases of wheat began to drive up its cost and cause a temporary but unpleasant rocketing of other food prices. American reserves of grains and soybeans became depleted, thus sharply increasing and unsettling food prices all over the world. The situation in India and other Southeast Asian and African countries became increasingly bleak. The dramatic decline in food reserves and increase in prices were asserted by experts to be the foretaste of a chronic world food problem, especially high-protein food. Meanwhile, a prolonged (several years) drought and famine in sub-Saharan Africa went largely ignored by well-fed Americans (and many others).

• Then came the energy crisis. It would have come anyway, eventually, but its onslaught would not have been so dramatic had it not been for the Arab-Israeli War of 1973. The depletion of the world's oil resources was not a transitory problem that could be surmounted by technologists on the pattern of the successful American post-Sputnik efforts to outdo the Russians in space, as suggested by Secretary of State Kissinger to the nations of the European Economic Community in December of 1973. The profound and permanent upward turn in the cost of oil and, in consequence, in the cost of almost all goods and services throughout the world, was unpleasant for the West, but the effect upon poor agrarian nations, trying desperately to increase their own food supplies, was bound to be vastly more serious. Low-cost oil and gas are essential to even moderate-priced fertilizer, and oil is needed to drive tractors and irrigation pumps, all of which are essential to a continuation of the Green Revolution in Southeast Asia. High-cost energy will bring closer the foreseeable period of famines in the underdeveloped world, possibly massive famines. In the high-energy technological societies of the West, the prices of virtually all physical products of the economy, as well as transportation, have been driven up steeply.

• Thus, hand in hand with the energy crisis came rampant inflation. To millions of Americans living close to the margin, inflation was of greater concern than the availability or cost of gasoline or the need to turn their thermostats down several degrees. Millions of households could no longer afford the high prices of meat and turned to cheaper foods, only to find that these, too, had skyrocketed in price.

• In 1974, the real Gross National Product (after correcting for the effects of inflation) declined, as a result of a recession in the midst of the second-highest inflation of the century. Normally, inflation induces high economic activity—people converting their money into goods in anticipation of still higher prices later. Yet, despite great anticipation buying, the GNP fell, leaving the economists confused and divided, as inflation and recession demand diametrically opposite remedies.

THE POLITICAL WOES OF THE UNITED STATES

These startling changes, which came about with bewildering rapidity in the 1970s, created consternation throughout the United States and much of the world. As fate would have it, the economic woes were compounded in the United States by two giant-sized political and moral calamities: the Vietnam War and Watergate.

The longest war in American history, the Vietnam War affected every aspect of American life. The ill-considered and even contrived manner in which the United States got into that war, the misinformation the public received about it, the pattern of overkill and ecocide employed by the military in the conduct of the war, and our protracted delay in pulling out after it became evident that military victory was impossible led millions of people—and particularly a generation of youth—to develop strong doubts about the fundamental moral sensitivity and capacity for judgment of their elected leaders of both parties. The effects of the Vietnam War on the psyche of the American people will inevitably be felt for decades. While not solely attributable to Vietnam, the drug culture, the sharp increase in disrespect for law, the spread of all kinds of violence and crime, the rapid rise in largely unpublicized and unpunished white-collar crime—these were manifestations of a general decline in moral restraint upon the uglier forms of human behavior that was aggravated by the stresses of the war.

Then came the unfolding of the shocking and sad spectacle of Presidential abuse of power—in the Watergate hearings, the House impeachment hearings, and ultimately the resignation of President Nixon and the indictment and conviction of some of his closest associates. The one hopeful thing about Watergate was that it came to seem a "bottoming-out" of the nation's deteriorating moral climate. The behavior of the President and his men could not, unfortunately, be viewed as a singular aberration of one small group of power-hungry politicians. Corruption among elected officials at all levels of government, as judged by the number of prosecutions and convictions, reached new highs in the first half of the 1970s.

Thus, public confidence in the institutions of government and in elected officials and lawmakers reached new lows at the same time that the economic and social problems of the nation and the world demanded leaders of the greatest talent, wisdom, and integrity. Moreover, many intellectuals and reformist liberals who had invested much of their lives in trying to achieve a greater measure of social and economic justice became increasingly skeptical about the prospect of solving the nation's problems through new Federal laws and funding. As they saw it, President Johnson's War on Poverty, as well as his effort to raise educational standards for the deprived minorities and to improve housing and community services, never had a genuine chance after the escalation of the Vietnam War in 1965. And deep down was the nagging and growing doubt that, even with proper financing, their programs could solve the social problems. Many activist sociologists admitted that they "simply did not know how to solve these problems, no matter how much money was available."

The decade of the 1960s also saw a loss of confidence in the basic manageability of urban agglomerations. There was some bounce back from the dark days of rioting and burning in Los Angeles, Detroit, Washington, Newark, and other cities, but the disenchantment of urban residents with the style and conditions of their life continued unabated. By 1972, only 13 percent of a nationwide sample of Americans said they would prefer to live in a city rather than in a nonurban area. Nostalgic and exaggerated though this may be, many felt imprisoned in the nation's cities because they had no economic alternative. Mayors and city managers could not express publicly the true depths of their pessimism, but they could see no solution to the problem of the escalating costs of urban services.

By the mid-1970s, many Americans began to wonder whether the nation, or indeed Western society, knew where it was heading, and more and more of them were beginning to reject the work ethic and deferred gratification, as well as the achievement syndrome. Some of the literature of the early 1970s reflected this gloomy and apocalyptic mood; *The Limits to Growth* and other works conveyed by their very titles the extraordinary degree of apprehension about the future that had seized many articulate members of the intellectual community: *The Doomsday Book* (1970) by Gordon Rattray Taylor, *The Closing Circle* (1971) by Barry Commoner, *The Coming Dark Age* (1973) by Roberto Vacca, *The End of the American Future* (1973) by Peter Schrag, *An Inquiry into the Human Prospect* (1974) by Robert Heilbroner, and *The End of Affluence* (1974) by Paul and Anne Ehrlich.

Not only were writers and artists raising alarums about the hazardous course of technological society, but increasing numbers were demonstrating by their manner of living a newly acquired conviction that the only way to combat the curse of bigness was to opt out. To many young people, and some not so young, almost any manner of making a living that would take individuals out of their organizational mazes and bring them closer to other people in small, informal group relationships—and into the open air, if possible—seemed preferable to much higher incomes gained from a high-rise rat race. Modest as the numbers of such people may be in relation to the total work force, the significance of their actions probably greatly exceeds their relative numbers.

How much of this change in mood from the 1960s to the 1970s derives from transitory causes, and how much from profound trends that might have brought the nation, in any event, to both a philosophical and a practical downward revision in its expectations? Is the era of high-energy technology nearing its zenith, to be followed by a decline and perhaps by the birth of a different kind of civilization? Are those who are opting out of big corporations and big government and seeking satisfactions in smaller units of human association just an insignificant fringe of intellectuals and esthetes who will remain an unimportant minority, or are they the intuitive and bold forerunners of a mass movement? Has the prospect of a world of plenty been permanently converted into a neo-Malthusian specter? Has the complexity of governing a society outrun the capacity of leaders to govern, or of citizens to choose wise leaders?

Any attempt to provide even tentative and partial answers to such difficult questions requires that we try to establish how we got where we are. What are the dominant forces that brought American society from a loose confederation of agrarian colonies with some 3 million members to the dominant technological society of the world in less than two centuries? If we can sort out the major factors that produced what we think of as the extraordinary American standard and style of living and examine them to see how much power remains in them, we should then be able to judge better what our future may hold.

II. The Fortuity of American Affluence

Two decades ago, a distinguished but not adequately appreciated American historian, Walter Prescott Webb, made an important contribution to the understanding of modern history in *The Great Frontier*, a book that reflected a larger and longer view of the role of the American frontier than that of the better-known Frederick Jackson Turner, who had initiated the frontier school of American history more than a half-century earlier. Professor Webb's theme was that the windfalls from the discovery by Europeans of the Western Hemisphere and Australia, and the subsequent exploitation of these continents, created a condition of economic boom not only among those who settled the new lands, but in varying degrees among all of Western Europe. The entire period from the 16th to the 20th centuries should be regarded, Webb thought, as one continuous frontier boom for the Western world—a boom that he saw as nearing its end in 1952. The extraordinary economic advantage conferred by the profligate use of the resources of the Western Hemisphere could not be much longer sustained, he implied, and Americans would need to seek new goals.

One aspect of his theme that Webb did not explore in as much depth as one might have expected from a Texan was the subject of oil—not oil alone, but oil as the most important source of energy of the modern world. For energy, directed by technology, has been the second great frontier, comparable in scope and influence to the discovery and exploitation of the Western Hemisphere. Especially in the quarter-century following the end of World War II, most Western intellectual and political leaders proceeded on the assumption that large amounts of low-cost energy would provide the basis for long-term economic growth of both the developed nations and the Third World. Their premise was shattered in 1973 by the quadrupling of oil prices and the lack of any realistic prospect that energy would again be cheap in the foreseeable future. *The second economic frontier may thus have been closed, just as the first one was closed when all the world's good land was occupied and either cultivated or mined.* For when energy is no longer cheap, nothing else is cheap— except human labor in certain major areas of the world.

Despite the symbiotic relationship of energy and technology in the development of modern Western civilization, social scientists have paid scant attention to the relation of energy to the operation of society. They assumed that science and technology had permanently mastered the technique of producing cheap energy. For their part, the scientists and engineers were happy to accept credit and medals for the improvements in the human condition resulting from high-energy technology while giving nature no credit for having stored 200 billion trillion joules of energy in the form of fossil fuels and yielding them up with remarkable generosity. One may look in vain for any discussion or even reference to energy in the most widely used economics texts used prior to 1973. But it seems unlikely that energy will ever again be ignored.

The double quantum jump in the use of energy from fossil fuels in the 19th and 20th centuries is almost certainly the single most important explanation for the affluence of highly modernized societies. Despite its central role, however, the early availability of low-cost energy and its consequent use in massive quantities is not, by itself, a sufficient explanation for the rapid emergence of the United States onto the world scene as both the most affluent and the most powerful nation in the world. The explanation lies in a fortuitous confluence of a score of forces. The causation is complex, too complex to be adequately covered in a single chapter. Yet it seems essential to the rest of our analysis of how we came to be where we are, and where we are heading, at least to sketch what seem to me to have been the strongest secular forces involved.

THE SOURCES OF AMERICAN TECHNOLOGY AND WEALTH

Listed below are 22 elements that seem to me to have been primarily responsible for the extraordinarily rapid growth of the American economy and the nation's consequent political power. A major purpose of the analysis is to see whether each is self-propelling or self-limiting. With respect to the factors that are self-limiting, the inevitable questions are: Are the limits proximate, or far in the future? To what extent were these elements the result of sheer luck, unprecedented in history and unreplicable in the future by any developing nation? How sustainable are they in the coming decades? Let us now examine each factor with these questions in mind.

1. A virgin continent. Settlers of the North American continent found incalculable riches—seemingly inexhaustible sources of food, fiber, hides, wood, and minerals with which to fashion all the necessities and most of the amenities of life. In what now constitute the 48 contiguous states of the United States lay more than 3 million square miles of virgin land with an average of 9 inches of rich topsoil over most of it, with magnificent timber and animals to be had for the taking from only a million or so Indians with neither land titles nor guns with which to defend their homeland. Never again can human beings stumble upon so mammoth an area of rich, sparsely populated, uncultivated, and easily exploitable land.

Approximately half of the rich topsoil the first settlers found in this area is now irretrievably lost, for centuries to come. It has been washed down the rivers and blown skyward after having been torn loose by the plow and shredded by the harrow. It takes 300 to a thousand years for nature to build back an inch of topsoil. Man may accelerate this process through careful nurture of the land, but not when he plants soil-depleting crops and seeks to wrest from it the maximum harvest. And now that the world is approaching a chronic food shortage, the pressures have become irresistible to put to the plow most of the remaining, semi-arid prairies in the West and Southwest. Soil-conservation experts estimate that in the crop year 1974 nearly 9 million acres of unfarmed land succumbed to the tractor and its manifold appliances, of which some 3.6 million acres were untouched natural grassland. According to the Soil Conservation Service, less than half of the new land is being farmed with adequate erosion control, and in 1974 alone some 60 million tons of topsoil were lost from the added area. Production may go up temporarily, but such abuse of land digs into organic capital and spends it like current income. A high percentage of the land in the United States that is suitable for agricultural cultivation, as well as much grassland whose cover should never have been turned under, is now being farmed. Increasing agricultural productivity, insofar as it depends on putting more land into production, has essentially run its course.

2. Vast space: an undervalued asset. In the 17th and 18th centuries, the gigantic size of the New World enabled the settlers to separate themselves as far as they chose from the authoritarian governments they had left behind, and to avoid unwanted conflict with their fellow colonists if they came too close and became too abrasive. The luxury of space and the open frontier became inseparable components of the fierce sense of independence that developed as one of the hallmarks of the American character. For well over a century after the War of Independence, the open frontier and Westward migration continued to draw upon the great reservoir of space and kept the size and cost of government low. Eventually, though, America was bound to lose this advantage over the more crowded world.

Space is now a greatly depleted resource. The United States is not crowded in the sense that Bangladesh or India or Japan are, but there is now intense competition for living and recreation space. Space is a relative matter. In a highly mobile culture like the United States, people need more space per person than they do in an agricultural village society. If Indians were to develop anything approaching American mobility, chaos would ensue. Conversely, if the United States were to develop one-quarter of the population density of India and still preserve its recent rate and style of mobility, physical and psychological collisions and destructive competition for space would become intolerable.

Already, many communities and states are girding themselves to protect the space they still have. Some—although still a small minority of them—have thrown away their welcome mats and are now resorting to legal actions to impede the development of more condominiums and shopping centers. Spatial limitations, therefore, act as an inconspicuous brake on both the growth of the economy and the growth of population. The more resistance there is to the continuing proliferation of urban sprawl, the more intense the zoning fights become, and the greater the delay in construction.

With their high level of mobility, Americans now are pressing against the limits of their space, and in doing so, are slowing down their economic and population growth.

3. A religious heritage encouraging exploitation of natural resources. Europeans who occupied the North American continent brought with them a Christian religious heritage that explicitly justified and even seemed to make it an ethical duty to go forth and "subdue the earth." This was in great contrast to the beliefs and practices of the American Indians, the custodians of the land for countless generations, who saw themselves as a part of nature, not its master. Thus the Indians took from the land only what they needed for a modest living; to the Christian settlers, they appeared primitive and benighted.

The dominant force in American culture became not merely Judaeo-Christian but Calvinist in its devotion to hard work as one of the highest of all virtues, leading to what has come to be known as the Protestant work ethic. That ethic, combined with the Biblical sanction to "subdue the earth," unleashed an era of almost unlimited exploitation of the natural wealth of the untouched continent. This binge lasted until the late 1960s, when the voices of the ecologists and environmentalists were suddenly heard. It is hard to find precedents, other than calamities of monumental proportions, that have brought about so sudden a change in social values by a significant and influential segment of the public as that represented and engendered by the environmental movement, which has had remarkable success in making Americans understand that their habits of conspicuous consumption, waste, and pollution have led to a deterioration of the quality of life.

A major effect of the environmental movement has been to slow down the great momentum of high-energy technology. At every turn, incursions into what remains of the nation's relatively unspoiled environment are met with protests and law suits, aimed either at halting the effort entirely or modifying it so as to minimize its effects on the ecology. The delays in the Alaska pipeline, the protests against the location of new generating plants, especially nuclear plants, the efforts to stop further development of the interstate highway system, the insistence on much stricter air pollution standards—these are but a few examples of the retarding effect of the new ethos on further large-scale technological development. All this happened in only half a decade. The ethical support of exploitation has now collapsed, with a consequent slowing of economic growth.

4. Racial exploitation: a temporary economic advantage with a delayed heavy price. So eager were the European settlers to turn the vast land to their profit with all possible speed that they imported more than 2 million slaves to cut the forests, farm the land, and ship the agricultural products, especially cotton and tobacco, to Europe in exchange for machinery and finished goods. Slaveowners were thus responsible for a double form of exploitation—of the slaves and of the land. While slavery was formally abolished in 1863, exploitation of the liberated Blacks continued, and the United States is still struggling to overcome the effects of the blight of slavery. The tensions and the human and economic costs involved are incalculable. The delayed bill, now falling due and being paid by American society for the practice of slavery, has years yet to run as a claim upon the Nation.

5. Economic and political doctrines encouraging rapacity. Adam Smith's *Wealth of Nations* was published in the same year as the Declaration of Independence, and both documents emphasized individual freedom and de-emphasized social responsibility. Thus both documents worked together, and were later given added support from the Constitution, to provide a philosophical framework of freedom for energetic entrepreneurs to undertake whatever business they chose and to accumulate as much wealth as their ingenuity allowed, with an absolute minimum of interference from government.

Economic and political support for this "free enterprise" was greater in the United States than elsewhere in the Western world from 1776 until the Great Depression of the 1930s. Not until the early 20th century did the Federal Government begin to put curbs on the barons of big business and to enact a Federal income tax. Total taxes remained low as compared with those of European nations until World War II. Public services were limited, and business was correspondingly free from the costs of such services. Free to exploit the natural wealth of the country as rapidly as possible, Americans produced more self-made millionaires than the rest of the world combined.

Out of the national desperation of the Depression, the New Deal, and the unavoidability of heavy deficit financing to pay for large-scale work and relief programs came the beginning of a great upsurge in expectations for government programs and services. The Federal budget rose from some $5 billion in 1930 to over $350 billion in 1975-76, not including another $50 billion or so in nonbudget expenditures on the part of government corporations. Even after one makes an adjustment for the depreciation of the dollar, that is an astounding jump. And the costs of state and local government grew even faster than Federal expenditures during the quarter-century after the war's end. The free-enterprise system was efficient in the rapid development and exploitation of the American continent, but it did not pay its way in social costs. Eventually it had to be replaced by a mixed economy, the costs of which are increasingly high. The economy of the United States that was minimally burdened with social costs in the years leading up to World War II is no longer in an advantageous position in this respect.

6. A free late start on the Industrial Revolution. As the U.S. economic and population booms of the early 19th century began to take shape, based largely on agriculture and deforestation, the Industrial Revolution was well under way in England. James Watt had produced a practical steam engine in 1776, and England quickly began to apply steam to the turning of factory wheels, as it had already done with water power. Soon some of Britain's cleverest machine designers were lured to New England, where factories sprouted almost overnight. The American late start in the Industrial Revolution became, in fact, a great advantage, since the nation did not have to waste capital on the trial-and-error process of developing new machines. The looms of New England represented a form of freeloading on British inventiveness and technological development until the Yankees finally developed competitive technology.

The flow of knowledge that inevitably occurs from more advanced to less advanced nations has now reversed direction. Since the end of World War II, country after country has acquired American technology and, with lower wage levels, converted that technology—often improving upon it in various ways—into competitive advantage in world markets. Japan has been the most conspicuous copier of such techniques (from the whole world, not just the United States), producing what may have been the most rapid economic growth over a period of two decades the world has ever seen. U.S. investments in research and development are far greater than those of any other nation, and the effect is to subsidize world technological development, since it is impossible to keep more than a fraction of the results of such research and development secret. Gradually, other nations are thus enabled to elevate their technologies to levels more comparable to our own, as Japan has done. The American comparative advantage has largely disappeared.

7. Millions of immigrants, bringing their skills. From Europe, too, the United States drew another form of wealth: millions of immigrants, most of them with well-developed skills as farmers, artisans, and tradesmen, as well as intellectual outcasts from Europe's revolutions (not to mention convicts and ne'er-do-wells who were sentenced to come to America). Much of the work force of the rapidly industrializing America came from Europe, especially from 1840 to 1910 (with the exception of the Civil War period). Once the frontier was gone, and in the wake of the Depression, the demand for restrictive immigration policies to limit the competition for jobs became strong. Congress cut immigration back sharply, and it is now at a level of 300,000-400,000 a year (plus the many illegal aliens who slip through the net of the Immigration Service). Immigration can no longer be characterized as an important contributing factor to sustaining and further developing America's unusually high standard of living (although it is worth noting that without the large number of foreign interns and residents in American hospitals, the health of the nation, especially of the poor, would probably have suffered considerably).

8. The 19th-century marriage of science and technology. For centuries, science and technology lived in two different worlds. The earth-shaking theories of Copernicus, Galileo, Kepler, and Newton were of no value to the toolmakers and technicians of their times, men whose arts were empirical rather than theoretical. But under the impetus of Faraday and others, science came down from the skies to earth in the 19th century. Bell and Edison and scores of other men interested in putting the world of science to practical application, drew on the science of England, Germany, and France and developed the telephone, the electric light, and a thousand other inventions. With space and freedom and capital, and with material sources and power sources and a laissez-faire system, America had the most fertile territory imaginable for achieving productivity with this new marriage of science and technology, which occurred, fortuitously, at a time when Americans were ideally situated to put to use the inventions that were its progeny.

That marriage is still intact and still productive, but there are signs of decreasing fertility. The employment market for scientists and various types of technologists is getting tighter, and the cost of educating them is becoming higher. Governmental support for research and development lessened in the late 1960s, and the public's enthusiasm for such expensive scientific and technological spectaculars as the SST and a manned Mars landing has dwindled. The power of science and technology remains substantial, but it no longer seems to be accelerating; in fact, it is now struggling to maintain its dominance, but is clearly losing ground.

9. Great stores of mineral wealth and fossil fuels. With the Industrial Revolution came America's discovery that it possessed fabulous riches below as well as above ground—in the form of coal, oil, gas, iron, copper, silver, gold, and numerous other minerals. Again, American laissez-faire encouraged the most rapid possible extraction and sale of these treasures by anyone who could get them out of the ground, with no thought given to the future industrial needs of the nation or how long the resources would last. Thus enormous supplies of comparatively cheap energy were provided to fuel the machines of industry, and cheap ores of the metals to build them.

Then, in 1973, the energy crisis brought the sudden realization that the nation's oil needs had outrun Western Hemisphere sources of supply and that by 1980, if oil use were to continue to increase at past rates, the United States would be depending on the Middle East for some 40-50 percent of its total oil requirements. Fortunately, the United States possesses about 20 percent of the coal and lignite reserves in the world, enough to fuel an industrial machine of current magnitude for a few centuries, but coal is not nearly as flexible a fuel as either petroleum or gas and it has the disadvantage of much higher sulfur content, a principal cause of atmospheric pollution.

It is clear that in respect to both fossil fuels and minerals, the extraordinarily advantageous position occupied until recently by the United States is fast dwindling. American consumption of these resources has been so profligate that we have suddenly become a dependent nation in respect to oil; we will soon become a have-not nation in respect to gas; and since World War II we have been a net importer of most metals.

10. Cheap raw materials and oil from the rest of the world. When the American industrial machine reached unprecedented levels of production and consumption during and after World War II, it became apparent that despite its remarkable sources of oil and minerals, the United States would have to rely on other nations for an increasing proportion of its needs. Since fossil fuels and high-grade ores are irreplaceable and limited natural capital, a country that industrializes early and buys and uses them when the supplies are plentiful gains a temporary advantage over all other nations. Because it buys when the price is low, it can build its own industrial plant at lower costs than those who come later and must pay higher prices as quantities diminish. This is what the United States has done.

But there is a reverse twist to this apparent good fortune. Building an industrial machine and, indeed, a total economy on the general assumption that low prices would continue into the indefinite future is like building an expensive house upon the shifting sands of an eroding beach. The American economy is not built upon a firm foundation of continuing low-cost energy and minerals; it is built upon a gradually and sometimes rapidly declining supply—and therefore rising cost—of *irreplaceable* fossil fuels and high-grade ores and a simultaneous, long-term increase in demand for them. Only in the 1970s did Americans begin to come face to face with this extraordinarily uncomfortable fact. The prices of oil, gas, and high-grade ores of almost all kinds are now headed inexorably upward. Consequently, the American economy, by virtue of its having become accustomed to more spendthrift ways than any other country in the world, may be in for a more extensive and uncomfortable revision of its life style than those whose per capita consumption of oil and minerals has been more modest.

11. Intense ambition, competitive spirit, and social mobility. One of the most powerful formative influences in the building of the

United States was surely the zeal to "get ahead." Expatriates from the Old World who sought freedom and fortune in the untamed New World were self-selected risk-takers, unhappy with their lot in Europe and confident that if they had an opportunity to prove themselves in fair competition they could improve their status in society. Pulling up their roots and transplanting them in foreign soil was far from easy, and many found it was even harder than anticipated; more went back than most American histories record. The majority of those who stayed must have felt that they had proved their fitness to survive and rise in a keenly competitive world.

With no landed aristocracy in the North and Midwest and, after 1776, no other formally recognized aristocracy, money became the principal measure of success and status. All that was needed to acquire social standing was wealth. Nowhere else was there such social mobility, and nowhere was there such eagerness to climb the ladder of success and fortune—or such confidence that hard work and smart trading would get you there. Probably at no time or place in history was there a greater opportunity for human beings to engage in unrestrained competition or stronger inclination to do so than in the United States during the 19th century. The restraints on competition increased markedly thereafter, but the competitive spirit and the desire for upward social mobility did not seem to flag much.

The compulsive effort to amass money is by no means uniquely American, but there seems little doubt that the amount of energy devoted to this purpose throughout the 19th and much of the 20th centuries has been one of the key factors that led to the nation's trillion-dollar GNP. By the 1960s, the Japanese had replaced Americans as the world leaders in competitive spirit, and their rate of increase in GNP reflected their new status. By the mid-1970s, more and more Americans had begun to wonder whether intense competition for the nonessentials and for status was worth the wear and tear on their weary minds and bodies; the college generation had become not only unusually egalitarian but less interested in being business entrepreneurs or managers than any of its predecessors; and the American competitive spirit had been substantially deflated. None of this augured well for a resurgence of American preeminence in industrial production and world trade.

12. The two-ocean moat and a century of cheap national defense.
Often recognized—but rarely adequately—is the "free ride" the
United States had from 1812 to 1917 in military defense. The separation provided by the Atlantic and Pacific Oceans, plus the power of
the British Navy to keep those oceans open to commerce and unavailable to any other nation bent on military aggression, made it unnecessary for the United States to tax its citizens heavily for military
defense, as did the major powers of Europe. This freed large
amounts of capital and energy for the production of peacetime goods
and services and sped the acquisition of foreign exchange with which
to buy raw materials and machinery, giving further impetus to
economic growth.

But the era of the two-ocean moat is now over, and it is the United
States that bears the burden of patroling the seas. It is the United
States that bears a disproportionate share of the defense burden of
the Western world, draining foreign exchange, causing inflation at
home, and otherwise squeezing the economy. War and defense have
been spurs to high-energy, capital-intensive technology, but the net
comparative advantage from military defense activities has turned
against the United States since World War II.

*13. Public schools and universities: the educational springboard
for American technological superiority.* Although the United States
lagged behind Germany and Scandinavia in the development of
compulsory education, free public schools and compulsory attendance laws spread rapidly after Massachusetts enacted the first such
law in 1852. The system of agricultural and mechanical colleges,
which was an integral part of the land-grant college system, was
launched in 1862; as its name implied, it was in major degree utilita-
rian, much different from the classical approach of European higher
education. Publicly financed education thus became the scientific, engineering, and management training ground for American
high-energy technology, at little direct cost to the technostructure itself.

The positive advantage of the American higher educational structure to the American economy lasted until sometime between 1960
and 1970, when the educational system became overextended. By
1970, some eight million students were engaged in some form of
post-secondary education, most of them in two-to-four-year colleges,
or in university graduate and professional schools. This was four

times as many as had been enrolled a quarter-century earlier. Students and their parents thought of college as the gateway to a better life, in terms of earnings and social class. Such a large number of students went to college that the supply of college-trained job applicants began to exceed the demand, while the demand for persons with various manual skills outran the supply. The gap between the salaries of college-educated white collar workers and the wages of blue collar workers narrowed. Meanwhile, the social cost of providing college education to large numbers of students who could not, or chose not to put their college training to vocational use was high. It was high for the students, for their parents, and for the taxpayers who footed a large part of the bill. Funds which might otherwise have gone into the capital needed for the creation of new jobs was siphoned off to operate expensive universities on a larger scale than was optimal. Leaving aside the assumed cultural advantages that some of these students gained, the economic result, when compared with a nation like Japan, was to hasten the end of American productive superiority.

14. Agricultural technology: a special American expertise. The agricultural production system in the United States became, in the latter part of the 19th and more fully in the 20th century, the focus of substantial amounts of both scientific and technological effort, something that did not occur in anything like the same degree in other nations affected by the Industrial Revolution. The active research programs of agricultural and mechanical colleges, coupled with the nationwide agricultural extension service to disseminate the rapidly developing scientific and technical knowledge, were a unique and brilliant American invention. The fields of agronomy, hydrology, genetics, and bacteriology laid the groundwork for long-term increases in agricultural productivity, while mechanical engineers teamed up with private industry to develop new machinery that could plant, cultivate, and harvest crops on America's huge flat and gently rolling fields on an unprecedented scale. American agriculture led and continues to lead the world in productivity per man hour by a wider margin than does its production of hard goods.

Until the large Soviet purchases of wheat and soybeans in 1972, resulting in the disappearance of reserve stocks and the sudden skyrocketing of various food prices, the American public assumed that its vaunted agricultural productivity would keep well ahead of demand and assure a good-quality diet at acceptable prices. But world financial capacity to buy American food had been going up rapidly while world supplies of food went up more slowly, and American agriculture began to be strained. The net effect was intense world demand for grains and soybeans and inevitable price inflation. There is now far less opportunity for further increases in agricultural productivity than is commonly assumed.

15. Two world wars waged from sanctuary. When the 19th century had run its course with free enterprise in the saddle, using up resources with little thought for the future, and after the barons of industry and transportation had distorted the market system through monopoly controls, the nation began to suffer increasingly severe economic depressions that did not seem to have effective self-correcting forces, as classical economics assumed they would. As chance would have it, war intervened to bolster the floundering economy. Not once but twice, war on a grand scale, fought on foreign shores with no destruction to the U.S. industrial plant, led to economic booms, the second being one of the greatest industrial developments in the country's history. Tragic and destructive as these wars were, it is undeniable that they conferred important comparative advantages on the United States.

The Great Depression had almost put an end to the deep faith of Americans in the unlimited growth potential of the American economy, but World War II resuscitated that faith. Enormous government expenditures for research and development laid the technological bases for surges in air transportation, television and other electronic communications, computer technology, and numerous other major technical and industrial achievements. And the enormous buildup of savings laid the foundation for the postwar baby, building, and educational booms.

While the Korean and Vietnam wars were also fought from sanctuary, with American civilians protected from the horrors of war (except as seen on their TV screens), these wars did not confer any comparative advantages on the United States in relation to the other modernized and competitive societies, as the two World Wars had. The Vietnam War was, in fact, a disaster in all respects, bringing internal dissension and demoralization and planting the seeds of inflation. Nor did there appear to be valuable spin-offs from military research and development into the civilian economy, as there had been during World War II.

Since 1965—the year of heavy American military intervention in Vietnam—war and its aftermath, and continuing preparations for war, have become a major drag on the American economy, contributing heavily to inflationary pressures, and with few offsetting economic aids to help the industrial component of the economy compete on favorable terms with other modernized societies.

16. The automobile culture. Future historians will surely record the domination of the automobile over American culture as one of the most, if not the single most, influential factors on both the economy and the total society in the 20th century. It is variously estimated that somewhere between one-fifth and one-sixth of all jobs in the United States during the post-World War II period have been associated with the automotive and highway industries. While American fascination with the automobile does not distinguish this nation from various others, the size of its industrial commitment and the degree of its dependence on the auto is certainly without compare. No other nation has spent nearly as much money on automobiles, created as many jobs, directly and indirectly, as a result of the automobile, or had its urban centers suburbanized and exurbanized by the auto, as has the United States. No other industry has had so great an influence on the psyche and mores of the public. No other industry has established so pervasively the principle of contrived obsolescence, investing enormous sums in new model changes every year and making people proud to have the newest product or dissatisfied if they do not. The growth of the American economy in the post-World War II years was predicated upon these mores, far different from those of earlier centuries.

Then the sudden quadrupling of the price of oil undermined the foundation of America's most basic industry. Prospective automobile buyers were thrown into a state of consternation as they waited in long lines at gasoline pumps in the winter of 1973-74 and wondered what was to happen next. Project Independence was launched by President Nixon and later embraced by President Ford, but even the most optimistic estimates are that heavy dependence on OPEC oil will extend for decades. While the automobile industry had sold some 11 million cars in 1973, buyer confidence was so shattered, and the public resources so depleted, that sales dropped to 7 million in 1974 and a spokesman for one of the four auto manufacturers asserted that he did not expect the industry to sell more than 6 million cars a year in the foreseeable future. The rug has been pulled out from under the largest and most domineering influence over the American economy, and there seems no prospect that the industry will ever regain its lost position. Nor is there any substitute on the horizon to take up the resulting slack in the economy.

17. A mass home market, without tariffs between states. Under the Constitution, no state may levy tariffs on imports from other states; thus no legal or jurisdictional impediment exists to the free flow of goods and services among the fifty states. Such a unique situation has given many industries the opportunity to take maximum advantage of the economies of scale. They produce for a large unified market, using a single language, a common system of weights and measures, a common system of money and credit, and nationwide advertising. These conditions gave Henry Ford and his numerous imitators and successors the chance to demonstrate the enormous advantages of mass production. America became the world leader in mass-production techniques because there was such a large home market to build upon. The home market then became the foundation on which exports of similar products could achieve additional economies of scale.

This advantage contributed much to American preeminence in the production of automobiles, trucks, earth-moving machinery, air-planes, generators, turbines, business machines, computers, and a number of other products that still account for a substantial share of American industrial exports. It was a major factor in America's rise to the position of economic leadership in the world. But the significance of this advantage is now declining in respect to a number of products. In the days of Henry Ford, nobody in the world produced cars so cheaply, but when the auto industry shifted to larger and heavier turnpike cruisers, these became unsuitable for foreign export and both the international automobile market and a substantial part of the American market were yielded to the Europeans and the Japanese. The United States still maintains its international dominance in commercial aircraft production, as it does in turbines and generators. Where very large aggregations of capital are required, and where the units of production are very expensive and are bought by commercial users (for example, large aircraft, turbo-generators, and oil-drilling equipment), the United States retains much of its comparative advantage over other nations of the world, by virtue of its head start in a large domestic market, but where the units of production are much less expensive and complex, and the products are useful to consumers all over the world (for example, transistor radios, small automobiles, small electric motors and devices), the American comparative advantage has disappeared.

18. A remarkably efficient transportation and distribution system. The American system of transporting agricultural products and manufactured goods from producer to consumer has been uniquely efficient. The transportation of perishable agricultural products by refrigerated truck and containerized freight, and their distribution through supermarkets has enlarged choice and reduced costs for consumers. Similar economies have been achieved in respect to canned, frozen, and dry-packaged food products, and a wide variety of nonfood products. Supermarkets and shopping centers surrounded by huge parking lots—by-products of the automobile culture and the Federal highway program—facilitate mass production and distribution of nationally advertised products, as well as mass buying by consumers. Americans can purchase large quantities of groceries at one time, pile them into their station wagons, parked free within a sea of other cars outside the supermarket, drive home via a superhighway, and transfer much of what they have bought into their king-size refrigerators and freezers. It is a characteristically American system, and by traditional cost-accounting methods, an extremely efficient one. It has also had the countervailing effect of contributing heavily to the destruction of the cohesive force of the urban neighborhood.

In France and England, the beginnings of the supermarket system are beginning to clash with the traditional mode of distribution through small, neighbor shops and markets. Shops and markets, together with such other gathering places as the English pubs, are social institutions, instruments of social cohesion by which neighborhoods are held together as communities. They yield psychological and social values that cannot be measured. But they cannot be preserved if the raw economics of the supermarket system are

assumed to take precedence over these intangible values, unmeasur-
able through standard books of accounts and generally unmanageable
by most political systems.

When we speak about and measure the American superior standard of living in relation to other nations, using the GNP per capita as
the standard of comparison, it is important to bear in mind that we
include only tangibles measurable in dollar terms. It is a peculiarly
one-dimensional, unqualitative method of assessing our individual
and social welfare. But that is the way our accountants, economists,
businessmen, and politicians, and most of the rest of us continue to
think and talk about the nation's economy, the foremost element of
the national welfare.

In any event, most American small neighborhoods have now been
superseded by shopping centers and the supermarket culture is so
pervasive that further economies through improvement of the efficiency of the distribution system seem very difficult to achieve.

19. A high-powered advertising industry. Annoying, expensive,
and unesthetic as it may seem to many Americans, the advertising
industry must be listed as one of the major contributing factors that
has generated the American style and standard of living. It has
awakened and even created desires for material goods among the
public where they hardly existed at all before. Through every means
of mass communication, it has drummed into the minds of all who are
exposed to its messages the idea that new products are superior to
those they are intended to supplant. By its special brand of manipula-
tive psychology, the advertising industry has caused the American
economy to be built on the foundation of rapid obsolescence—and
helped to propel the GNP to the trillion-dollar level.

With the coming of the environmental movement, high-cost
energy, and inflation, Americans are devoting more attention to
making their money go further instead of relying on the expectation
that they will have more income next year with which to buy—on
credit—the new and better products that the advertising industry
dangles before them. To the extent that Americans do change their
attitudes in this direction, high-powered advertising will become
correspondingly less effective, and it will probably contribute less to
any further increase that may occur in the GNP.

20. The credit system of governmental, corporate, and personal finance. Until the 1930s, it was widely believed that debt was undesirable and to be avoided if at all possible. But with the advent of John Maynard Keynes's new theories of economics, governmental debt became an instrument for managing and stabilizing the economy, and a rising government debt was a contributing factor in a rising GNP. This profound change in attitude toward borrowing gathered momentum in the late 1930s and during and after World War II. The debt of the U.S. Government rose from $43 billion in 1940 to $259 billion in 1945, and then reached $425 billion in 1974; far from causing the nation to go bankrupt, this stimulated an enormous postwar boom in purchasing power that eased the transition from war to peace with comparatively little unemployment.

The new fiscal ethic was transferred to the personal sphere in the postwar years, with savings from World War II rapidly spent on new cars, refrigerators, TVs, and the like—and a consumer credit boom of massive proportions began. Personal saving was no longer high on the list of meritorious behavior patterns. Consumer credit went from $4.9 billion in 1935 and $5.6 billion in 1945 (an actual decrease when correction is made for value of the dollar), to $39 billion in 1955, $56 billion in 1960, and $159 billion in 1973. Shifting from an economy based largely on consumer saving to one based on borrowing in anticipation of income had a tremendous stimulatory effect.

Such a shift in economic mores could occur only once, but when spread out over a period of years it could and did convey the false impression of a steadily ascending curve of consumer purchasing with no visible upper limit. This stimulation was given added impetus by the deficit spending brought on by the Vietnam War, without any accompanying tax increase, and aggravated by the tax reductions of 1969. And as we have seen, the domestic market for the products of American technology does not have the indefinite expansibility that had been assumed, so with the onset of the energy crisis, not only was the automobile industry in trouble, but so also were all other products that depend heavily on credit financing and consume substantial amounts of energy.

Credit is not a magic source of wealth, but we have treated it, for the last 30 years, as if it were.

21. Enlargement of the production and distribution system through the employment of large numbers of women. World War II brought large numbers of women into the work force and thus began not only a significant alteration of the dynamics and economics of the American family, and the life-styles of women, but the permanent expansion of the labor force as a proportion of the total population—from 13.8 million women in 1940 to 33.9 million in 1973. Such an increase in the numbers of people earning wages and salaries, supporting the nonworking, dependent population, obviously greatly enlarged the consumer market and was a boon to the economy and the per capita GNP. Although the expansion has almost certainly not completely run its course yet, it is physically impossible for another similar jump to occur in the ratio of women workers to the total work force. This, then, was a nonrepeatable expansion of the economy.

22. Shooting for the moon. America's space program, the largest single investment in research and development in nonmilitary programs in the 1960s, gave an important boost to the national economy. The indirect effects on the advancement of American technology, particularly its computer industry, were of major value in giving the nation a still greater technical lead than it had had over other Western nations. In the 15 years from 1958 to 1973, more than $30 billion was spent on the Apollo program to explore the moon and other aspects of the space effort. It seems unlikely that we shall again see, in this century, so large and complex a technological and management feat.

During the 1960s the comparative advantage of American technology, highlighted by its space program, began to look to the Europeans (but not to the Japanese) almost as beyond competition. This was the dominant concern of European technologists as they observed large appropriations of government funds being poured into research and development in the United States—vastly more than European governments could afford. Massive infusion of government funds into applied research is a form of forced saving and investment that accelerates new product development to a greater degree than exclusive reliance on the free market. But the European apprehension did not turn out to be long-lasting. As the decade ended, both the public enchantment with the space program and Congressional support for peacetime research and development were in a state of decline. Faith in the products of science and technology, temporarily boosted by the Apollo program, could not be sustained.

The space program had, in fact boomeranged. The most lasting effect of the Apollo program was to turn our vision around, to begin to make us realize how barren is the rest of the solar system, and how full of life, but lonely, is "spaceship earth," floating in a jet-black infinitude. We now know that man has but one option in the foreseeable future, and that is to see that his earthly home is preserved and that nature's various and variegated forms of earthly life are protected from destruction. The universe is incredibly vast, but our universe, we suddenly saw, is much smaller and more limited than space science had led us to believe. How well we learned the lesson, only the future will tell.

As the space program declined, NASA sought hard to find ways to transfer its organizational and technical expertise to the solution of man's earthly problems, particularly the management of the cities, but few thought the skills were transferrable. The problems of the cities are overwhelmingly those of managing complex human relations in a nonhierarchical setting, not the orderly management of complex technology in a clearly structured organization. The future of NASA, therefore, remains unclear. Its potential stimulus to the national economy does not appear to be very promising.

THE POTENTIAL FOR FUTURE GROWTH

I have tried, in this summary of the sources of American technological supremacy and wealth, to examine the dynamics of each to see how much potential for further growth remains. No pretense is made that the list is either comprehensive or definitive, and differing interpretations of the various items will surely occur. Nevertheless, it is suggested that the very making of such a list, and the effort to assess the kinetic energy left in these contributing causes to American high-energy technology, cannot help but illuminate the noncontinuous nature of many of them.

Looking over these 22 factors makes one realize how unfirm a foundation they provide for projecting the pre-1973 rates of economic growth into the future, even if and when the nation should surmount its recession, inflation, and energy crises. As a group, the elements almost certainly had a synergistic effect, but such mutual reinforcement can easily turn toward negative interaction if some of the elements turn sour, as they have done since 1973. None of the trends was on an accelerating curve even in the early 1970s, while many had already peaked and were declining. American technology is still a vital force, but the combination of advantages that brought the United States to world pre-eminence—a few decades during which its political leaders proclaimed over and over again that the nation had become the strongest the world had ever seen—appears, on closer examination, to have been much more fortuitous than was realized. And the durability of this fortuitous combination may be considerably briefer than euphoric politicians, economists, and historians thought probable.

Even though high-energy technology still has enormous momentum, it faces two overwhelming problems: It is running out of goals that have strong appeal to the human family—strong enough, that is, to warrant the investment needed to permit it to keep on accelerating—and it is much nearer to running out of oil and gas than was realized. Science fiction could provide us with numerous goals, but few of these would combine the necessary size with sufficient social utility and popularity to gain support. Large appropriations by the Federal Government are needed for the development of major technological innovations, and competition for the Federal dollar is intense. Except for certain developments in the armaments industry and the effort to produce economical, reliable, and safe new sources of energy, no such projects appear on the horizon.

Transportation, communications, construction, war, and aerospace have been America's boom industries for the first three quarters of this century. High-energy technology has been key to all five and has produced mammoth derivative effects that have shaped our total society. Now these industries are in varying degrees of difficulty, and none seems set for any new boom that will sustain what we thought of as the accelerative thrust. The communications industry may have more life left in it than any of the others since it is more economical in its use of energy—that is, the amount of energy needed to store, retrieve, and transmit bits of information has declined enormously in recent years. Improved communications techniques are likely to make it more feasible and economical for many currently centralized commercial operations in urban areas to be handled in much smaller and more decentralized organizational units in suburbia and exurbia, a trend that is already strongly in evidence but could increase substantially in coming years. However, the techniques to accomplish such purposes may reduce transportation requirements sufficiently so that total industrial and commercial activity will not be significantly increased and may indeed be decreased.

The abrupt end of the era of cheap energy seems likely to stymie any resumption of the accelerative thrust. Only the development of inexpensive nuclear power seems capable of launching us on another accelerative trajectory, and it is the consensus of nuclear experts that this could not have a major effect before the 21st century, if then. Some of the most distinguished nuclear scientists are dubious that fusion energy will ever become practical for peacetime use.

IMPLICATIONS FOR THE THIRD WORLD

The end of the accelerative thrust has important implications for the nonmodernized, low-energy societies. Development economists, policy-makers, and much of the internationally minded public have tended to assume that if we could but transfer our technical knowledge base to the developing countries, they should be able to enter the modernized world and achieve a reasonably high per capita GNP. But having examined the confluence of factors that brought a high standard of living to American workers, it seems abundantly clear that such a convergence can never again happen anywhere else in the world except, conceivably, in the oil-rich nations. The United States hit upon a bonanza and skyrocketed to wealth at a time when its resource base was enormous and the population was sparse and did not press hard against that resource base. Many of the Third World nations are now confronted with a situation in which their rapidly growing population is pressing harder and harder against their comparatively limited resource base. Meanwhile, with the high-energy societies increasingly dependent on the dwindling natural resources of the world, resource-poor nations will have a very difficult time competing in world markets for the high-priced energy and materials needed to industrialize, and there is little they can do to earn foreign exchange with which to buy the capital goods needed for industrialization. Technical knowledge is essential to modernization, but it is just one element and hardly suffices alone.

It would be an unfortunate error, however, to conclude that because low-energy, nonmodernized nations have no genuine prospect of even approaching current American levels of affluence, they therefore have little chance of developing or retaining creative and durable cultures with adequate psychic rewards for their members. In fact, as we shall see later, a high-energy society may have greater difficulty in sustaining itself and providing such rewards to its people than a moderate-energy society.

III. The Closing of the Second Frontier

If most of the factors that have given the American economy both its preeminence and its illusion of unending growth are, indeed, fortuitous and nonsustainable, what, then, is to become of the American economy? Has the nation already reached or come near the zenith of its affluence, measured in material terms? This question is being asked by increasing numbers of thoughtful citizens.

In his presidential address to the American Economic Association in December 1973, Walter Heller told his colleagues, "We have been caught with our parameters down and we have to go back to the drawing boards." Only an economist would use the word parameters as a euphemism for pants. The era of cheap energy had come to an abrupt end, undermining the capacity of economists to use Keynesian theories to keep the economy on its exponential growth track. To be sure, other factors were involved in the simultaneous double-digit inflation and near double-digit unemployment—the decline in the world fish catch, a bad crop year, the devaluation of the dollar, and the decontrol of prices—but the huge increase in oil prices was the critical influence.

The sudden end of the era of cheap energy and its brake upon further exponential growth took virtually everyone by surprise. Not even the pessimists had expected it so soon. Its jolting impact recalls a fable from *The Limits to Growth*:

A French riddle for children illustrates another aspect of exponential growth—the apparent suddenness with which it approaches a fixed limit. Suppose you own a pond on which a water lily is growing. The lily plant doubles in growth each day.

45

If the lily were allowed to grow unchecked, it would cover the pond in 30 days, choking off all other forms of life in the water. For a long time the lily plant seems small, and so you decide not to worry about it until it covers half the pond. On what day will that be? On the twenty-ninth day, of course. You have one day to save your pond.

This lesson was the essence of the message of *The Limits to Growth*. The last quarter of the 20th century, by implication, was the thirtieth day. The reaction of economists was almost uniformly deprecatory, principally because of the primitive quality of the predictive model, but also because of their profound disbelief that we could be nearing the limits to growth. The title of economist Carl Kaysen's review, "The Computer That Printed Out Wolf," typified the reaction of his colleagues, some of whom took consolation in the number of doomsday predictions that had been made over the years and been proved wrong; there was no wolf. But with apologies to the much-maligned wolf, the principal moral of that fable is that no matter how many times there may be false cries of wolf, one should not be lulled into the false notion that the danger no longer exists. The wolf—the physical limits of the earth—was and is indubitably still there. The crucial question is how long we will keep on behaving as if the wolf has disappeared.

The world oil situation is now beginning to change the perspective of some economists. In fairness, they cannot be faulted for not having foreseen the Yom Kippur War of 1973 and the resultant economic-political-military action of the Arabs in using oil as their major lever of power. But there is little evidence that they recognize the enormous implications of what I earlier referred to as "the closing of the second frontier"—the end of the era of cheap energy. Without cheap energy, their previous growth models are obsolete. They must not only go back to the drawing boards; they must re-examine their basic premises.

THE ASSUMPTION OF CHEAP ENERGY

Virtually all economic growth models of the quarter-century preceding 1973 assumed that the era of cheap energy would extend far into the future. Such an assumption was critically important in respect to all kinds of resources, especially metals, which require a steadily increasing amount of energy for their extraction and refinement.

As economists point out, under all but the most extraordinary circumstances, we are likely to run out of any resource gradually rather than abruptly, so that as this occurs, we should have time to adjust and substitute other, lower-grade but more plentiful resources. But lower-grade ores require far more energy for their extraction and refinement than high-grade ores, so that a sudden, major price change in the cost of energy has a disproportionately large effect on the cost of metals that are now "energy intensive." This is likewise true of other resources and commodities that have become increasingly energy intensive, including agricultural products, and especially the further extraction of fossil fuels.

Until recently, we have given little thought to the matter of "net energy." Obviously, it takes a substantial amount of energy to extract and convert fossil fuels to usable form, and some potential sources of energy require enormous amounts of energy for their extraction and refinement, so that the net energy is low, as, for example, oil from shale. The more of the remaining fossil fuels we consume, the higher the cost of locating and extracting each additional barrel or ton. The cost escalation of indigenous fossil fuels will be rapid.

The limited resources of the earth thus constitute a much more important contributing factor to inflation than we have heretofore been led to believe. The prices of many metals and other resources have not genuinely reflected their approaching scarcity in relation to world demand, or the increased cost of the energy that will be needed for their conversion to useful products. Prices may fluctuate substantially and unpredictably in the short run—until cartels are formed to stabilize them upward—but their long-range direction is inescapably up, and at a significantly faster rate than the general rate of inflation.

In contrast to the slow awakening of most economists to the full implications of the still rising costs of energy and materials, the physical scientists, or at least a significant number of them, are becoming deeply concerned about the need to re-educate the American people to the physical limits of the earth and the urgency of a fundamental shift in social policy and life-styles. In April 1974, Glenn Seaborg, then president of the American Association for the Advancement of Science, strongly counseled his colleagues and the general public to begin thinking in terms of converting American society rather rapidly to a "recycle society," emphasizing conservation of materials, their reuse wherever possible, the production of goods that are genuinely durable, and a general reversal of our wasteful ways. It was to be the beginning of a series of speeches and other efforts by Seaborg to get the American people to rethink their course.

A few months later, the Energy Policy Project of the Ford Foundation made similar recommendations in its preliminary report (and later in its final report) and foresaw the practical possibility of meeting the energy needs of the nation with considerably less energy than had previously been assumed to be necessary if only the American people would follow Seaborg's advice and abandon their wasteful habits. In February 1975, the Committee on Mineral Resources and the Environment of the National Academy of Sciences, in a special report, echoed these ideas with vigor, asking policy-makers and the general public to face squarely the need to steer the national economy away from continued growth and toward a new era of conservation. "Growth in a material sense," said the report, "has long been such a bedrock of conventional economic wisdom that it may seem heretical to suggest that it will be less valid in the future. But our study strongly suggests that, for purely physical reasons, at least the material consumption part of the economy will increasingly encounter limits to growth. Material economics follow S-shaped curves more nearly than rising exponentials. In our view, national policies exhorting and based on ever greater growth rates in the material economy will become increasingly shortsighted and inconsistent with human aspirations."

The contrast in viewpoints between people who are trained to think in terms of energy and materials, as scientists are, and those whose major preoccupation is the flow of money, such as financiers and macro-economists, is well illustrated by an old but widely repeated story about the Houston banker Jesse Jones, who was in charge of stockpiling of scarce raw materials at the beginning of World War II. Natural rubber was one of the scarcest and most urgently needed of war materials. One morning a distraught aide rushed in to tell Mr. Jones that a huge warehouse containing a significant portion of the natural-rubber stockpile had just gone up in flames. "Don't be so upset," Mr. Jones was reported to have said, "it's all insured."

Such a perspective is further illustrated by the fact that the economics curricula of most universities contain amazingly little on the subject of where energy and basic resources come from, how they are extracted, processed, and distributed, and the physical dynamics of their past, current, and future supply patterns. But only through such studies is it possible to comprehend adequately the physical basis of economics. The world energy crisis should bring the macro-economists down from their mathematical theorems about managing the economy through fiscal and monetary policy to the imperative of grappling with the implications of petroleum geology, the genetics and ecology of hybrid grains, the hydrologic problems of meeting the critically important demand for water in various parts of the nation and the world, the substitutability of materials, the political limitations on capital formation, and dozens of other such vital subjects.

That there is recognition of this need is evidenced by the recent comments by two distinguished economists, very different in their approaches. In an interview at the time of President Ford's convocation of a series of conferences on inflation, Nobel laureate Wassily Leontief, an accumulator and student of vast quantities of detailed information about economic relationships and interactions, observed: "The macro-economists work by disregarding details. This aggregate approach was developed for pedagogical reasons—so that even the President could understand the economy. There's a lot of fancy methodology, but the macro-economists get indigestion if you give them the facts." And Kenneth Boulding said: "I have been gradually coming under the conviction, disturbing for a professional theorist, that there is no such thing as economics—there is only social science applied to economic problems. Indeed, there may not even be such a thing as social science—there may only be general science applied to the problems of society."

CAN ECONOMIC GROWTH CONTINUE?

As we have already noted, it is the judgment of the best-informed scientists that cheap energy will not again be available in the 20th century. For the next quarter-century, therefore, and probably for the indefinite future, the energy frontier has been closed, just as the

land frontier was closed when essentially all the world's easily culti-
vable crop land was plowed up. But we may say to ourselves, perhaps
it will be possible to continue our economic growth and well-being in
spite of the diminishing supply of energy and its increased cost. It
will not be easy. It would mean a profound change in private attitudes
and public policy—a redefinition of what we mean by economic
well-being, new methods of allocating the jobs and income of our
society.

Let us approach this crucial question by first considering four
related questions: (1) What does technology have up its sleeve? (2)
Can the service sector pick up the slack in the economy? (3) Can
increasing productivity continue to raise the standard of living? and
(4) Can the capital shortage be overcome?

1. What does technology have up its sleeve? We have been so
conditioned to the assumption that there is a great treasure chest of
inventions waiting to be brought forth when the time is ripe that we
must inquire whether these will not furnish the basis for a renewal of
past economic growth trends. Following World War II nothing
seemed beyond the ingenuity of the brilliant young physicists, chem-
ists, biologists, and engineers who were electrifying the world with
nuclear energy and who, with the coming of the space age, began to
talk of such scientific advances as programmed dreams, genetic
control over the basic constitution of individual human beings,
interplanetary travel, permanent undersea colonies for humans, and
even a solution to the earth's population problems by space coloniza-
tion.

In 1967, futurists Herman Kahn and Anthony Wiener (in *The Year
2000*) listed a hundred technical innovations that seemed very likely
in the remainder of the 20th century. Included were: "intensive or
extensive expansion of tropical agriculture and forestry . . . new or
improved use of the oceans (mining, extraction of minerals, controlled 'farming,' source of energy) . . . new improved plants and
animals . . . inexpensive road-free and facility-free transportation
. . . very low-cost buildings for home and business use . . . home
computers to 'run' the household and communicate with the outside
world." Their forecast showed no premonitions of the coming
environmental movement or the energy crisis. Over and over, they
repeated variations on the theme of "inexpensive" and "low cost"

new methods of producing both the necessities and the amenities of life, but with little to back up their optimistic forecasts. There have been no recent forecasts that share such optimism; in fact, more and more analyses are tending in exactly the opposite direction.

One area that seems to hold greater promise than most others is miniaturization, stimulated by the space age and the necessity for compressing mechanisms into extremely small space. The development of tiny computers, improved, low-energy, reliable communication systems, feedback information systems, and the like opens a wide range of opportunities for the substitution of such low-energy communication systems for higher-energy transportation systems. Peter Goldmark, among others, is now concentrating on the use of communication techniques to permit business conferences to take place with the participants separated by wide distances. This could facilitate the physical dispersion of the headquarters operations of giant corporations, and inexpensive conference television would accelerate the process. While this may not be a happy augury for New York or other urban centers, such technology seems likely, over the long run, to make it possible for more people to live closer to nature and at the same time not have to spend a large part of their lives commuting. Anything that reduces energy demand and simultaneously reduces the wear and tear on people must be counted as an advance.

2. Can the service sector pick up the slack? Economists have assured us that over the long haul, as the demand for manufactured products declines, the service sector will contribute an increasing share to the dynamics of economic growth. This trend has been pronounced for the past two decades: we are not supposed to worry if the manufacturing sector weakens (except when it does so abruptly); the GNP can and will continue to rise. Unfortunately, the service sector now seems shaky, too.

Outside of the service components of the transportation and communications industries, the principal service "industries" that have boomed in the past decade are education, health, and state and local government. The first and third of these are now in financial difficulty—in some cases, dire straits—and the prospect for their revival as growth industries is bleak.

Education is the victim of the falling birthrate and the overinflated expectations as to how many of America's youth would consider a college education indispensable. The baby boom reached its peak in 1957 and then fertility rates resumed their long-term decline. The elementary schools were beginning to feel the effects by the mid-1960s, and the secondary schools by the early 1970s. Children born in 1957 reached college age in the fall of 1975, and from that point forward, almost every graduating high-school class will be smaller than the preceding one for at least eighteen years.

College enrollment had quadrupled in a quarter-century, from 2 million in 1946 to 8 million in 1972. Thereafter, the proportion of college-age youth who opted for college began to decline, as a result of the high cost of college and its declining economic value. There seems little possibility that the proportion will increase in future years; it is more likely to continue to decline. There is thus an added reason to expect declining college and university enrollments after 1977, with the decline picking up speed in the 1980s. The education boom has begun to turn into a long-term decline.

State and local governments are experiencing the same kind of fiscal difficulties as education. The demands for police and fire protection, for environmental protection, for recreational services, and especially for public assistance and welfare services have increased over the last decade at such a rate that budgets have risen by 14 percent per year—doubling in five years and quadrupling in ten. By 1975, however, the income of state and local governments had stopped rising or begun to decline to such a degree that substantial numbers of them were finding it necessary to stabilize or decrease the size of their work forces. Taxpayer revolts against further expansion of services and construction of new facilities seemed to be putting an end to the upward climb in public-service jobs except those financed by the Federal Government. Meanwhile, state and local governments had committed themselves to large payments to their civil-service retirees without making adequate financial preparations for these obligations. The day of reckoning is looming.

Only health services seemed to offer the possibility for continued and significant growth. On the theory that during stringent economic times most people would rather have cash than health services, President Ford recommended that the national health insurance plans, which had seemed headed for enactment before the 1976 election, be put on the back burner. But they will probably be moved forward eventually and result in some form of national health insurance or nationally mandated insurance which will almost surely bring about further growth in the health-service industry. Major efforts will be made, however, to hold the growth to moderate proportions.

3. Can increasing productivity continue to raise the standard of living? If Americans' material standard of living is to continue to increase, industrial and agricultural productivity must go up *not per man-hour and not per worker, but per person.* Let's use, as a hypothetical example, a country that has a population of 1 million people and is entirely self-contained agriculturally. Its farm-labor population is 100,000; thus each farm worker feeds 10 people on the average. Now let us assume that the output per farm worker improves by 3 percent per year. If the population were stable, and the full product of the farm workers were purchased, the food consumption of the people would increase by 3 percent each year. But now let us assume that the population increases 3 percent each year without any increase in the number of farm laborers. There is then no opportunity for the populace to increase its per capita food consumption. Agricultural productivity per man hour continues to increase but with no improvement in nutritional welfare per person.

One may make the same set of assumptions with respect to manufacturing, construction, and other material aspects of the nation's economy. If the number of consumers per worker goes up faster than the productivity per worker, then the amount of the product per capita clearly goes down. One may well ask, where do all these additional consumers come from, and why are they not contributing to an increase in the number of production workers, so that productivity would increase enough to keep pace with the larger number of consumers?

The additional consumers, of course, come from the increase in population, which grew at a rate of 1.7 percent a year (including immigration) during the 1950s but is now down to about 0.8 percent a year. In the two decades from 1950 to 1970, the population went up by more than a third, from 150 million to 203 million. At the same time, the number of agricultural workers supplying the nation with its basic foodstuffs declined from 8 million to 3.3 million. But so great was the increase in the productivity of farm workers that the 3.3

million workers in 1970 could provide more food per person for 203 million consumers than 8 million did for 150 million consumers in 1950, and still have a large amount left over for export. Such a remarkable increase in productivity can hardly continue much longer, and it may already have ended with the bumper farm crop of 1975. A report of the Department of Agriculture in 1975 showed a rise in the number of people supplied farm products per farmer from 14 in 1950 to 44 in 1971, but projected a leveling-off by 1975. With oil, fertilizer, and capital costs rising at prodigious rates, and with an end to the improvement in productivity per farmer, consumers must expect that food costs will continue indefinitely to rise at a faster rate than their incomes.

Mining and manufacturing seem to have followed somewhat similar patterns, although productivity per worker has not increased as rapidly as in agriculture. Composite indexes of productivity going back to 1950 are not available in mining and manufacturing, but an inspection of selected trends indicates a significant slowing down in productivity improvement (per worker) in the early 1970s and an actual decline in 1974. This does not imply that there is no likelihood of further productivity increase per worker, but the rate of increase is likely to be slow and much harder to achieve than in the past. And in an industry like oil, which is exploring for new sources, the productivity per worker will certainly go down, since it is now necessary generally to drill deeper and longer for each thousand barrels of oil extracted.

If we group together the industries that produce farm products, that extract fossil fuels and minerals, and that manufacture goods, we find that from 1950 to 1970 employment increased by barely a million workers, while employment in service-related industries increased by more than 20 million (out of the population increase of 53 million). The service components of the economy include such diverse operations as the telephone system, resorts, airlines, restaurants, golf courses, doctors and hospitals, lawyers, and government services. Productivity in most of these areas is difficult or impractical to measure, but with the exception of parts of the communications industry, it seems to be either declining or at least not significantly increasing. The service sector in its totality is not a promising area from which to expect major future increases in productivity.

Another factor affecting the capacity of the economy to keep the standard of living rising is the proportionate size of the work force producing the goods and services people want to buy with their disposable incomes. To take a simple example, if all married women with children were to drop out of the work force, and those among them eligible for welfare were to begin to collect it, total productivity as well as productivity per consumer would drop markedly, and, other things being equal, the general standard of living would plummet correspondingly. The same is true when the proportion of retired people and other dependents increases in relation to the work force. An increase in services per person in the dependent group (such as education, Medicare, and Medicaid), a marked trend in recent years, has the same effect—that is, to reduce the goods and services that members of the work force can buy with their disposable incomes. Thus, the standard of living of the dependent groups (not to be equated with the poor) has been rising proportionately, although most of them are not conscious of it, while the standard of living of the workers is falling proportionately, a fact of which they are painfully aware.

A similar effect occurs when the proportion of people in the work force who are rendering services nobody wants to buy with their disposable income rises, or if their proportionate buying power increases. Policemen and firemen are good examples. Few people can afford private bodyguards, and still fewer would choose to spend their money that way if they could afford it. But if the condition of society is such as to demand a steadily increasing proportion of policemen and firemen to maintain basic standards of protection, then, other things being equal, the standard of living goes down. The same is true of numerous other, less conspicuous functions of government. The more complex the society, the more regulatory functions are required, the more lawyers are needed to argue about equities, the more administrative personnel are required to plan, supervise, and audit. Most of these people are necessary to manage an extremely complicated society, but they inevitably drain away vast numbers of tax dollars and thus reduce the disposable income of the workers who are producing the goods and rendering the services for which people enjoy spending their disposable incomes. This is the reason so many people rail against the costly bureaucracy. High-cost government is an unfortunate but inescapable condition of life in high-energy technological societies.

This fact must be borne in mind: If the standard of living is to continue to rise, the productivity of that part of the total work force that produces the goods and services that people wish to buy with their disposable incomes must continue to increase fast enough to sustain the rising proportion of the population that are either dependents or workers in other sectors of the economy. It is getting harder and harder to keep productivity rising to that degree. We are nearing or have reached the end of the fortunate era in which technology could keep productivity climbing fast enough to yield a seemingly continuous rise in real, disposable per capita income.

4. Can the shortage of capital be overcome? One of the basic reasons for the troubled economy, it is frequently pointed out, is the deteriorating state of the nation's plant and equipment and the difficulty of acquiring sufficient capital to modernize production facilities and launch new ventures. Without such capital and equipment, American industry cannot improve its efficiency much in absolute terms, and it falls behind in competition with nations whose machinery is newer and more efficient, especially Germany and Japan, and whose workers are either more efficient or lower paid or both. In an economy geared so heavily to the expectation of continuing growth in total production and in productivity per man hour, such capital shortage is a serious matter.

Because of high labor costs, the American comparative advantage in international markets is with products that are capital-intensive (that is, that use large amounts of labor-saving machinery). To manufacture competitive products, therefore, Americans collectively must save more and invest more per unit of production than other nations. But they are not doing so. The largest part of the saving in the last two decades was through the process of withholding profits from dividends by the nation's major corporations and using those undistributed profits for expansion, modernization, or overseas investment. A smaller proportion came from the floating of new stock issues or corporate bonds and debentures. As long as profits were high during this period, and especially in those industries that occupied a central place in the American economy, the reinvestment of a significant part of the profits was a reasonably dependable source of saving, but as foreign competition increased in the automobile industry, for example, profit margins fell, and inevitably the investment by the auto companies in modernized equipment declined. Having lost a significant part of its market, and profits, to foreign competition, the automobile industry had less ability to re-establish its comparative advantage over foreign products by developing still more efficient, labor-saving machinery. Their inclination then was to invest more and produce more in American-owned subsidiaries abroad, thereby still further diminishing the funds available for modernization of plant and equipment in the United States, and to let their American plants deteriorate further.

This tendency to shift investment capital from the United States to foreign nations has been a general one among the numerous multinational corporations. In economic terms, it is entirely rational to invest capital where it will yield the greatest return, but the long-run effect is to accelerate the decline in the condition of American plant and equipment compared to foreign competitors, reduce the demand for American labor, and speed up what may be an inevitable long-run reduction in the disparity between American and foreign living standards.

To a greater degree than is commonly realized, the rate of capital accumulation is affected by political factors. This is particularly evident in the case of energy. Huge new investments will be needed in coming decades to convert the energy of fossil and nuclear fuels and the sun's rays to meet the energy needs of the nation if its appetite for energy continues to increase. But the body politic opposes price increases that seem to create profit bonanzas for the oil companies or the public utilities, even if most of the profits are promptly reinvested. In the short run, the public would suffer by such price increases; in the long run, it is expected to benefit. Under such circumstances, "'Gresham's Law of Human Behavior" ("The urgent drives out the important") becomes operative. The time horizon of the body politic is short and its expectations, encouraged by politicians with similarly short time perspectives, are not geared to the sacrifice and deferred gratification needed for long-range investment, especially when price increases are perceived to yield high profits to the titans of industry.

The implied imperative is that the Federal Government must become the "investor of last resort" to a much greater extent than in the past. It has adopted this role in the field of mass transit, but the demands upon it in the field of energy will exceed anything it has heretofore contemplated. The competition for funds will be intense. Budgetary requirements for urgent, current needs are so great as to generate unprecedented peacetime deficits, and large additional expenditures for capital investment would add to inflationary pressures. It will not be easy, therefore, even with government aid, to increase markedly the savings of the American people directed toward new capital formation and thus overcome the nation's serious capital shortage. Without large infusions of new capital, even the slow growth rate of recent years will be difficult to regain. The political limits to growth are being strongly felt.

WHERE WILL THE JOBS COME FROM?

Where do we go from here? How can a society continue to progress without continuing to increase its energy production and consumption? There seem to be only two options: (1) devise ways of achieving its central purposes with less energy per capita, and/or (2) change some of its central purposes from those that require high-energy consumption to those requiring less. Examples of the first would be a shift from using heavy, overpowered automobiles to lighter, more efficient cars and the greater use of public transportation. Altering life-styles so as to travel substantially fewer miles is an example of the second. Both, in the superficial sense, lower the American standard of living, but neither needs to make life less meaningful. In fact (as I will develop in Chapter VI), less energy consumption could help to restore some of the lost cohesion of American society.

It is easily imaginable that we might, if we were sufficiently wise, face forthrightly the closing of the energy frontier and begin rapidly and not unhappily to create a society of conservators. It is much more likely that we shall do so grudgingly out of sheer necessity. The degree of reluctance with which we face this prospect will determine how much social breakdown accompanies our shift from a growing energy society to a stable or declining energy society.

The single greatest difficulty in this shift is that we have no very good idea how to do it while at the same time maintaining high levels of employment, or low levels of unemployment. Even before the recession, America had the highest level of unemployment among the major industrial nations. Both conservative and liberal economists agree that even at best, prospects are bleak for any near-term return to pre-recession rates of unemployment. If, in fact, there is validity to the foregoing analysis, it seems extremely unlikely that unemployment rates can ever be brought back to 4 or even 5 percent by the use of conventional fiscal and monetary policies, unless we are willing to accept large deficits and double-digit inflation. Other means will thus have to be found to cope with the crucial problem of unemployment.

Shifting to a society of conservators will mean a reduction in the physical volume of goods and services per person. With the price of energy rising more rapidly than per capita income, people will be more cautious about buying goods that require a great deal of energy. They will buy smaller cars and drive them longer. They will buy fewer new air conditioners and use them less. They will be less likely to buy large freezers and self-defrosting refrigerators. They will take fewer long-distance trips. They will build fewer single homes and more garden-type apartments and condominiums that use less energy. This is only the beginning of a much longer list of changes that are surely coming. But it is enough to indicate that their purchases will not sustain as high a level of employment in these industries as heretofore.

Nor, as previously pointed out, will the service sector pick up the slack left by the decline in demand for energy-consuming goods. Taxpayers, understandably, are now strongly opposed to additional public spending, particularly at the state and local levels. Where, then, are the jobs to come from? Therein lies the most difficult and perhaps the most crucial domestic question our economists have ever faced. It can be solved neither by allowing the self-corrective forces of the system free rein, nor by manipulating the levers of fiscal and monetary policy. Waiting years for the unemployment rate to work its way back to what Americans used to think of as a tolerable level—4 percent (a level the Europeans and the Japanese have never regarded as acceptable)—would be a perilous course. Some alternative, or combination of alternatives, must be found. It will take extraordinary leadership, especially if the end of the era of growing affluence has actually been reached, to alter the attitudes of those who have jobs, status, and income toward the needs and the legitimacy of the claims of those who lack them. Yet the society is likely to be in increasingly deep trouble if this does not happen.

To exclude from full membership in our society millions of able-bodied people who are eager and ready to work, and hundreds of

thousands of others who are so defeated as to have lost their motivation to work, would be a perilous course for the nation. The failure of
the system to provide jobs for youth is particularly short-sighted. The
period from the time young people reach physical maturity until they
establish themselves in reasonably steady jobs is frequently the most
difficult time of adjustment in their entire lives. For many who have
grown up in the subcultures of poverty and near-poverty, the hurdles
are high and the failures numerous. Even in the best of times, these
disadvantaged have grave difficulty in getting jobs without experience, and none can get experience without jobs; in the worst of times,
the vicious circle closes tight around them. It is no wonder that so
many of them drift into the drug syndrome and from there into
crime. Society's neglect of this group is more costly every year—not
just in billions of dollars, but in terms of the pervasive deterioration
of lives.

Urban youth unemployment rates in 1975 exceeded 20 percent,
and in some cities Black youth unemployment exceeded 40 percent.
Youths without jobs are normally not entitled to unemployment
insurance, since they have not yet been established in the labor
market, the prerequisite to such insurance. If they are not living with
their families (and many come from broken homes and have become
alienated from what may be left of these "homes"), they are not, in
many states, eligible for welfare unless they produce a child. Stealing
or dope peddling are almost the only options for a substantial proportion of the impoverished, unemployed, detached males. The employment and training programs of the Department of Labor are far
too limited to cope successfully with such levels of unemployment as
were reached in 1974-75—and are predicted for the balance of the
1970s. A system that encourages irresponsible parenthood and drives
unemployed youth into crime is about as poorly designed as can be
imagined.

If it is to survive, there must be major modifications in the
American economic system's methods of allocating jobs and income.
There must be a realization that reasonable social stability demands
that the Federal Government take the leadership in providing the
financial underpinning for a subsidized nationwide program of useful
employment for both youth and adults. While new approaches to the
supplementation of income for the working poor and rationalization
of the welfare programs are also of high importance, they take second

place to the all-important matter of providing jobs—the only avenue to full membership in the society—to those who need and should have them.

It is not my purpose to present a comprehensive plan for the Federal Government to encourage greater employment by the private sector and the provision of Federally financed public-service jobs. Opportunities abound, but they require imaginative leadership, design, and exposition. Payment for useful work would make vastly better social sense, even though the direct and immediate monetary cost is greater, than continuing to try to cope with income-maintenance problems through the extension of unemployment insurance, provision of welfare after the unemployment insurance runs out, or the devising of a new program that would put more dollars in the hands of recipients without giving them greater access to jobs.

What will happen if there is a failure of leadership and the people with jobs, status, and income (especially that top one-fifth, who receive more than 40 percent of the national income) do not realize they must consent to being taxed more heavily in order to bring much of the excluded subculture of American society into full membership? To provide a partial answer to this question, it is necessary to seek to understand the social dynamics of such exclusion.

In these first three chapters, we have analyzed the economic limitations and vulnerabilities of our high-energy society. It is no less important to examine the counterpart, its social vulnerabilities. The next two chapters are an effort to probe some of the central aspects of these social vulnerabilities—weaknesses frequently observed but rarely examined in relation to the essential operating requirements of a successful society.

IV. The Internal Vulnerabilities of Modern Technological Society

Under the impact of the 1974 coal miners' strike in Britain, the English public became keenly aware of the fragility of human relationships formerly taken for granted. Unspectacular though they are most of the time, these webs of mutual trust, spun of invisible fiber into organizational form, are as important to the functioning of high-energy technology as its supplies of oil and coal. These webs consist of a number of requisite behavior patterns to which the human operators of a technological society must adhere. Many of them have been taken for granted and barely recognized for what they are—the connective tissue of that society.

FOUR REQUISITE BEHAVIOR PATTERNS

Four such patterns are: (1) a high order of compliance on the part of the vast majority of members of the key organizations of the society with the decisions of authorized supervisors, managers, and officials; (2) a low percentage of acutely alienated persons willing to take major personal risks to sabotage such organizations from within or the larger technostructure from without; (3) a sufficient supply of specialized and qualified manpower, and especially of talented managerial leadership, able and willing to design complex systems and knit together the component operations of the major enterprises; and (4) least appreciated of all, a supportive social structure and body politic on which the separate organizations of the technostructure can depend to furnish the needed reservoirs of manpower, credit, social order, and other requisites of success.

1. A high order of compliance. That a high order of compliance with management and governmental decisions is essential to any successful system may seem self-evident, but some elaboration will clarify its imperative quality. Consider the Apollo program, in which some 300,000 people, working through thousands of contractors and subcontractors, were successfully meshed into an extraordinarily complex technological enterprise. It is inconceivable that NASA could have put the astronauts on the moon, enabled them to explore it, and brought them back to successful splashdowns right on target, time after time, without an unusually high level of discipline and compliance with decisions. Although there was significant opportunity for inventiveness within many participants' orbits of responsibility, there was little tolerance for failure to carry out key decisions and instructions issued by those at higher echelons. And despite the multiplicity of electronic feedback mechanisms to help the human organization, the importance of sufficient discipline to guarantee compliance with agreed-upon decisions could hardly have been greater. The more complex the technology and the human organizations needed to support it, the more important becomes the principle of compliance with duly constituted decisions and willingness to respect and abide by the rules of the system.

In contravention of law, the sanitation men of the City of New York went on strike in 1968 and stayed off the job long enough to create a serious public health hazard. What occurred was a system breakdown similar to, but not as serious as, the British coal miners' strike. The use of raw economic and social power—a form of social blackmail— superseded traditional willingness to operate by the agreed-upon rules. Nothing could be more self-evident than that the total society would degenerate into chaos if each segment in a position to exercise such blackmail were to decide to use that power to the hilt.

A high-energy, high-rise society is immensely more vulnerable to social blackmail than a low-energy one. There are scores, probably hundreds, of specialized occupations that are so essential to the functioning of a large, modern city that their practitioners hold a powerful threat over major segments of the public. Compliance with a set of rules that precludes the collapse of urban systems has so far been achieved, but by a thin margin. The hazard of that margin, and the difficulty of maintaining it under the conditions likely to prevail for the balance of the century, are grounds for grave concern.

Within industry, there are numerous forms of noncompliance with the rules and disciplines essential to good and competitive production, and they have increased over the years to an astounding and hazardous degree. It is disturbing to run down even a very incomplete list of such forms of noncompliance with what in former years would have been considered basic standards of organizational behavior: organized slowdowns on factory production lines; "job actions"—organized failure to report to work on the part of large segments of a particular work force; wildcat strikes, contrary to union contracts; boredom and carelessness on the production lines and in numerous other parts of the production system; alcoholism and drug use on the job; large-scale absenteeism on a casual, unorganized basis; high turnover of personnel, resulting in substantial numbers of workers with subminimal training; and the almost total disappearance of pride in craftsmanship.

All of these behavior patterns slow down the nation's economic growth and some of them create serious safety hazards for consumers. As we shall see later, the problem of compliance becomes even more serious when we look at the whole society in relation to the technostructure.* Noncompliance with the imperatives of the system has for some time been cutting into productivity and making American products more expensive and less attractive in comparison with foreign competition.

2. A low level of sabotage. This is a companion to the first requisite. The goals and methods of the various organizations that are key to the operation of the technostructure must be such as to avoid intense alienation from within or animosity from without. A tiny percentage of intensely alienated employees who are willing to take major risks to sabotage the system can either slow it down or bring it to a temporary standstill. Similarly, nonemployees bitterly opposed to the purposes or methods of the enterprise can obstruct its operation in various ways.

---

*Technostructure is a term used here to mean the collective operation of the nation's large private corporations.

Saboteurs are often psychotic, and high-energy technology gives unprecedented scope for those with destructive tendencies. Many of them have so little to cherish and so much to envy and hate that they care little for life, either their own, or anybody else's. Lesser forms of destructive activity are perpetrated by unemployed and disaffected youth, addicts, and others whose aberrations fall short of psychoses. Among the forms of destructive behavior to which technological society is especially vulnerable are: the planting of bombs, throwing of Molotov cocktails, and sending of letter bombs; arson; the cutting of power lines and sabotage of generating plants; derailment and the wrecking of trains; assassination, kidnaping, and the murder of key members of governmental and business organizations; burglaries, assaults, and other felonies which reach such a numerical level as to cut markedly the productivity of the technostructure; and white-collar crime at a similar level.

All of these and other forms of destructive activity have been resorted to increasingly by alienated members of society. When the threshold of restraint within the surrounding society falls, the number of psychotics who feel they can achieve their moment in the sun through dramatic acts of perverted heroism sharply increases. About 1 percent of the population are estimated to manifest psychotic symptoms in varying degrees—some 2 million people. Not all or even a substantial proportion of these are potential saboteurs, but if conditions should increase their alienation so that even one-tenth of them became saboteurs, they could bring our fragile technostructure to a grinding halt. Imagine tens of thousands of angry and unhinged men and women like the "Mad Bomber" (who was released from a mental institution in 1973 at the age of 70), an intensely disgruntled employee of Consolidated Edison in New York, who planted bombs both in the company's power plants and elsewhere some forty times before he was apprehended and committed.

The trial of Arthur Bremer for the attempted assassination of George Wallace in 1972 revealed the mind of a man who wanted his name to go down in the history books for something, no matter what; he wanted to blast the system he blamed for making him into a cipher. The two attempts on President Ford's life in 1975 revealed similar mental aberrations. How many more such people are there walking around in society, and how much impetus will it take to push them over the brink into similar action? It is not a pleasant thought, but if unemployment should continue for some time at or near its 1975 level of 8-9 percent the number of such persons will undoubtedly increase and their threshold of restraint will drop.

While political assassination may not appear to be directly related to the ability of the production system to keep functioning and achieve higher levels of productivity and complexity, it is important to keep in mind that the effectiveness of the technostructure is so closely related to the effectiveness of the political system that the two are inseparable in system terms. One cannot help wondering whether the appeal of high political office under current conditions has diminished to a dangerously low point for men with the capacity and balance to become statesmen, while it maintains its appeal to men whose ambition and search for glory greatly exceed their wisdom and capacity for cogent analysis.

3. Adequate supplies of qualified manpower. The supplies of specialized manpower and talented managerial leadership, able and willing to knit together the component operations of an enterprise have generally been assumed to be automatically available. At least, it has been assumed that with government-subsidized education and training for a wide variety of skills, the market mechanism will operate to produce an adequate supply of appropriately skilled manpower, and to provide both the technostructure and the surrounding society with the skills needed when they are needed. It has, in fact, worked this way in many respects, but now the demands for unusually qualified manpower are greatly outrunning the supply.

By "qualified manpower," I mean people with the knowledge, character, imagination, and foresight needed to make decisions that will benefit the members of the system not just for the short run, but for the longer range. Knowledge is needed to deal with both short- and long-run decisions. Character is needed to shun the opportunism of short-run advantage for the long-run benefit of all (or most) persons related to the system. Imagination and foresight are needed to comprehend the widespread ramifications of each decision and to help distinguish between short-run illusory advantage and long-run genuine advantage. Let's look at a hypothetical situation involving these elements.

George Baxter, a corporation executive with headquarters in New York, is approached by the mayor of a midwestern city in which the corporation's largest plant is located. He wants the corporation to undertake a program to train and employ 50-100 out-of-school youths, most of them Black, each year as a contribution to the upgrading of the skills, employment, income, and stability of the community. The mayor has previously approached the plant manager, who has told him that there is no room in his budget for such a program.

The company has eight plants, four of which have been built in the South since World War II. The Southern plants have higher productivity per worker, less absenteeism, and less labor trouble. The productivity in the Midwestern plant has been deteriorating for some time as the older workers, some of them first-generation Europeans, have retired and been replaced by younger, poorly disciplined workers who have high rates of absenteeism, error-ridden performance, and higher wage rates than the Southern plants. The company's board of directors has been urging the executive to consider phasing out the midwestern plant entirely and enlarging the Southern plants to absorb the workload. What should George Baxter's response to the mayor be?

As it happens, Baxter grew up in this particular Midwestern city and worked his way up to plant manager before being promoted to an executive position in the New York headquarters office. He has fond recollections of the community as he knew it and is sad that the central city is deteriorating, but he does not see how his company can do much to help overcome the city's problems. Agreeing to the mayor's proposal would be contrary to the financial interests of the stockholders, and he would be criticized for it by his board of directors. Another factor in the picture is that his company may soon be taken over by a multinational conglomerate, and he has a chance of becoming a high official of the larger corporation. He does not wish to jeopardize that possibility by throwing good money after bad in a plant that is now barely profitable. Baxter's loyalty to his home town has sharply diminished since his move to New York, and in any event he rationalizes that he should not allow nostalgia to bias sound business decisions. His general interest in the preservation of central cities from further decay is slight, and his vision of or concern for the future of American society is limited. In his suavest, most courteous, and most reluctant manner, Baxter tells the mayor that he has no choice but to say no. The company's financial situation cannot stand the added burden, and furthermore, it would be a disservice to the youth of the city to train them for what could become nonexistent jobs.

Let us suppose that Baxter had more imagination and foresight, and a stronger character. He might respond to the mayor quite differently: "Mr. Mayor, I understand what you are trying to do, and I admire you for it. Our plant manager in your city was absolutely right that his budget cannot stand the cost of the training program you propose. The fact that you have not taken his 'no' for a final answer and have come to New York to talk to me about it is itself a most helpful sign for your city. You tell me that you have approached several other plants and only one has been at all receptive. Let me make a suggestion to you.

"None of the executives of the plants in your city wants the city to continue to deteriorate, but none can afford to make a large charitable contribution that will go down the drain. I suggest you do the following things, and then I will tell you what we will do. I suggest you convene a conference of the major business interests in your city, including the executives of locally owned companies and top executives from the parent companies of those plants that are not locally owned. Invite appropriate representatives of organized labor, the state labor department, and the Manpower Administration of the Department of Labor. Ask the governor to give the opening speech. Then get down to the business of working out a plan for maximizing training and employment in the city. You are going to need a planning office you don't now have, and you will need some help in setting up a good one, not just for this conference but for the long range. Then you will need some help in estimating how many training slots it is reasonable to try to get each company to agree to sponsor. You will have to dicker with them to do more than they originally offer, and the more information you have with which to do the dickering, the better off you will be. You are also going to need all the help you can get from your Congressional delegation to get as much money out of the Labor Department as possible.

"Now I'll tell you what my company will do and what I will do personally. I will come to your conference. If you want me to, I will make a short speech urging the parent companies to allocate money from their central budgets for this purpose as a part of the imperative national need to save the nation's central cities. Not only that, but if some of the parent companies are reluctant to send representatives to the conference, or plan to send low-level functionaries with no authority, I will call any of the top executives whom I know personally and urge them to come. If you want to set up a planning office—which I strongly urge you to do, because without it, I do not think the plan will work—I will lend you our top planning man for a short time to advise you on how to staff it and even, perhaps, give you some tips on how to get money for it. He can also show the men in the planning office, when you get it set up, how to get the information needed to deal with some of the big companies.

"One other thing you will need to do is to talk with uncommon candor to the union officials of your city, and perhaps even some at the national level, to gain their cooperation and support for a concerted effort to raise the productivity and the quality of workmanship of the union members so that the plants in your city can compete successfully in national and international markets. You might even be able to develop a model educational program that would have applicability elsewhere in demonstrating to workers what they and management are up against in terms of increasing competition from lower wage sectors of the nation and from abroad. I think I know where you could get some financial help for such a program if you've got the nerve to try to get it organized. Now, how does all this strike you? It will take a lot of doing, but nothing less is likely to pay off."

Which kind of a Baxter do we have in most executive positions? The question answers itself. The supply of Baxters of the second type in relation to the need is very small. This applies with equal or greater force to the Baxters of the political world, as well as various other "worlds" within our society. Is it in the nature of things that we cannot produce enough people with the qualities needed to become effective leaders of the organizations and institutions of our society? If so, why? Does it have something to do with the inherent nature of technological society, or is it our particular economic system or social structure? These are key questions to which we shall return, but let us take a brief look here at the impact of science and technology on our educational system and on the production of leaders.

The increasing compartmentalization of knowledge requires more and more people to become specialists of one kind or another, to the point where most members of technological society are employed in narrow specialties. But specialized training, followed by specialized technical and professional work, only increases the complexity of the technostructure and the larger society, making it more difficult to mesh the ever more numerous specialists into a durable social fabric. This is where the role of management and executive leadership comes in.

If we analogize the specialized occupations to the warp of the fabric of our society, then the legislators, the judges, the public administrators, and others who perform integrative social roles are the woof, and in a business enterprise it is the managers and the executives. When the warp of a fabric is comparatively strong and the woof relatively weak, the fabric quickly becomes frayed. This is precisely what is happening to our social fabric: The men and women who fill the integrative occupations are not strong enough to hold the social warp together. Business organizations are having the same difficulty, though not yet to quite such an intense degree.

The "Peter Principle" is relevant here: Dr. Laurence Peter said that each person tends to rise to his level of incompetence within any organization. That is, when he does a job well, he is promoted again and again until he reaches the point where he is over his head—his "level of incompetence." Then he is no longer promoted, but neither is he demoted; he remains, therefore, at his level of incompetence. This principle is applicable to supervisors and executives of large organizations and, distressingly, just as applicable to the totality of American society.

Politicians tend to be promoted to their level of incompetence rather faster than members of large corporations or bureaucracies for several reasons. The first is that elective positions of major responsibility—especially big-city mayoralties, governorships, and the Presidency—are the most difficult to perform well. One's level of competence or incompetence has to be judged, of course, in relation to the difficulty of the job undertaken; the more complex the job, the smaller the potential supply of persons who could fill it competently.

Second, the unpleasant aspects of politics deter many people who may have the talent. The electoral process is so demanding on the physical and monetary resources of most politicians, particularly those who are scrupulous and conscientious, that the most competent young people thinking about careers are loath to consider politics. If and when they should select such a career and if they are elected, the legitimate demands on their energies are so enormous, and the presumptions on their time and on their personal and family privacy by insensitive members of their constituency so great, that it makes life close to unbearable for many an elected official with a sense of public purpose. For those who stick with politics, the enjoyment of prestige and power, and a sense of dedication to public service, may manage to overcome the disadvantages. But the supply of politicians with first-rate abilities and real sensitivity is markedly curtailed by the all-consuming nature of the occupation.

Third, our complex technological society has not yet learned how to develop its own leaders. It knows how to develop scientists, engineers, doctors, lawyers, and scores of other professionals, but it has no schools for politicians and no professional standards, either self-imposed or achieved by general consensus. It does not even have any good means for aiding voters to distinguish between those who are genuinely competent and the politicians with meretricious answers to complex social problems.

I have emphasized here the acute shortage of people with high talent for "making a mesh of things," to use the phrase of the late Paul Appleby, a skilled public administrator. This is where the manpower shortage can have and is having its most severe effect on the operation of the total society. If the technostructure and the surrounding society are symbiotic—as they surely are—it is evident that the complexities being generated by the technostructure are outrunning the capacity of the political leaders to comprehend and redress the problems created by them. The technostructure is therefore undermining itself in this respect, as in various others.

4. A supportive surrounding society. The society that surrounds the technostructure, is, to a large degree, the unplanned product of that technostructure. No one in business or industry ever willed the creation of New York or Los Angeles as they exist today, but these cities are the indirect effects of the development of electric motors, elevators, skyscrapers, automobiles, airplanes, and the like. Nobody designed them; they just grew by accretion. They might, in fact, have turned out to be more dysfunctional if they had resulted from an attempt at comprehensive governmental planning. The complexity of these and numerous other cities has now become so great that it staggers the imagination and defies efficient management. Latter day attempts at city planning—both physical and operational—have sought to make some sort of order out of increasing chaos, but with rare success.

Beyond the limits of the major cities lie their independent satellites, some industrial and commercial, some "bedroom" and TV-watching communities, held together principally by school, water, and sewerage systems, and zoning authority. These, too, are the unplanned products of the technostructure, along with the real-estate developers, the Federal highway lobby, and the desire of commuters for at least economically stratified segregation. These suburban subsystems are obviously not supportive of the central cities, nor are they basically functional in respect to the technostructure—the productive heart of technological society. Quite the contrary; they complicate life for the core cities, taking more money out of them than they put back into them, while placing a disproportionate demand for public services on the cities. Most commuters take little or no responsibility for the improvement of the central cities in which they work. They fiercely resist most efforts to incorporate their suburban communities into larger units of government, or to levy or increase state taxes and pass funds back to central cities to fight urban blight.

Cities and their suburbs cannot, therefore, be regarded as mutually supportive subsystems of technological society, but are in fact destructively competitive subsystems. Nor is it possible for city planners to alter these basic relationships.

It is not only urban and suburban disorganization that causes the surrounding society to be nonsupportive of the technostructure's objectives of production and growth, but the lack of any pervasive sense of responsibility on the part of the technostructure for the welfare of the society as a whole. As emphasized by John Kenneth Galbraith, the overriding motivation of the technostructure is corporate growth and feathering the nests of the corporate bureaucracy. Its officials should not allow themselves, they believe, to spend more than token amounts of the income that would otherwise be shared by their stockholders and themselves for the purpose of shouldering undefined responsibilities for the public interest. When their corporate efforts to grow and make profits conflict with a vague sense of responsibility to help make the surrounding society more viable, the corporate interests come first. As with cities and suburbs, businesses and cities are not mutually supportive subsystems either.

For the technostructure, the realities of international competition seem to force a course of action that contributes to the deterioration of the surrounding society. In international markets, where products compete with those of low-wage economies, American sales can only be maintained by capital-intensive and automated production. The more complex the machinery and the more automated the production process, the less unskilled and semi-skilled labor is needed, and the greater the number of persons made surplus to the needs of the technostructure. As the proportion of persons employed by the technostructure declines, a correspondingly larger proportion must either be employed by the private-service sector or the government or be unemployed. The same tendencies are at work in the service sector, which is becoming more and more mechanized and capital-intensive. Gradually, a higher proportion of the population is becoming surplus to the needs and profitability of the production system, and it is hard to see where the jobs will come from to absorb these workers.

Defenders of automation have often argued that the total number of jobs has been going up, recessions aside, and that automation's effect is actually to increase the number of jobs elsewhere in the economy, principally in the service sector. While it is true that the number of jobs has risen substantially during the last two decades, it is also true that the number of low-skilled people who can find no niche in the economy has likewise risen rapidly. Unemployment figures, serious as they are, mask the large and growing number of people who regard themselves as outcasts from the production economy and are no longer looking for work. The dismaying rise in the welfare rolls is one of the best indicators we have of the number of these outcasts. Between 1960 and 1975, the number of adults covered under the Aid to Families with Dependent Children program rose from less than 1 million to over 4 million, and the number of children receiving benefits climbed from 2 million to 12 million. While many of these families have not completely given up, many others have. And large numbers of these children are growing up under conditions that will encourage them to become members of a permanent underclass, unable to find any avenue into the mainstream of society.

How could a society that excludes such large segments from

genuine membership and active participation expect to avoid intense
alienation, one of the most serious vulnerabilities of high-energy
technology? All sorts of counterproductive activity can be expected
from a major segment of society that has been excluded from membership. Crime must be regarded as an expected reaction to such
exclusion and it is happening at an ever rising rate.

Not only do we witness counterproductive and antisocial behavior
from those who are excluded from membership in the society, but we
are also dismayed by what appear to be antisocial actions from various
components of the central majority of American society, and even
from the leaders of American society. If the prevailing ethic is
"What's in it for me?" from the top to the bottom of society, how can
we expect the system to work in the broad public interest? In times of
economic adversity, many labor leaders would rather allow a factory,
a newspaper, a theater, or any of a thousand enterprises go under
than accept a cut in wages, or even a continuation of wages at current
levels. Unions and others keep pressing to raise minimum wages
even when it is demonstrable that to do so will accelerate the substitution of machines for people, with no new employment opportunities in sight for the energies of the people thus rendered surplus
and obsolete. Corporation executives keep raising their bloated
salaries with no regard to the restraints expected of their employees.
Truckers block the highways with their huge rigs in protest against
the national lowering of the speed limit and the increase in the cost of
diesel fuel during a world energy crisis because their take-home pay
has decreased. Each looks upon the economic system, including its
crises, as a power struggle and seeks to protect his direct and
immediate self-interest. Just imagine what a nationwide strike of
computer programmers and console operators may be able to do a
decade hence at the rate we are being computerized.

I have sought here to highlight the inherent vulnerabilities of
high-energy technology that might limit its future development. We
have been accustomed to think that the fruits of high-energy technology, relieving the human family of all kinds of onerous burdens, are
strongly positive in their net social effects. We have been accustomed to measuring and talking about those beneficial results by
pointing to a constantly rising GNP. The idea that the adverse
side-effects of high-energy technology might some time become

sufficiently serious to outweigh the beneficial effects is new to us. The idea that the time when those adverse side-effects overtake the direct favorable effects might be now—in the mid-1970s—rather than in the 21st century, as suggested by the authors of *The Limits to Growth*, is no longer unthinkable.

V. The Chasm Between Rights and Responsibilities

Beginning with the New Deal, and especially since World War II, a rapid growth has occurred in legally guaranteed rights and in the assertion of additional claims to moral rights, without corresponding acceptance of added responsibilities. This has been a pervasive trend throughout all segments of society, and a resulting chasm has developed between rights and responsibilities—in great contrast to nonmodernized agrarian societies, where rights are few and inconspicuous, while responsibilities are the foundation of family and community life. How solidly grounded and durable a society can be when its citizens demand and are granted legal rights that vastly outweigh the responsibilities assigned to them or voluntarily assumed by them is, to say the least, a troublesome question.

Simply to list the principal rights that have accrued to American citizens over the last two centuries via the Constitution and Federal laws, and others that are asserted to be morally justified and seem to be moving toward legal status, and then to seek to find corresponding responsibilities is to realize the enormous imbalance:

Constitutional rights:
Right to freedom of speech.
Right to free assembly.
Right to freedom of religion.
Right to a free press.
Right to own private property.

Right of private economic enterprise (implicit).

Right to choose one's occupation and place of abode, and to travel without hindrance within the country (implicit).

Right to be secure in one's person, house, papers, and effects, against unreasonable search and seizure, and from arrest without a warrant.

Right to a speedy trial by jury of all persons accused of crimes.

Right to freedom from excessive bail, excessive fines, and cruel and unusual punishment.

Right to counsel in any criminal trial.

Right to freedom from *ex post facto* laws or bills of attainder.

Right to freedom from state laws that would abridge the privileges and immunities of citizens of the United States or that would deprive any person of life, liberty, or property without due process of law.

Right of citizens to vote without abridgment on account of race, color, or previous condition of servitude.

Right of citizens to vote without regard to sex.

Right of citizens to vote if they have reached their eighteenth birthday.

Rights established by Federal statute:

Right to bargain collectively.

Right to strike (with limited and often ignored exceptions).

Right to a "decent" minimum wage, unrelated to productivity.

Right to unemployment insurance when employment is terminated through no fault of the employee (a *de facto* right under a Federal-state system of unemployment insurance).

Right to public assistance (welfare) when other sources of support do not exist (also a *de facto* right under a Federal-state system of public assistance).

Right to equal opportunity for employment without regard to race, national origin, or sex.

Right to equal pay for equal work.

Right of persons over sixty-five to an old-age benefit annuity and Medicare.

Right to government guarantee of protection against loss of funds deposited in banks and savings and loan associations.

Right to information about the government's conduct of its legal responsibilities.

Asserted moral rights, with varying degrees of legal force:
Right to necessary medical care without regard to ability to pay.
Right to a decent and adequately paying job.
Right to an assured basic income sufficient to avoid privation.
Right to adequate housing.
Right to safe consumer products.
Right to clean air and water.
Right to elementary and secondary educations of good quality on a
    nonsegregated, nondiscriminatory basis.
Right to as much education beyond the secondary-school level as is
    necessary to develop the full potential of each individual.
Right of women to the means for controlling pregnancy and to
    obtain abortions during the first two trimesters.
Right of privacy (freedom from wiretaps, electronic eavesdrop-
    ping, noncriminal dossiers, etc.).

Other asserted rights:
Right of workers to participate in management decisions.
Right of citizens to participate in local government decision-
    making by means other than voting.
Right to accessible child-care centers.

This is not, of course, a full list, but it should be sufficient to test
the comparative weight of rights and responsibilities in the social
balance scale. Responsibilities appear to be limited to four basic
peacetime duties, the first two of which are to be performed during
the shortening period—hardly even a half-life—between the com-
pletion of education and the age of voluntary or involuntary retire-
ment: (1) working and earning the wherewithal to support oneself
and one's dependents, if any, assuming there is no independent
income—a responsibility in which the underlying moral force rapidly
diminishes when the opportunity to work is not provided by the
private and public sectors of society; (2) obeying statute laws (mainly
prohibitions) and fulfilling contracts voluntarily entered into (the
common law); (3) paying taxes; and (4) voting.

Self-support and family support, more implicit than explicit in our
legal system, have undergone considerable erosion, particularly in
the past decade. Obedience to statute laws has also been declining as
such laws have proliferated, and their enforcement has become more

difficult, more time-consuming, and more ineffective. Taxes, of course, are never ending, except for the poorest, and even they are heavily hit by sales and indirect taxes. Voting is commonly regarded as an obligation, but as the difficulty of sorting out the complex issues increases, and as more citizens become cynical about the capacity of government to govern, voting seems to an increasing number of citizens not so much a responsibility as a waste of time.

As a general proposition, therefore, it can be said that the only enlarged affirmative responsibility that the government has laid upon its citizens in order to support and balance the numerous and expensive new rights they have been accorded since the mid-1930s is to pay more taxes. In the minds of most citizens, rights are rights, and taxes are discriminatory and unnecessarily heavy burdens upon hard-working citizens to support a bloated bureaucracy, with no understandable connection between them.

FOUR DECADES OF RISING EXPECTATIONS FOR GOVERNMENT BENEFITS

Even if the tax burden were borne without a grumble, it is hard to see how a society could go on indefinitely granting more and more expensive legal entitlements without building a corresponding foundation of responsibilities for the structure of rights. Even the one presumably sturdy component of the foundation—the tax base—is weakening. Let us review briefly how Americans came to expect more from the Federal Government than it can possibly provide.

For nearly a century and a half after the Constitution and the Bill of Rights were adopted, the disparity between rights and responsibilities was not sufficient to be of great consequence. Federal programs included neither cash payments nor costly services to individuals. The rights established by the Constitution were, for the most part, enforced by the courts, and hardly any administrative bureaucracy was necessary. Only when the role of the Federal Government began to change drastically as a result of the Great Depression did the imbalance between rights and responsibilities start to generate problems, barely perceptible to begin with, but developing rapidly in the 1960s and 1970s.

At the time of the Depression, with somewhere between a quarter and a third of the work force unemployed and businesses and banks crashing, there were no government-operated safety nets to protect people against bankruptcy and starvation and the Federal Government was the only institution capable of rescuing them. The major role of Franklin Roosevelt and his New Deal was to build both short and long-term economic safeguards. The short-term rescue operations—the Civilian Conservation Corps, the Federal Emergency Relief Administration, the Works Progress Administration, the Public Works Administration, and the National Youth Administration—served their purpose and disappeared when the defense industries of World War II took their place. Long-term legislation began the process of putting the Federal Government in the permanent role as principal agent of the people in guaranteeing economic rights. The laws included: the Social Security Act, establishing old-age, survivors', and (later) disability insurance, a system of Federally mandated, state designed and administered unemployment insurance, and a system of Federal matching grants to states to establish programs of public assistance to the needy; the National Labor Relations Act, guaranteeing the right of labor unions to bargain collectively and the right to strike (with certain exceptions); the Federal Deposit Insurance Act, guaranteeing the security of bank deposits, and a companion act for savings and loan associations; the acts establishing the Home Owners Loan Corporation and the Farm Credit Administration to prevent homeowners and farmers from losing their homes and farms through foreclosure; and the Securities and Exchange Act to protect stock investors against fraud and other financial malpractice, and to some extent against their own imprudence. These formed the basic framework of what came to be regarded, rather informally, as a new economic bill of rights, later to be supplemented with other measures, foremost among them the Employment Act of 1946, which stated: "The Congress hereby declares that it is the continuing policy and responsibility of the Federal Government to . . . promote maximum employment, production, and purchasing power." It did not establish the right of every able-bodied person to a job, but it began to build a presumption in that direction which might eventually be converted into a claimed right.

From the 1930s onward, the public's expectations of the Federal Government grew by leaps and bounds. When World War II demanded their total commitment to a great national effort—a temporary responsibility they willingly shouldered—they found the Federal Government running their lives, drafting them for the armed forces, rationing their food and gasoline, controlling the wages they could receive and the prices they had to pay or could charge, and taxing them heavily. With its seemingly beneficial effect on the American economy and the economic status of most Americans, the war carried the public a long step further in the direction of regarding the Federal Government as a powerful and effective instrumentality of the people to accomplish whatever their leaders decided was necessary or desirable. Under the President's leadership, the government had waged and won a two-front war; despite the annoyances of wage and price controls and rationing, the government had demonstrated its ability to manage a wartime economy and improve the relative economic condition of vast numbers of Americans; it had aided numerous businesses to build up their plant and equipment and to acquire new techniques and expertise. The Federal Government had been converted in a little over a decade from a remote conductor of foreign affairs, aloof and impotent in most domestic matters, to a potentially benign and extraordinarily potent intervener in domestic affairs. Thereafter, it was expected to be the guarantor of the nation's economic health.

With another turn of the wheel of time came the Supreme Court's decision invalidating school segregation by race, and then, after a few years, the painful process of enforcing it. Probably no act of Dwight Eisenhower's Presidency was more distasteful to him than having to call out the National Guard to reinforce the power of Federal marshals to carry out the court order to integrate the high school in Little Rock, and probably no act was more symbolic of the steadily enlarging role of the Federal Government as a guarantor of social as well as economic rights. During the next decade, that responsibility was expanded enormously by both the courts and the Congress. The early 1960s was the period of the most prolific enactment of legislation in the nation's history, imposing duties upon the Federal Government to guarantee rights and to create programs that placed heavy and continuing claims on the Federal budget. It was the era of the Great Society: the War on Poverty (which turned out to be a series of skirmishes); the Civil Rights Act; Medicare and Medicaid; aid to elementary, secondary, and higher education; increased old-age, survivors', and disability benefits; liberalized public-assistance laws to include families with unemployed parents; and many other expensive laws. It was an unprecedented burst of claims upon the Treasury, claims which were often asserted as moral rights that should be

recognized as such and converted to legal status. Meanwhile, there
was no increase in Federal income tax rates. It seemed magical.
Group after group successfully prevailed upon the President and the
lawmakers to support their claims to a basic requirement for survival
—Federal subsidy. And all without the need to put Congressmen
in the awkward position of voting for a tax increase. How could this
be?

It could be, of course, for a simple and politically painless reason.
As the national income rose, individual incomes rose—because of
both increased productivity and inflation—and as incomes rose,
people paid more taxes. This would have occurred even with a
flat-rate income tax, but with the graduated income tax, people
moved up into higher brackets and paid higher rates. *De facto*,
therefore, tax rates were going up for individuals without any change
in the law or the rate scale. No Congressman or Senator had to face
his constituency and defend himself for having voted for a tax
increase. The added revenues seemed to come effortlessly, and
Congress came to look upon the "fiscal dividend" as a source of
endless opportunity to meet the steadily rising demand from the
public for more services from the government and more rights to be
guaranteed by it. The public, by and large, saw no relationship
between these services and rights and the taxes it paid. Social responsibility seemed to have been almost totally shifted from the individual to the Federal Government. Public expectations, converted to
asserted moral rights, soared.

In only one program—Social Security—was there a clear linkage in
the public mind between taxes paid and the accrual of rights. In this
case, Congress did regularly vote for an increase in tax rates, knowing
that the recipients of Social Security benefits would strike them
dead, politically speaking, if they did not raise the taxes sufficiently
to cover the steadily increasing outgo from the Social Security Trust
Fund. Workers might grumble, but they could make no headway in
organizing political support to hold payroll tax rates low, since there
would then not be enough money to pay the legally assured retire-
ment, survivors', and disability benefits. Much has been written in
recent years attacking the Social Security system, and behind many
of these objections lies the dislike of accepting the full responsibility
that is the inescapable concomitant of the rights granted by the
system.

The Federal income tax for individuals has, with very minor exceptions, never been raised during peacetime. Since the first and very low rate schedule was enacted following the approval of the 16th Amendment to the Constitution in 1913, significant general rate increases have occurred only during wartime. If taxpayers had been able to foresee the amounts that their children and grandchildren would have to pay in income taxes, they might never have agreed to that amendment, but they were assured that this was to be a means of raising moderate amounts of revenue from the minority blessed with substantial incomes. Circumstances alter commitments, though, especially in politics, and two world wars released Congress from even the memory of such assurances. Income tax rates were increased during World War I to help pay for that war, and were not reduced to their prewar level after the war was over. In fact, the income tax yielded consistent surpluses during the 1920s, even after paying for amortization of the Liberty Bonds, veterans' benefits, and the generally higher cost of a still small Federal establishment. The surplus that troubled Federal budget directors in the 1920s disappeared, of course, with the stock market crash of 1929, and the Depression that followed. Keynesian deficit financing became the order of the day. Then came World War II, creating an unquestioned need for high and steeply graduated taxes, ranging up to 90 percent at the topmost increments. No Congressman or Senator was faced with any serious political recrimination for having voted for such a huge tax increase; taxpayers with high incomes could hardly compare their sacrifices adversely with the 11 million men and women in uniform. It was at this time that the Ruml Plan, requiring employers to become tax collectors and withhold from their employees' pay checks the estimated tax for which workers were liable, was instituted, making taxpaying relatively painless for the millions of persons who had never been subject to income tax but who suddenly became the backbone of the Federal tax system. Thus, workers never saw their full pay, and they were not faced with the shock of having to pay their taxes in a lump sum after the year was over, as had previously been the case. Because of the good wartime wages and premium pay for overtime, the public accustomed itself to the new high tax rates with comparatively little complaint.

After the war was over, taxes were readjusted downward to some degree to accommodate to the lower Federal budget, and in the thirty years since then there have been a number of significant reductions in the rate schedule while the Federal budget rose. For the graduated tax structure contained the inherent dynamic that enabled the tax yield to increase steadily and substantially, without an increase in the rate, as long as the economy grew. It was a golden era for Presidents, Congressmen, and Senators bent on solving the nation's problems through the addition of new social programs.

Despite the enormous increase in the Federal budget since 1945, the GNP has risen fast enough to provide most citizens with a higher net income after taxes each year than they had the year before. Meanwhile, great numbers of citizens and institutions came to depend on the Federal Government for transfer payments, subsidies, grants, and contracts as a critical source of income. This applied to Social Security beneficiaries, public-assistance recipients, civil service and military retirees, state and local governments, all levels of educational institutions, research institutes, defense industries, and numerous others. Many of these had escalator clauses geared to the cost of living. The budget could go in no direction but up, even if the economy went down. Standing in line in 1976, waiting to be added to the budget and treated as permanent rights of all citizens, are such expensive programs as national health insurance and a minimum assured income (some variation of the negative income tax) to take the place of the unsatisfactory welfare (public assistance) program. These and others are expected by their proponents to be added without any general increase in income tax rates. But by now public expectations greatly exceed what is economically possible; rights have outrun fiscal responsibilities.

THE DIFFICULTIES OF ESTABLISHING LINKAGES BETWEEN RIGHTS AND RESPONSIBILITIES

It probably never occurred to the authors of the Bill of Rights to write into the Constitution a Bill of Responsibilities. If it had occurred to them, they would probably not have found it feasible, since it would have been an extremely awkward thing to do, from a legal standpoint. It was taken for granted that each citizen would be responsible for his and his family's support, and for such support of the community and nation as each required. Since all 13 colonies were made up of farms and small towns, with only a few cities of consequence, responsibilities, to the extent that they went beyond the family, were cooperatively determined by one's neighbors in a town meeting or its equivalent. Neighbors, individually and collectively, could observe the manner in which agreed-upon responsibilities were carried out, whether they involved assigning work to, and feeding, landless paupers, doing one's share of the road maintenance, or whatever. Since citizens and their families were remote from their national government, and largely self-sufficient within communities where they knew almost everyone else and could observe their behavior, responsibility was implicit in daily life.

The essence of community and of social responsibility are one and the same: common roots in a place and a common feeling of mutual support among a group that trusts and is basically loyal to one another. When communities are small enough so that each person recognizes by sight and knows the names of most of the persons he or she sees each day and feels that he or she knows or has some sort of meaningful access to the leaders of the community and role in it, the concept of responsibility can be and usually is inextricably integrated with daily living. The larger the social unit, the more difficult it becomes to achieve this mesh, and when the political unit becomes a huge city, where people live in mammoth high-rise apartment complexes, shop in supermarkets, know few of the people they see on the streets, have no way of distinguishing "neighbors" from strangers and therefore belong to no community, the voluntary exercise of social responsibility becomes more exceptional and heroic than normal.

For an extended period, as cities grew, the neighborhood became the partial substitute for the community. Although neighborhoods were not political units and its members did not have control over most community services, they were somewhat cohesive segments of cities, segments in which people paid attention to each other, took pride in the appearance of their property, greeted each other in the small stores and shops that were frequently owned and operated by people who lived upstairs and treated customers as trusted friends, sometimes trusting them too much. Children usually went to neighborhood schools, and churches and synagogues were neighborhood institutions. In short, city neighborhoods were important partial substitutes for communities, and large numbers of people in them voluntarily accepted a substantial degree of responsibility for looking out for one another.

As the automobile culture developed, and as suburbs, shopping centers, and circumferential highways sent the middle classes spinning out of the central cities, leaving behind the poor and the rich, and as both of these groups became increasingly housed in high-rise apartments, neighborhoods lost their earlier cohesion. Fewer and fewer urban dwellers felt as though they owed any concern or loyalty to those who lived nearby, except for a few close friends who might or might not live within walking distance. As neighborhood cohesion went down, the opportunity for unpunished crime increased. Friends who did live within walking distance often became afraid to walk even a few blocks. In many cities, conditions have now reached the point where people who observe street crime taking place often turn away for fear of becoming involved. The mutual support that was the essence of community and neighborhood has thus melted into nothingness.

Mutual defense and support are the *sine qua non* of community and social responsibility. If societies are so structured—physically, socially, economically, and politically—that individuals are deterred from, and made afraid of, participation in a system of mutual support, as has become the case in many areas of large cities today, then it seems hard to see how such cities can hope to contribute to an improvement in the human condition.

Some small number of citizens of every city and subdivision have a strong inner drive to create social order out of the intricacies and complexities that are inherent in the operation of local government. When they try to bring about such social order, however, they find it incredibly difficult. At the root of the matter seem to be several interlocking sources of frustration, to which we have been alluding. The first is the steady erosion in the voluntary acceptance by citizens of various types of responsibility for improving the operation and maintenance of their cities. Most citizens know their rights and assert them, while few even recognize their responsibilities, much less accept and discharge them. The second is the continuing centrifugal effect of the out-migration of businesses and people as the cohesion of central cities diminishes. The third is the rapidly growing interdependence among local, state, and Federal governments; among the vast number of different parts of local governments; among these different parts and the businesses, institutions, groups, and individuals that make up each city; among local governments and semi-autonomous authorities, regional planning organizations, and the like, and so on, *ad infinitum*. The complexity, which defies human understanding and effective management, generates the fourth and most intractable of the sources of frustration: the powerful drive of vast numbers of participants in the process of governmental operation and management to establish and defend "territorial rights." Given the degree of complexity that has been created, it would be impossible for most people to think in terms of the effective operation of the total system, about the interrelationship between their assigned functions and those of the larger system and subsystems, of which their particular role is only a sub-sub-subsystem. In consequence, it is only natural that each participant should overvalue and overdefend the importance of his function as if it were physical territory that belonged to him.

These systems and subsystems constitute a social centrifuge of enormous proportions. No centripetal counterforce of sufficient strength to create among the body politic a sense of cohesion and mutual support at the local, state, and Federal levels appears close at hand. Despite Marshall McLuhan's assertion that with the coming of television and communications satellites all the world had become a village, in terms of direct personal responsibility for persons who live in close physical proximity, the trend has been quite the opposite. High-energy technology has been driving us toward anonymity and a diminished sense of community. Extreme complexity, accompanied unavoidably by extreme specialization and powerful special interest groups generate uncontrollable centrifugal force. These are incompatible with a manageable society.

It seems likely that social breakdowns will gradually increase. As they do, people are likely to develop inventive devices of group self-protection, thereby beginning the process of re-creating the essence of community, even while general national policy continues to move in the opposite direction—toward more centralization. Eventually, one or the other tendency is likely to become dominant. It is even conceivable that the two trends may be rationalized, with the Federal government taking full responsibility for certain functions which states and local communities cannot reasonably be expected to handle, and with states and local governments given much wider latitude, opportunity, and encouragement to use their imagination and initiative to see if they can re-create the essence of community and citizen responsibility. But that would take remarkable statesmanship, a commodity currently in short supply.

One cannot help but wonder, when we look at the degeneration of neighborhoods and communities, whether national policy, especially Federal court decisions—perhaps unavoidably—may have undervalued the importance of neighborhood and comminity in seeking to redress the inequalities of educational opportunity that seem to flow from racially unbalanced neighborhood schools. Neighborhoods have no legal status and therefore no rights and no standing in court. The fact that neighborhoods have helped to carry into the city some of the sense of mutual responsibility that was formerly the essence of small rural communities, is not a factor weighed in the judicial scale. The authors of the Constitution could not conceivably have foreseen the degree or character of the urbanization of society. Even if they had, they would not have known what to write into the surprisingly foresighted document to give some legal assurance that the desirable aspects of responsibility for mutual support that are the essence of community and neighborhood would be preserved and encouraged. Equality of educational opportunity is a social value that deserves very high ranking on any value scale, but so, too, does the opportunity of people to develop mutually supportive neighborhood and community groups. A better method needs to be found for recognizing and giving proper weight to the latter while seeking to achieve the former.

If political scientists were to identify any single subject that deserves to be placed at the center of their study and concern, one might suppose that it would be the question of how the exercise of responsibility by the body politic can be brought into better balance with its rights and expectations. Yet this receives pitifully small attention. It would be a great step forward if a significant segment of political scientists and a corresponding number of economists were to join together in re-establishing the once flourishing discipline of political economy, and add to it a group of anthropologists, sociologists, historians, and philosophers, with the intent of seeking to make use of the knowledge of their respective disciplines to bring human rights and responsibilities into reasonable balance so as to make society more manageable.

VI. The Centrifugal Social Effects of Energy

Is there any dominant cause of the disruptions in technological society that might be within our power to control, assuming we have the wisdom to take the necessary action? Astonishing as it may seem, the excessive consumption of energy may be just such a cause. Energy is the central dynamic of our society, the taproot of affluence, but it powers a social centrifuge, spinning people apart. Its effects deserve the closest analysis.

Ever since Prometheus stole from Athena and Hephaestus the gifts of fire and tools, man has regarded energy as an unmitigated blessing. Until the modern age, most of the energy he employed to augment the power of his muscles came from strong and docile animals, from the burning of wood, and from interruption of the flow of wind and water. In such modest quantities as these sources yielded, energy could hardly be considered anything but a boon. Only when men learned to convert the stored energy of fossil fuels on a massive scale did the combination of energy and technology begin to remake the physical face of the earth in dangerously adverse ways and generate an incomprehensibly complex society. Only in the smidgeon of history represented by the lifetime of today's senior citizens have there been societies that were overwhelmingly urban and suburban, where the typical citizen guides himself several thousand miles each year over streets and highways in a machine that consumes millions of joules of energy and others are transported tens of thousands more miles through the air. Only in this recent, thin slice of time has most work been performed not by humans or

89

domesticated animals, but by machines using fossil fuels or electricity generated from fossil fuels.

That energy from such fuels was the foremost factor in converting American society from being nearly three-quarters rural in 1880 to nearly three-quarters urban in 1970 can hardly be doubted. Advanced technology had existed for centuries—how else could St. Peter's basilica have been built?—without producing any large, predominantly urban societies. It was the coupling of fossil fuels with the steam engine, the internal-combustion engine, the turbine, the turbo-generator, and the electric motor that produced America's technological society. Without these, modernization would have been impossible; with them, it appears to have been inevitable—as long as fossil fuels, and particularly petroleum, existed in plentiful supply. These were the engines of urbanization, high-rise buildings, suburbanization, freeways and shopping centers; ultimately, they could be considered the unindicted subverters of the traditional foundations of society. Modernization would have been possible without the automobile, but not American-style modernization.

Just what is it that this symbiosis of fossil fuels and technology has done to society? To begin with, it has created an intense energy addiction. Without huge amounts of energy, every modern city would come to a mechanical stop and turn to chaos; every mechanized farm would be unable to plant or harvest its crops; every industry would come to a grinding halt; every apartment building and virtually every home would be paralyzed. In the short run, there is no conceivable way a highly modernized society can kick this energy addiction, and not much evidence that it wants to, although the numbers of individuals who would like to do so are growing daily. More important still, the high consumption of energy has had a profound impact on the two most fundamental institutions of all previous societies: the family and the community.

THE IMPACT OF ENERGY AND MODERNIZATION ON THE FAMILY

That the family has been the basic building block of all prior societies seems well established. In any essay summarizing the most general propositions about which sociologists should be able to agree, Princeton sociologist Marion Levy has this, among other things, to say about the fundamental role of the family: "There are no known societies lacking in family structures. . . . Until relatively modernized societies developed, the vast majority of all people in history spent the majority of their time and had the majority of their interrelationships in a family context. Ideally and/or actually—even if not ideally—the family context was the major focus of organizational behavior. It still is for a large proportion of the people of this earth." The words, "until relatively modernized societies developed" imply, of course, that modernization was responsible for demoting the family from its position of centrality. If we accept, for the purposes of this analysis, the contention that modernization's foremost characteristic is the consumption of large amounts of energy coupled with advancing technology, then energy can be said to be the driving force behind the demotion of the family as a social institution.

The centrifugal effect of energy upon the family accords with common observation. The strains created by urbanization and the wage economy, the sharp diminution in the amount of time spent by fathers and mothers with sons and daughters in joint economic and survival efforts, as compared with agrarian societies, and by grandparents with younger generations, has obviously loosened family ties. When children became economic liabilities and hindrances to alternative forms of self-fulfillment, the gradual decline in the importance of the family became inevitable. Children became luxuries, often more expensive than Cadillacs.

To the extent that energy is responsible for the extreme urbanization and modernization of society, therefore, it seems fair to say that it is responsible for the decline of the importance of the family as the central building block of society. And to the extent that families are valued, either for their own sake or as an institution believed to be essential to the stability and durability of society, the use of large quantities of energy—large enough to produce extreme urbanization and modernization—can be said to have a negative effect.

Just how essential a healthy family structure may be to the preservation of a reasonably durable society, we can only speculate since no society has ever tried before the 20th century to operate without building upon the family as its most fundamental institution. This fact alone would seem to create a fairly strong inference that creating conditions unfavorable to the family without developing an assured and tested substitute might be a hazardous course. So far, the capacity of highly modernized societies to create effective substitutes or collateral institutions which can, in conjunction with weakened families, provide an equally firm foundation is not evident.

The educational system has been unsuccessful in serving, for our current society, in the role formerly performed successfully by the family in a low-energy society—that is, to prepare young people for adult life. If it cannot succeed in this vital role under current conditions, one must wonder what other social institution or system can. The damage done to the family by high-energy technology may be irreparable within the context of a society that is as overwhelmingly urbanized, as specialized and compartmentalized, as highly centralized and bureaucratized as is America. It may be necessary to face the almost inescapable conclusion that only a basic change of direction might reverse the deterioration of the family as an institution.

The family deserves consideration as much or more for its past and potential contributions to basic human psychological satisfactions as for its function in helping to make societies stable and durable. The two are obviously closely related. It is impossible to measure objectively the comparative psychological satisfactions that are gained by people within and outside of family contexts. There are so many variables, most of which lie in the social and economic settings within which families operate. One major factor is how hard it is to make a family a functioning and cohesive unit within the surrounding society. If the conditions of the milieu strongly discourage the possibility of a family's functioning as a cohesive unit, the satisfactions gained can hardly avoid being low and the price people are willing to pay for the marginal satisfactions that come from noncohesive families—both in dollars and in forgone alternative satisfactions—will be correspondingly low. Lower marriage rates, higher divorce rates, deliberately childless marriages, and subreplacement fertility rates are, in some degree, indicators of lessening psychological satisfaction derived from the institution of the family. They may also be indicators that society has thoughtlessly created conditions that frustrate the opportunity of people to have and to cherish cohesive families.

Social policy in the United States has rarely been designed to promote family cohesion. Quite the reverse. One of the most disgraceful chapters in the history of American social policy was the inadvertent creation and thoughtless perpetuation of a Federal-state welfare program that contained powerful pressures toward the breakup of destitute families. Daniel Patrick Moynihan has been especially critical of such schemes. Farm policies, too, were just as callous to the values inherent in cohesive families. The family farm was treated as having no other value than that of a production unit, and if it could not make its way in competition with highly capitalized industrial farms, its members had no choice but to migrate to cities and try to adjust. The centrifugal effect of low-cost energy and high-cost equipment on millions of farm families in this country is incalculable. The creation of the highway trust fund, although hardly anybody foresaw it at the time, also turned out to be an extremely destructive influence on the institution of the family and the viability of the city neighborhood, with its stimulation of suburbanization.

THE EFFECT OF HIGH-ENERGY USE ON THE COMMUNITY

The second building block of all earlier societies—the community—was, like the family, cast into the high-speed centrifuge of modernization and spun to its perimeter. Community is used here to mean a group of people with cohesion growing from a common bond to a place, a common pride in it, and group loyalty stemming from familiarity with and substantial trust of each other. Thus the concept of community is meant to apply to groups of people who live in a sufficiently circumscribed area so that each recognizes by sight and knows the names of most of the others he sees each day within that area and feels that he knows or has some meaningful access to the leaders of the community and role in it. By this definition, a small proportion of Americans live in communities, while a large proportion of the people of China live in communities. (This is not to suggest that the type of communities the Chinese live in would be suitable for Americans.) How important communities are to the fulfillment of the psychological needs of people and to the stability and durability of societies is a matter to which insufficient attention has been given. There may well be such wide variations between cultures and between individuals within the same culture as to make generalizations of little validity and value. Nevertheless, speculation is useful.

The community and its partial urban substitute, the neighborhood, have, over the years, served affirmative psychological as well as economic and protective purposes. They establish human connections with other people who have roots in the unique place in which they live and from which they take psychic nourishment. Those associations develop into varying degrees of trust and affection and frequently of unspoken loyalty to the common bond and humanity of the group. Membership in a genuine community has a strong tendency to enlarge the capacity of each member for accepting and extending mutual trust. In this sense, it provides a depth of meaning to life that is difficult to obtain by any substitute means. When trust is extended, so too is responsibility. Some people, of course, in any environment, shrink from both trust and responsibility; the more inhospitable the environment, the greater the proportion of such people.

The community and the neighborhood also provide a source and form of security. People look out for one another. If they see strangers doing unusual things, they become suspicious and usually take whatever protective action seems called for under the circumstances. If a lone individual falls sick or is injured, his neighbors come to his aid. If a family has a catastrophe, the community pitches in and helps. Such mutual support is the essence of community or neighborhood.

The use of ever larger amounts of energy has the unfortunate effect of diminishing both the affirmative and the protective aspects of the community and the neighborhood. Even without the automobile, an affluent, high-energy society—dependent on trains, buses, and jets for transport, living in high-rise apartments, fed by an agricultural industry that uses large amounts of energy but employs only 5 percent of the work force—would have difficulty preserving the cohesive force of the community or the neighborhood. If little conscious realization existed of the importance of these institutions, and social policy were not specifically designed to preserve and enhance them, the general tendency would be toward their dissolution.

When the economics of land costs, construction, and maintenance drive builders and housing authorities to erect high-rise structures, the effect is to make neighborliness more difficult and neighborhoods less viable. It is immensely more difficult for people to be neighborly when they live in high-rise apartments than when they live close to the ground and move about horizontally and conspicuously on their own two feet rather than vertically in self-operated elevators. High-rise apartments also diminish the inclination of people to take responsibility for each other because of the sheer numbers involved. Residents may get to know a few other people in the building, but the bigger and taller the structure, the less likely they are to have any feeling of roots in the place or loyalty to its inhabitants. An anonymous vertical city is substituted for a horizontal association of people who recognize each other and develop some sense of trust and loyalty toward each other, a feeling of belonging.

THE PLACEMENT OF THE AUTOMOBILE AT THE CENTER OF SOCIETY

Each step toward urbanization, suburbanization, and exurbanization has been accompanied by an increase in dependence on energy and an escalation in its consumption. Different methods of using energy have different degrees of centrifugal force upon communities and neighborhoods. The automobile heads the list both in terms of the amount of energy consumed and as an agent of demolition of community.

In a perceptive book entitled *Energy and Equity* (1974), Ivan Illich discusses the use of energy to enable people to move from one place to another. He uses the word "transit" to mean those movements that put human metabolic energy to use, and the word "transport" to cover that mode of movement that puts other forms of energy to use. Transit applies principally to walking and bicycling, transport to whatever mechanized modes may be widely used. So far as the United States is concerned, transport means primarily the automobile.

At the rates and range of movement that are possible in walking or riding bicycles, people are relatively equal, friendly, and communicative. Their movement is also highly efficient in the use of energy, and best of all, the cost is low in terms of time and money. In contrast, Illich paints this picture of the use of time and energy in the American automobile culture:

The typical American male devotes more than 1,600 hours a year to his car. He sits in it while it goes and while it stands idling. He parks it and searches for it. He earns the money to put down on it and to meet the monthly installments. He works to pay for petrol, tolls, insurance, taxes, and tickets. He spends four of his sixteen waking hours on the road or gathering his resources for it. And this figure does not take into account the time consumed by other activities dictated by transport: time spent in hospitals, traffic courts, and garages; time spent watching automobile commercials or attending consumer education meetings to improve the quality of the next buy. The model American puts in 1,600 hours to get 7,500 miles: less than five miles per hour. In countries deprived of a transportation industry, people manage to do the same, walking wherever they want to go, and they allocate only 3 to 8 percent of their society's time budget to traffic instead of 28 percent. What distinguishes the traffic in rich countries from the traffic in poor countries is not more mileage per hour of lifetime for the majority, but more hours of compulsory consumption of high doses of energy, packaged and unequally distributed by the transportation industry.

The automobile culture determines the configuration of social space, breaking up communities and urban neighborhoods; the more rapidly people can be transported from one place to another, the more economically insupportable neighborhoods become. Neighborhood shops and services become scarce, often nonexistent—a sure sign of the decline and perhaps imminent disappearance of the neighborhood. Traffic arteries split neighborhoods apart, and high volume, low margin shopping centers make neighborhood shops nonviable. The further one can travel in an hour's time, the greater the impetus of the huge retail corporations to achieve economies of scale and provide services on a mass, impersonal, non-neighborhood basis.

Ivan Illich's greatest hope is that the combination of walking and bicycling, in conjunction with whatever mass transport may be required, will permit a "social restructuring of space that offers each person the constantly renewed experience that the centre of the world is where he stands, walks, and lives." Bicycles permit great flexibility of movement, the ultimate in efficiency, and the means of healthy exercise. Walking is in many ways superior to bicycling—it completely removes people from dependence on any mechanical contrivance and is the ultimate in flexibility—but the feasible radius of transit is more limited. In any event, it is not necessary to opt for walking or bicycling as a general mode of transit; each can be used to fit the need of the occasion.

In a tract entitled *Autokind vs. Mankind* (1971), Kenneth R. Schneider picked up and expanded upon a set of concerns expounded earlier by Lewis Mumford. Schneider coined the word "automobil-

ity" to describe the uniquely American dependence on the automobile for basic mobility:

> Automobility—particularly in cities—entrenches itself in con-
> crete, monopolizes movement, then congeals it, makes every
> roadway a barricade, reduces choice, hogs resources, increases
> costs, ravages the landscape, endangers and oppresses the
> pedestrian, boxes and deforms the body, contaminates the
> breath of life, enrages the ears, insults the eyes, makes an
> automaton of the nervous system, puts every citizen nearer the
> clutches of the law, denies casual association, rigorizes organiza-
> tion, distorts the public purpose, and dulls human sensibilities.
> Oh yes, and it kills half a million people each decade and maims
> millions more.

Overdrawn and caustic though it may be, such a critical characteri-
zation of what the automobile has done to both people and their social
institutions is substantially deserved. To make a balanced evaluation
of the automobile's costs and benefits, one would have to list its
notable contributions so that they might be fairly compared with this
heap of "disamenities" (only an Englishman like the economist Ezra
Mishan would think to apply such an understated term to such angry
complaints, but he is one of the few economists who has not accepted
the automobile as a self-evident contribution to human progress).
These would include: democratizing the exhilaration of power and
speed; the opportunity to travel and thereby be broadened (the boon
that Francis Bacon thought would flow automatically from travel—
but that was before hundreds of millions of people came to be manic
and competitive travelers); a more flexible means than mass transit of
transporting people from a place where they are to another place they
would rather be; and the chance to economize by buying things in
large quantities in supermarkets. Other items could be added to the
list, but still when it is weighed against Schneider's indictment, one
can only conclude that the impetus that has propelled the automobile
to the center of American society, converting the human to an
auto-man, is in no sense rational; it is the sheer magnetism of power,
speed, and mobility.

Rational or irrational, our society has now been structured in such a
way that the automobile is indispensable to most people. With few

exceptions, most new construction in the last quarter-century outside of New York City has been built on the assumption that people
would be transported to or from the new buildings by automobile. A
person without an automobile—a person who wishes to move about
by walking and by public transportation—is tantamount to a cripple.
The environment has been consciously designed and constructed
around the automobile; people are clearly secondary. Amazingly, as
Schneider points out, the United States has built a society in which
one cannot drink without driving—that is, most of the sociable
drinking that occurs requires most drinkers to drive home afterward.
Is it any wonder that our automobile accident rate is so high?
Schneider is no less interested than Illich in the social restructuring
of space to put human beings back at the center and restore the use of
their feet.

The American love affair with the automobile has been so ardent
that most of its devotees have been disposed to ignore its iniquities.
The killing of fifty to sixty thousand people a year and the injury of
some four million more seems to most people a tolerable price to pay
for a couple of hundred horses in their garage, ready to leap into
action at their command. The fact that the totality of highway deaths
has exceeded American fatalities in all wars, and that injuries vastly
exceed war casualties apparently does not disturb them. The spewing
of more pollution than all industry combined seems of minor concern. That automobiles choke cities and foul the countryside with
trash, junked cars, and neon signs is unfortunate, to be sure, but
seemingly just another cost and by-product of progress. But we can
hardly ignore the facts that they engender disrespect for law (rare is
the driver who does not violate speed limits when he thinks he can
get away with it), clog the courts to such a degree that judicial
decisions are delayed interminably, thus frustrating one of the most
important purposes of the judicial process, and entice juveniles into
theft and adults into going into debt over their heads.

On any given amount of paved street or highway, the more cars,
obviously, the more likelihood of a traffic jam, and the more speed,
the more likelihood of collisions, casualties and fatalities. With the
drivers of a hundred million automobiles trying to transport themselves somewhere else as expeditiously as possible, a kinetic crowdedness (that is, having one's movements constrained by others competing to occupy the same space) is created that far exceeds that in a

much denser, slower-moving non-automotive society. Studies of the effects of crowdedness on the human psyche and soma are only in their infancy, but when they become more sophisticated they will probably reveal that the American automobile culture creates a greater sense of crowdedness than is felt by many of the citizens of China and India whose physical density is much greater. Such psychological tension cannot fail to have adverse social and physical effects.

ENOUGH IS TOO MUCH

In a widely anthologized essay entitled "The Tragedy of the Commons," the biologist Garrett Hardin called attention most persuasively to the adverse social effect caused when herdsmen who make use of open and commonly held pasture for grazing their cattle, raise so many cows that the common pasture is overgrazed and the capacity of the land to feed the herds collapses. Hardin develops an analogy with human populations that may not be entirely valid but is useful in relation to the automobile population of the United States. There is a certain threshold up to which additional cows or cars do not seem to do any great harm to the common area within which each may roam. Beyond that point, however, the capacity of the land is overstrained and additional units have a strongly negative effect. Yet no single individual is constrained thereby to cut back on his number of cows or cars in the interest of the other users of the commons, since cutting back on his own use of the commonly held space injures him and aids others. Why, therefore, should he do it? Hardin concludes that the only conceivable answer to this difficult problem is "mutual coercion, mutually arrived at." That, of course, is what government is all about. But in a society that operates through representative government and the consent of the governed, the only way that such mutual coercion can be achieved is for the body politic to become sufficiently convinced of the imperative nature, or at least the desirability, of laws and penalties as applied to themselves as well as others, that they are willing to have such coercion universally applied.

The national park system is an example of the commons of which Hardin speaks. A half-century ago, the magnificent Western parks were the Mecca for a limited number of nature lovers, but with the democratizing effects of the automobile the parks came within reach of the average American. Picture, then, the teenage girl who had seen Yellowstone and Yosemite after a transcontinental trek in the 1920s and vowed that when she had a family of her own she would bring them to see this greatest of natural wonders. Three decades later, she piled her four teenage children into a station wagon and headed West. When she arrived at the grandest of the grand sights, as she thought of Yosemite, the family was caught in a traffic jam, competing with some 40,000 other people who wanted to share the same inspiration. They spent hours, bumper to bumper, inching along or not moving at all for long periods. The family became restless, annoyed, and tired. What was to have been a supreme life experience turned out to be a disappointment. Yellowstone was not quite so bad, but it, too, was seriously overcrowded. The proliferation of the automobile had degraded the best parks.

The jets have visited upon much of the world what the automobile has inflicted upon the choicest natural areas and historical and cultural spots of the United States. Transporting and disgorging millions of tourists around the globe, the jets have brought commercializing and homogenizing influences to bear on the tastes and hostelry of the people of exotic lands, persuading the placid, noncompetitive Fiji Islanders, and millions of others, that their culture is backward and that they should modernize—but keep just enough of the old ways to attract tourists. Tourists now overrun natural and cultural landmarks on all continents, vulgarizing many areas.

In recent years, about two million people a year have been touring the Acropolis to view what remains of the Garden of Eden of Western thought and culture. They have so eroded the steps of the Propylaea that planking has been installed as an emergency measure. The same is happening to the Parthenon. In a variety of other ways, the overwhelming tourist traffic is degrading the Acropolis. '"Tourism is good to a certain point," said Dr. George Dontas, Director of the Acropolis Museum. "Then it becomes a plague." It seems obvious to him and to others that that point has been reached and passed. The problem is how to bring matters under control. In dozens of ways, the jet age has carried the automobile age one step further in reducing the diversity and interest of the multiple cultures of the earth.

Thus we see the basic paradox of affluence: Enough for everybody turns out to be too much for anybody. If the world were to become steadily more affluent, with more and more disposable income available to be spent on travel, the world would become vastly more homogenized and uninteresting and the very purpose for which affluence was presumably intended would be defeated. The natural and cultural environments would be degraded beyond recognition, and, worst of all, so would be the people who expected to be enriched by travel.

As in the case of so many other matters in the physical world, there is a threshold effect here. We may be approaching the threshold at which disenchantment with international travel exceeds its enchantment. That point will, of course, vary widely between countries, with greater travel still ahead to selected countries where pleasure still outweighs discomfort, but in some others—especially those where crime, hijacking, begging, and anti-Americanism flourish—international tourism by Americans may already have passed its peak. In any event, it seems rather clear to anyone who examines recent trends that international air travel cannot regain its earlier accelerative thrust in the foreseeable future. High costs are, of course, an important factor, but kinetic crowdedness is taking a major toll.

"Kicking" the American Addiction to the Automobile

Five years ago, one would have said that there was no reasonable possibility that Americans would have any interest during this century in "kicking" their overwhelming addiction to the automobile. But today, the prospect that Americans may take major steps in the next decade—certainly before the year 2000—to bring their dependency under manageable control appears substantially greater. The OPEC countries suddenly made the habit annoyingly expensive, but that is not the only stimulus to change. As described earlier, large numbers of people are finding driving less and less enjoyable under the conditions that require them to contend and compete with traffic at both ends of the day and at other times as well. Their bodies are deteriorating for lack of exercise and their tempers and nerves are deteriorating from too much exercise. They are becoming psychologically ready to reduce their dependence on the automobile, but it will not be easy.

Society conspires against the person who wants to free himself or herself from the automobile habit to a greater degree than it frustrates the smoker who decides to become a nonsmoker, for he is actively discouraged from doing so by public policies that overwhelmingly favor the automobile. The difficulties and dangers of riding a bicycle on main traffic arteries during rush hours make it imprudent for most people even to consider it. Even the few hardy souls that do face the problem of parking their bicycles in places where they will not be stolen. It is quite apparent that the automobile has hogged the streets. Does this mean that those who wish to will never be able to buck the automobile, that there is no way of kicking the automobile habit? Almost, but not quite.

In 1973, more than 16 million bicycles were bought—5 million more than the number of automobiles; in 1974, the bicycle sales continued to exceed those for automobiles. The American love affair with the 10-speed bicycle had begun to warm up at the very time that its enchantment with the automobile was obviously cooling. Bicyclists are probably already sufficiently numerous to have it within their power to obtain enactment of city ordinances and other legislation that will help them alter the transit mores of the society. If not, they soon will be. The creation of one-way bicycle streets during rush hours, as in Holland, the creation of systems of parking bicycles in protective custody at key points, including commuter train stations, and similar encouragements to the use of bicycles seem likely to develop in many U.S. cities and thus begin a gradual change in transit systems and habits.

Despite the lack of comprehension and support of Midwestern and Mountain state Congressmen for Federal aid for urban mass transit systems, it seems predictable that as the price of gasoline rises and as the deterioration of core cities becomes a matter of unavoidable national concern, the mass transit systems will cry out so loudly for modernization and operating subsidies that a reversal of the long degenerative process of these systems will slowly begin. The rebuilding of mass transit will be a long, slow process, but there is a certain inevitability about it as a public policy, for without it some cities—especially New York—would decline in a manner and to a degree the nation could not tolerate.

Slowly, a significant shift is occurring in a variety of public policies that should demote the automobile from its role at the center of society. Without the sudden jump in the cost of oil, and the sudden re-education of the American people concerning the future availability of oil and gas, and all the implications that flow from such abrupt changes, this lessening in importance of the automobile would have seemed unlikely in the foreseeable future. But with the end of cheap gasoline as a permanent fact of life came the real probability of a basic change in our automobile society. Smaller automobiles will gradually replace the 200-400 horsepower models, cars will sooner or later be built to last longer, and gradually new residential and commercial construction will be adjusted to appeal to people who choose to live without owning an automobile, renting a car for the limited number of occasions when it becomes indispensable. This may be an integral part of a major shift in the direction and values of American society (which I will discuss in the final two chapters). Needless to say, it will not be at all easy to make the kinds of adjustments required in the pattern of skills and employment of persons whose livelihoods depend directly and indirectly upon the automobile industry.

Reason, as we know, is slow to take effect in coping with an addiction. When external circumstances alter in such a way as to reinforce reason, change may come more rapidly than one would otherwise expect. The fundamental alteration in the world's petroleum market is just such an external factor.

VII. The Energy Trap:
The Search for
a Way Out

Many people inclined toward a conspiratorial view of history saw the energy crisis of 1973-74 as primarily the result of connivance among the big oil companies to create a profit bonanza. Others, including high government officials, saw it as a form of political-economic blackmail which could somehow be broken by the concerted action of the oil-consuming nations. Still others felt that scientists, technologists, and private enterprise, with strong encouragement from the government, would find adequate new energy sources. Few realized at the time that it might truly be the end of the era of cheap energy. As each year passes, this realization becomes more stark, but its implications and ramifications are too great for immediate acceptance.

The contrast in energy consumption between the so-called developed and less-developed countries is striking. There is a large gap between the United States and the other technologically advanced nations, and then a gulf between them and the less-developed countries of Asia, Africa, and much of Latin America. The increase in the use of energy by the United States between 1960 and 1968 was not nearly as rapid on a percentage basis as that of most other nations of the world, but on an absolute scale, Americans added some 50 million BTUs per year to their per capita energy consumption, bringing it up from 250 million to 300 million BTUs per person per year, while the countries of Asia and Africa (where two-thirds of the world's people live) were moving up from a per capita level of some 6 million BTUs to 12 million. Since most of the energy consumed in the world is from fossil fuels, whose supply is startlingly limited, it is not surprising that the less-developed countries have been increasingly concerned that the era of cheap energy may end before they have the opportunity to partake of its benefits in any significant degree. Unfortunately for them, it has probably now ended. Their problems of modernizing, Western-style, will be immensely compounded.

When depicted graphically, the growth in the consumption of energy from sources other than animal power and wood by the U.S. economy looks like a large segment of an exponential curve pointing and reaching toward infinity. Anyone with either an intellectual or an intuitive understanding of the finitude of the earth knew or sensed even before the energy crisis descended upon us that such a rate of increase could not, in any event, have continued much longer. The Arab oil embargo brought us to a recognition of both the limits of the world's petroleum supply and its distorted distribution in relation to the world's people. Some geologists had been attempting to alert us to this problem, but we were not listening.

The most accurately prophetic of the petroleum geologists—one who has for years been seeking to warn us of the overoptimism of the official forecasts—is Dr. M. King Hubbert. He has spent a lifetime studying the geology of fossil fuels, especially petroleum, and has made the most conservative and the most accurate of the generally used long-range predictions as to the future discoveries of oil. From the standpoint of human history, he points out, the epoch of fossil fuels will be quite brief. He developed bell-shaped curves to predict the discovery and use of oil and coal reserves over the coming decades which show the peak of world oil extraction occurring somewhere between 1990 and 2000, depending on whether one uses the low or high estimate of remaining oil reserves. Coal, being considerably more plentiful, will take over from oil after the flow of petroleum goes into decline.

Hubbert's projection means that if the world were to go on increasing its consumption of oil as it did up to 1973, within roughly two more decades half of all the world's oil would be used up, and from that point forward, no matter how much more exploring might be done, the amount of oil extracted would decline, at first slowly but within two more decades precipitously. Meanwhile, the demand for oil throughout the world would have reached levels that would cause cutthroat competition for the remaining supplies, and the consequent price increase could make OPEC's earlier quadrupling of prices seem mild by comparison. When looked at in this light, the action by OPEC may actually have been beneficial. It has slowed the consumption of oil, thus extending the petroleum era somewhat, and it has initiated the necessary adjustment to the post-petroleum era soon enough to ease the transition, as compared with the almost certain cataclysmic consequences of proceeding pell-mell to use up the world's oil as fast as we could pump it out of the ground.

Hubbert estimated that oil discoveries up to 1965 in the United States (excepting Alaska and Hawaii) represented about 82 percent of the prospective ultimate total, an estimate considerably lower than the official forecasts of the U.S. Geological Survey, but one that employed what experience has shown to be a much sounder methodology. Former Interior Secretary Stewart Udall discovered after he had left that post that he should have been listening to Hubbert—a lone geological expert within the Geological Survey—rather than to the euphoric predictions of the top officials of that organization (an agency of the Interior Department). The implications of Hubbert's projections are both clear and ominous—that the United States has not the slightest chance of becoming anything like self-sufficient in oil at current levels of consumption. U.S. oil extraction reached a peak in 1970 and has since been declining, and the more zealous we become in exploiting remaining reserves, the more rapidly we will exhaust them, and the more dependent we will become on OPEC oil. By 1975, we imported some 38 percent of our oil from OPEC, and the future direction is likely to be toward further dependence on OPEC oil. We are thus becoming more vulnerable, rather than less.

The only conceivable way we could lessen our vulnerability would be to reduce our consumption of oil *drastically*. And the only equitable way such a reduction could be effected would be by government rationing, probably similar to the system employed during World War II. Allowing the price to float free would distribute the hardship with great inequity. Strange as it may seem, OPEC has almost certainly done the United States a great favor by forcing a shift in policies well before Middle Eastern oil reached the point on the exhaustion curve already reached by our domestic oil supply. The only trouble is, neither Presidential nor Congressional leadership is equal to the problem of telling the American people in clear terms what major changes will be required in life-style, and what policies will have to be pursued to bring about those changes in a fair and equitable manner.

THE AWAKENING OF THE OIL-RICH NATIONS

Half of all the reserves of oil known to have been deposited within the earth lie under the waters of the Persian Gulf and the sands of the Middle East. The cost of extracting this oil is low—one well in the Middle East does the work of dozens in the United States. It was not until the Yom Kippur War of 1973 that Arab nations, which had been selling their oil at low prices and competing against one another in exporting oil to the world, acted collectively to set world oil prices. There is nothing like a war to bring out the advantages of alliances. In this instance, the OPEC alliance served a triple purpose—military, economic, and political—and is likely, therefore, to have more carry-over peacetime durability than most alliances. When the OPEC countries quadrupled the price of oil and turned off its flow entirely to selected adversaries, they caused the oil-importing nations suddenly to become far more respectful of their position and role in the world. Never again, at least not so long as they (wned half the world's oil, OPEC nations decided, would they play ,econd fiddle in world economics and politics. A fundamental chang e had occurred in world power overnight, a change whose reality would take a considerable time for the leaders and public of the Western world, particularly the United States, to comprehend fully.

President Nixon and Secretary Kissinger talked about not submitting to blackmail and intimated that they had t¹ e means to retaliate and make the Arabs regret having overreached themselves. They called a conference of the oil-consuming nations of Western Europe and formed a consumers' union called the International Energy Agency to develop a cooperative program as a basis for bargaining with OPEC. The initial agreement called for conservation of energy, development of alternative sources of energy, research and development on a larger scale, especially on new technologies, and the search for new and better ways to utilize uranium as a nuclear fuel, all of which the nations would have done in the absence of an agreement.

The fact remained that OPEC had the oil and the West had become addicted to oil. The withdrawal symptoms and trauma from any concerted effort to counter-boycott Middle Eastern oil were too horrible to contemplate, and the sheiks and shahs knew it full well. If the new price they had set for oil resulted in some reduction in its use, the OPEC countries would be happy, not sad. They would still accumulate more foreign exchange than most of them could spend for their own immediate needs, and a slowdown in the extraction of their exhaustible resource would mean that they could remain a world power center for a much longer period. Whether or not the preservation of oil for their grandchildren was in their minds, this may be one of the most important effects of sudden monopoly control of oil by OPEC.

The OPEC countries may conceivably ease, but they will not significantly back down from, their invulnerable bargaining position. Oil will never again be cheap.

THE AMERICAN RESPONSE: PROJECT INDEPENDENCE

The American response to the oil crisis was a typical blend of overconfident problem-solving and Madison Avenue hoopla. President Nixon announced the launching of Project Independence, setting as a target the development of sufficient alternative sources of energy within the control of the United States that would make it invulnerable to any sudden cutoff of foreign oil and gas by 1980. Project Independence was launched with the expectation that while conservation measures would be invoked, the basic American pattern of steady increase in the consumption of energy would not be more than temporarily impeded. An Office of Energy was quickly established not only to cope with the immediate crisis, but to devise strategies and R&D programs that would relieve growing American dependence on Middle East oil. The public was hoodwinked. Either an unacceptably drastic conservation program would have had to be undertaken, or the target date would have had to be set way beyond 1980, or both, for the goal to be reached. Profound technological and economic adjustments require a long period of development and adjustment, and the objective of making the United States self-sufficient in energy is one of the most pervasive and difficult adjustments the country could undertake.

The Office of Energy was faced with these basic questions: (1) How can the nation increase, as rapidly as possible, domestic extraction of fossil fuels and identify additional domestic reserves? (2) How can it make more efficient use of energy sources, particularly fossil fuels, and otherwise conserve them without significantly impeding economic growth? (3) How rapidly and in what manner should nuclear energy be substituted for fossil fuels in the generation of electricity? and (4) What other sources of energy have a reasonable chance of providing a significant share of our energy requirements? Let us briefly examine each of these questions.

1. Increasing domestic extraction of fossil fuels. At 1973 rates of consumption, U.S. oil would be exhausted by about 2010, give or take a few years—only as far in the future as the U.S. entry into World War II was in the past, not a very long time in the perspective of many middle-aged and senior citizens. Thus one can say that the petroleum era is moving rapidly toward its twilight years.

Additional exploration will locate more oil than geologists are now aware of, but experience shows that the amounts found in new fields are generally smaller than those already discovered and tapped, and the costs of extraction are progressively higher. The more aggressive the American efforts to find and use the remaining American oil reserves, the briefer the remaining years in which we can remain reliant on the gasoline-powered automobile as our principal means of transportation.

The supply of oil from domestic sources is neither elastic enough in the short run nor sufficiently expansible in the long run to extend the petroleum era far into the 21st century. This does not mean, of course, that in 2011 there will be no more domestic oil, but it does mean that well before then the price will have risen to such a degree as to cause a basic downward shift in our consumption patterns. Long before the end of this century, Americans will be paying more for gasoline than the $2 per gallon the French were paying for it in 1975, without making any allowance for inflation. A substitute fuel—such as methanol, methane, or even hydrogen—could take the place of gasoline as an automobile propellant, but even with such substitutes, the auto age will move into its declining years. In the light of our analysis of the adverse effects of the automobile on the basic institutions of society, this diminution of American dependence on the automobile would clearly not be so bad. In fact, in my own view, it is one of the more hopeful things about the future.

Oil from shale is often regarded as our insurance policy. Oil shale contains a beeswaxlike organic material called kerogen, which when heated releases vapors that condense to an amber-colored raw shale oil, a substance that can, in turn, be refined into petroleum products. U.S. oil shale reserves are said to be as much as eight times as large as petroleum reserves—more than any country in the world, so far as is known. But the problems of extraction and conversion are immense. Even in the best deposits, more than one and a half tons of rock must be processed for each barrel of oil produced, and enormous quantities of water are required that are unavailable at the mine sites. The processing, including the transportation (and possibly the desalinization) of water over great distances to northwestern Colorado, will therefore require a substantial part of the energy extracted and huge amounts of capital, sharply reducing the *net energy* thus made available. An appreciable part of the remaining net energy would be needed to redress some of the environmental damage done by the processing, damage that would greatly exceed that done in the strip-mining of coal. The potential hazard of heat and atmospheric damage from the consumption of enormous amounts of energy to yield a small proportion of net energy has not yet been adequately evaluated. Despite these difficulties, when the price of oil gets high enough, there seems little doubt that efforts will be greatly increased to recover oil from shale.

Recently, research on a new method of obtaining oil from shale has resulted in optimistic forecasts that it may be much simpler and less environmentally destructive. The method involves breaking up the shale deep underground with high explosives after excavating a site that can be used as a large retort. A burning process is then begun that forces out the volatile components of the shale, enabling it to be collected as oil underground. Some estimates were made that oil could be produced on a large scale by this method for $10 per barrel. It is well to remember, however, that early cost estimates are almost invariably low, and the difficulties and delays in bringing about a major technological development of this kind are inadequately recognized. Still, this could significantly extend the petroleum era, at a price that would almost surely require much more economical use of oil.

Oil from the Athabasca Tar Sands in northwestern Canada is another possibility. Like the Colorado shale, these sands have great amounts of petroleum intermixed with quartz sand; it is also difficult and expensive to separate, but probably less costly than the production of shale oil. Just how high the price of oil will have to go before Canada invests the large sums needed for the development of these resources is not clear, but the lead time would be substantial. Thus no short-term relief is in sight, and in the longer run it must be thought of as a source of rather expensive energy. But by the time it does become comparatively "economical" for Americans to use it, all energy will have become much more expensive than it now is.

Natural gas has about the same brief life span as oil. Hubbert's forecast of the peak of natural gas production in the United States was between 1975 and 1980, but the peak actually occurred in 1973. The demand for gas had accelerated because of its cleanliness. The importation of liquefied gas will no doubt increase in coming years, but by no means sufficiently to keep up with demand. It is predictable, therefore, that a steady shift will occur in the direction of coal, both used directly and converted to gas and liquid fuel.

Even though it is far from ideal, coal is undoubtedly the fossil fuel of the American future, simply because it is abundantly available. It is obviously dirty and its exhaust gases contain sulfur and fly ash, major culprits in the pollution of the atmosphere. (Air pollution in 1968, according to a study made by the Environmental Quality Council, did some $20 billion worth of damage.) Coal is also expensive to transport, increasingly expensive to mine, and when extracted by strip-mining, requires substantial and costly effort and government enforcement to achieve reasonable restoration of the surface land. It is not, therefore, as desirable a fuel as either oil or gas. Nevertheless, coal is not only available in much larger quantities than either oil or gas, but it can probably be made more useful than in the past through a variety of new technologies.

In the decades immediately ahead, coal will almost certainly have to be used in increasing quantities to substitute for oil and gas in the generation of electricity in conventional generating plants. In December 1974, the Environmental Protection Agency determined that the scrubbing technique for removing sulfur gases from smoke stacks had been determined to be safe and effective. This decision, plus others that will probably follow to open up various coal fields in the West to controlled strip-mining, will open the way to the greater use of coal in existing plants and probably the construction of new coal-fired plants. In the longer run, coal offers the prospect of conversion to various types of gas that can be transported by pipeline, the cheapest form of land transportation.

As the extraction of natural gas dwindles, the conversion of coal to a substitute form of gas becomes increasingly important. Much research is currently going forward on coal gasification, and it is certain that such research will continue to be financed by the government for an extended period. Synthetic natural gas can be produced from coal—with roughly the same heat content per cubic foot as natural gas contains—but the process is complicated and expensive. There is some possibility of developing a means of generating methane underground through controlled oxidation of coal that has been broken into small fragments by the use of explosives, but the research is not yet far enough advanced to predict success. In any event, some method of converting coal to methane gas is sure to be an important energy industry of the future.

· Coal may also be used to yield hydrogen from its hydrocarbon base. Hydrogen is a hazardous gas to handle, but if safety problems can be made manageable (they are not like those of nuclear energy), hydrogen could become an important method of transporting and converting energy to many of the numerous purposes for which both natural gas and gasoline are now used.

There is also the possibility that coal might be used to generate electricity more efficiently than at present through the use of its gases directly, rather than by steam turbines—an advance that would be analogous to the shift from the internal combustion to the jet engine in aircraft. Research is going forward—in Japan, the U.S.S.R., and several European countries, as well as in the United States—on a magnetohydrodynamic generator, which converts heat from combustion gases directly into electric power. This method might, if successful, eliminate sulfur dioxide and reduce nitrogen oxide emission from coal-fired power plants. As with so many other technological developments that may eventually have a major effect on energy methodology, even when, as, and if the technology is first proven successful, it would take well over a decade, perhaps a quarter-century, for it to have a broad-scale impact.

Coal-mining is not an attractive occupation and it will not be easy to get American workers to take it up as the coal-mining industry is expanded. Wage rates are likely to go up rapidly, and the power of the United Mine Workers may become as great as is that of their counterparts in Great Britain. Since coal is not easy to transport in solid form and is hard on railroad beds, the increased use of coal will make necessary a major improvement in the nation's railroad system, now in deplorable condition. Conceivably a method may be found for economically transporting coal by pipeline as slurry.

The more coal used, the lower the quality in terms of BTUs per ton, which means that more will have to be mined to produce a given amount of heat. The greater the weight of the coal per BTU, the higher the cost of energy. Coal will be the fossil fuel of the American future, but its BTUs are certain to be much more expensive.

2. Increasing the efficiency of fuel use. There are numerous ways in which energy could be more efficiently used. For example, the amount required to heat commercial buildings and homes could be substantially reduced by modifying construction techniques, eliminating vast heat losses through glass, improving insulation, and using heat pumps (normally operated by electricity, and for every BTU a pump uses in electricity, it produces two or three in heating a house or building; it can also be reversed and become an air conditioner in the summer).

Heat now wasted from the exhaust gases of industrial furnaces could be used for space heating. Similarly, waste heat from the condensers of electric generating plants could be (and already is) used for space heating, but not extensively.

Nearly half of the cost of electricity results from its transmission and distribution. Improved methods of transmission, especially over long distances, seem well on the way to realization, but these will not be nearly enough to offset the higher generating costs stemming from sharply rising fuel costs.

3. Energy conservation. Not only can energy be more efficiently used, but there are numerous ways in which it can be conserved without serious adverse effect upon the material comfort of Americans. The use of mass transit instead of private cars, the use of car pools instead of individual commuting, the use of bicycles where feasible, and walking are all means of saving gasoline; the last two are also promoters of health. Avoidance of heating unused spaces, keeping the thermostat down in winter and up in the summer obviously save energy. These and other methods have been used since 1973 and no doubt will continue to be.

The greatest energy wasters in the United States are, of course, oversized automobiles. Gradually, Americans will shift to smaller and lighter cars, on the European pattern. It seems predictable that the tax structure will be adjusted to speed up this shift. Large sums could be saved, too, by providing incentives to build durable cars instead of continuing the expensive practice of frequent model changes.

At some point, Ralph Nader or somebody like him and an aroused group of American consumers seem sure to bring enough pressure to bear to make the Federal Power Commission and state public utilities commissions shift their rate structure so as to encourage conservation rather than consumption. Users who are modest and careful consumers of electricity and gas, should pay the lowest rate rather than the highest, with progressively higher rates for profligate users, especially for lighting, air conditioning, and heating. Europeans have had far more intelligent rate structures than the United States, especially in granting low rates for off-peak use of electricity for such purposes as heating water. A variety of such steps is foreseeable in the future of American energy policy.

4. The nuclear option. While the age of petroleum is moving rapidly into its declining years, the era of nuclear energy is generally assumed to be in its youth, able to pick up the falling flag of petroleum technology and march vigorously forward into a new age of plenty, based either on splitting atoms or fusing them, or both.

All controlled nuclear energy so far converted to man's use has been based on fission as the source of heat used to produce the steam and spin the turbines of the currently operative nuclear power plants for the generation of electricity. Fusion energy, involving the combining of light nuclei, such as deuterium, would, if it could be harnessed, make use of the principle of the hydrogen bomb and would require the achievement of a fantastic combination of heat, pressure, and duration far exceeding anything yet approached. (The heat required exceeds that at the center of the sun.) Edward Teller, father of the H-bomb, sees no prospect that fusion energy can be made practical and generally available in this century, and some nuclear physicists seem to doubt that it will ever become feasible. The hopes of those who expect nuclear energy to launch a new epoch in high-energy technology rest, therefore, primarily on fission energy, at least for the next several decades.

The critical fuel of the currently operative nuclear-powered generating plants (light water reactors) is uranium-235, a rare isotope of uranium. Each 100,000 atoms of natural uranium contain only 711 atoms of uranium-235. As Dr. Hubbert points out, therefore, if nuclear energy depended entirely on uranium-235, the nuclear age would not last long since supplies of uranium now known to exist would be sufficient for only a few decades. Other discoveries of uranium are being made, and will no doubt continue to be made for some time, but the days of uranium-235, like those of oil, are comparatively short. The enrichment of uranium by a variety of methods is already going on, here and in Europe, and will become more intense as the supply of uranium declines, but it is no long-term solution to the problem of nuclear fuel.

If the supply of fuel for conventional nuclear reactors were to run out, the nuclear age would not, however, need to come to an abrupt end, provided nuclear scientists have their way. They have devised an ingenious means of breeding new fissionable material within nuclear reactors while the fission is producing heat for the generation of electricity. The breeder reactors seem to offer the world an inexhaustible supply of energy. The only trouble is that the fuel they produce and use in large amounts is plutonium, the material from which the Nagasaki bomb was manufactured and one of the deadliest substances known to man. Current nuclear reactors also produce plutonium but in much smaller quantities. Let us look first at the conventional nuclear reactors and return to the problem of the breeders in the next chapter.

In 1974, there were some 50 nuclear power plants in operation in the United States using U-235 as fuel and generating 6-7 percent of the nation's electric current. In spite of the uncertainty as to how long the supply of U-235 may be available, the Atomic Energy Commission was promoting, up until its mitosis in 1974, the most rapid possible construction of additional plants and had predicted in 1973 that by the year 2000 there would be 1,000 such plants in operation (a figure later reduced by one-third), generating 60 percent of the nation's electric power needs. Thus, nuclear power seemed well on its way to becoming the nation's principal source of electric energy. Notwithstanding the AEC's view of the future and the even greater reliance that several European countries—including France and Great Britain—are placing on nuclear energy, it is not at all clear that fission will rule the future. Too many problems remain, and some may be insuperable.

SAFETY AND RELIABILITY: THE NAGGING NUCLEAR QUESTIONS

Current nuclear power plants offer three inescapable hazards. The first is the possibility that human error or the failure of key components of the reactor mechanism could cause a disastrous nuclear accident, spreading plutonium and other radioactive material over a wide area. The second is the difficulty of disposing of the dangerous waste products, which even in the most minute quantities could be extraordinarily perilous to humankind. Kansas salt mines had been èxpected to serve as the deep disposal vault for these radioactive materials with a half-life up to 24,000 years, but they have now been determined to be unsuitable. And third, there is the worst danger of all—that terrorists might obtain (conceivably with the cooperation of a foreign government that had become antagonistic to the United States) enough plutonium with which to make one or several nuclear bombs and plant them in dense population centers or use it in other ways to poison vast numbers of people.

In March 1974, the *New York Times* carried an article describing the seventeenth major shutdown of the Vermont Yankee nuclear power plant over a period of 19 months, 15 of them because of accidents, failures of equipment, faulty parts, corrections of illegal or dangerous conditions, and (in one case) lightning. "We're not as bad as some," a Vermont Yankee spokesman was quoted as saying, "but we're not as good as others." Six months later, the AEC ordered 21 of the 50 nuclear reactors producing electric power in the United States to close within 60 days to determine whether cracks were developing in the pipes of their cooling systems. Most of them were reopened within two weeks, but the shutdowns emphasized the continuing apprehension that exists over the possibility of nuclear accidents. At about the same time, a leading nuclear safety expert, Carl J. Hocevar, quit his job with the Commission "in order to be free to tell the American people about the potentially dangerous conditions of the nation's nuclear power plants." Ralph Nader had earlier begun one of his crusades to tell the American people the same thing.

According to figures assembled by Professor Henry W. Kendall of the Union of Concerned Scientists—a group that is deeply disturbed about the implications of the proliferation of nuclear power plants— nuclear plants had a "deliverability factor" of 54 percent of their theoretical capacity in December 1973, and 46 percent in January 1974. Reliability and safety are inextricably intertwined. Although many New Yorkers took the famous 18-hour blackout of 1966 as something of a lark, it was, of course, a serious matter and could have posed real dangers if it had lasted much longer. All major cities, especially New York, must have reliable sources of electric power for their safety.

Since all nuclear power plants produce plutonium and other long-lived radioactive poisons, there is no conceivable way in an increasingly unstable world that nuclear plants can be made safe. The light water reactors (LWR) of conventional nuclear plants create far less plutonium than would the liquid-metal fast breeder reactors (LMFBR) now being developed, but still far more than enough to make nuclear bombs. The AEC, the utilities, and the big industries that produce the equipment for nuclear power plants have sought to assure the public that they have taken extra safety precautions and the chance of a serious accident is extremely small. But those members of the public who know the facts, and who are uncommitted to nuclear power, remain deeply concerned.

Despite multiple reassurances by nuclear engineers that all will be well in the new and bright nuclear age, there are indications that their confidence is not as great as they would have us believe. Edward Teller, in an article published in late 1974, proposed that in the future conventional nuclear plants be built 200 feet underground. That tells us something about the potential danger of nuclear accidents.

The high-energy societies are moving into the future with the apparent explicit intent that nuclear energy will be used and relied upon to meet the steadily enlarging electrical energy requirements of industrial and postindustrial societies. As the petroleum age fades, the LWR age takes over; when the supply of U-235 is gradually exhausted, the LMFBR age will step in and carry on. This third stage is intended to be assured by huge investments in the development of the new breeder reactor; the 1975-76 budget called for the expenditure of more than a half-billion dollars for just that—more than for the development of any other form of energy.

NEW SOURCES OF ENERGY

Other alternative sources of energy do exist, though none has as yet been extensively developed. Geothermal energy, wind energy, the burning of solid wastes, and, most important of all, solar energy could open new avenues for energy conversion. None of these should be denigrated, but none except solar energy offers the hope of long-range solution of mankind's energy problems and needs, and it will be slow in coming. Geothermal energy—tapping the subsurface heat of the earth—would be economically feasible in only a few localities. Wind is more widely available, and its energy will again be used, but the problem of conversion and storage of the energy for use when the wind is not blowing is sufficiently great as to make it a less than ideal source. The burning of solid wastes needs further research and development, but two factors militate against excessive reliance on it—the need to encourage industry and consumers alike to generate less solid wastes, and the need to encourage recycling of much of the burnable solid wastes. Paper and paper products are an example. The manure from feed lots is another. Feed lots will decline in the future, as a larger and larger proportion of the meat eaten becomes range-fed beef with less fat, and methods will probably be developed for recycling the manure of the remaining feed lots onto the land where it belongs. Organic fertilizer would thus replace part of the energy-intensive nitrogen fertilizers currently used.

Direct conversion of solar radiation seems to offer humankind the greatest possibility of an inexhaustible, nonpolluting, widely distributed, and safe supply of energy to meet the world's needs. Development of techniques for the conversion of solar energy to useful form is in various stages of development. In its simplest form, solar energy can be widely used in the heating of homes and low buildings—not as an exclusive but as a major source of heat. "Within five years," said a report of the American Association for the Advancement of Science in 1973, "many [of these] scientists believe, solar-powered systems for heating and cooling homes could be commercially available at prices competitive with gas or oil furnaces and electric air conditioners." Early in 1975, a report of the American Institute of Architects called for the creation of a new type of utility company to buy and install solar heating units, windmills, and other devices capable of turning natural energy sources to human needs and purposes. All types of structures, including office buildings and family dwellings, would be converted to become more economic users of heat, cool air, and electricity. Solar heating seems definitely in prospect, but like all major technological changes, it will take a good many years for it to become a major substitute for existing heating systems. A government development program to improve the techniques and to encourage and subsidize the use of solar heating (the government has heavily subsidized the development of nuclear energy for the generation of commercial and residential power use) would greatly accelerate the adoption of such methods, thereby reducing the drain on domestic oil and gas.

Converting solar radiation directly into electricity is practical but still expensive. Solar cells similar to those used to generate the electricity needed in space satellites are now commercially available. Their price has dropped dramatically, but it would require a great increase in the market and automated production (as occurred in the evolution of the transistor) to begin to make solar cells a significant source of electricity. Their greatest advantage is independence from central generating stations and transmission lines.

There are various ways in which solar energy might be converted into electricity on a large scale. One is through the use of numerous small, decentralized power turbines that would operate at temperatures far below those of conventional or nuclear power plants. The other is to build large, centralized solar thermal units that would require transmission of the electricity over much longer distances. Still another possibility would be to use heat collectors to concentrate the energy needed to separate the hydrogen and oxygen in water and transport the hydrogen over long distances by pipeline (an economical method of moving energy) to the points where it would be used as the fuel for the generation of electricity or in a variety of other ways. The first two of these methods are under active research and development, making use of a $60-million appropriation for this purpose to the Federal Energy Administration (1975-76)—a modest appropriation for so important a purpose.

Coal, nuclear energy, and solar energy are the potential sources of large scale energy production for the next several generations, and energy conservation seems increasingly necessary in any event. The relative degree of emphasis on these options will surely be one of the central themes of American and world politics for much of the balance of the 20th century.

VIII. The Ethics and Politics of Nuclear and Solar Energy

Our energy future will be decided not only by physical and economic factors, but by ethical and political influences. The supply and demand factors are clear: Other things being equal, those forms of energy that are most plentiful and cheapest during any period will attract the most users. But the price of energy is not controlled exclusively by the law of supply and demand. It is influenced in major degree by the President, Congress, governors, legislatures, public utility commissions, and the public itself. The public's perceptions of equity and its undefined feelings as to what constitutes right and wrong have a marked effect upon the actions of its elected and appointed representatives. These factors will generate lengthy and probably escalating debate as people become more conscious of the issues and more aggrieved by conspicuous inequities.

Non-economic factors will loom especially large as the public and its policy-makers are required to make decisions on nuclear energy, since the hazards are of such magnitude and uncertainty that they cannot be translated into economic terms. The lethal potential of radioactive fuels and wastes is almost unimaginable, and certainly not subject to cost-benefit analysis. If "efficiently" distributed, a ball of plutonium (Pu-239) the size of a basketball would be sufficient to kill all 4 billion of the earth's human inhabitants. And once created, radioactive materials retain their death-dealing potential for what might as well be an eternity; their rate of deterioration is so slow that much of the nuclear fuels and waste products would take more than 20,000 years—and in some cases more than 200,000 years—to

121

become safe for human beings to handle. Only a single-minded, shortsighted "economic man," bereft of all ethical sensitivity and ecological understanding, could consider the question of whether and to what extent we should now become heavily dependent on nuclear energy as if it were a purely economic calculation of comparative costs. More than any issue the public has ever had to face, national nuclear policy will increasingly have to be weighed in terms of such factors as the stability of social and political institutions, the vulnerability of the society to sabotage, the obligations of this generation toward its successors, and the relationship of humankind to the rest of the natural kingdom.

Such factors seem to be deeply disturbing to at least some of the nuclear scientists, particularly those who have taken time to ponder with care the long-range implications of a world energized by plutonium. One of the most distinguished members of the nuclear fraternity, Dr. Alvin M. Weinberg, for nearly a quarter-century the director of the AEC's Oak Ridge National Laboratories and the leading developer of the American version of the breeder reactor, became, like Oppenheimer, much concerned about the ethical implications of letting the nuclear genie out of the bottle, but managed to persuade himself of its net benefits to the human race. In wrestling with his conscience, he helped clarify to himself and others that the policy issue as to whether or not to use nuclear energy on a large scale for the generation of electricity was, indeed, a moral issue:

We nuclear people have made a Faustian bargain with society. On the one hand we offer—in the catalytic nuclear burner—an inexhaustible source of energy. Even in the short run, when we use ordinary reactors, we offer energy that is cheaper than energy from fossil fuel. . . . But the price that we demand of society for this magical energy source is both a vigilance and a longevity of our social institutions that we are quite unaccustomed to. In a way, all of this was anticipated during the old debates over nuclear weapons. As matters have turned out, nuclear weapons have stabilized at least the relations between the superpowers. The prospects of an all-out third world war seem to recede. In exchange for this atomic peace, we have had to manage and control nuclear weapons. In a sense, we have established a military priesthood which guards against inadvertent use of nuclear weapons, which maintains what *a priori* seems to be a precarious balance between readiness to go to war and vigilance against human errors that precipitate war. Moreover, this is not something that will go away, at least not soon. The discovery of the bomb has imposed an additional demand on our social institutions. It has called forth this military priesthood upon which in a way we all depend for our survival.

Dr. Weinberg's reference to the catalytic nuclear burner means, in our terms, the breeder reactor, but the thrust of his thoughts applies to all nuclear reactors. His views are strongly confirmed by two other nuclear scientists who were commissioned to make a study of nuclear safety by the Ford Foundation Energy Policy Project, Mason Willrich and Theodore B. Taylor. They concluded their report, *Nuclear Thefts: Risks and Safeguards* (1974), with these words: "None of man's previous discoveries compare with nuclear energy in terms of the demands placed on him to use it wisely. *Indeed, the widespread use of nuclear energy requires the rapid development of near-perfect social and political institutions. This is the unprecedented challenge before us.*"*

Resource economist Allen Kneese pointed out (in 1972) the illegitimacy of any special claim to expertise by the nuclear scientists to make judgments on society's behalf as to the appropriate future for nuclear energy:

This means that technical people, be they physicists or economists, cannot legitimately make the decision to generate such hazards based on technical analysis. Society confronts a *moral* problem of a great profundity—in my opinion one of the most

---

*Italics added. All three of these men are nuclear scientists, not students of social and political behavior. "Near-perfect social and political institutions" cannot exist without near-perfect people to design, operate, and support them. Are these scientists telling us that human beings can suddenly become—throughout the world—near-perfect? What gives them the slightest hope that this is possible in the face of thousands of years of historical evidence to the contrary? The only reassurance they offer us is that national leaders, with the aid of the military priesthood, have managed to accumulate a vast arsenal of nuclear weapons and still avoid a nuclear holocaust for all of 30 years—a statistically perfect record. Yet they seek to persuade us that the proper course of action is for human beings suddenly to become near-perfect rather than to reject the Faustian contract they have laid before us.

consequential that has ever faced mankind. In a democratic society the only legitimate means for making such a choice is through the mechanisms of representative government.

For this reason, during the short interval ahead while dependence on fission energy could still be kept within some bounds, I believe the Congress should make an open and explicit decision about this Faustian bargain. This would best be done after full national discussion at a level of seriousness and detail that the nature of the issue demands. An appropriate starting point could be hearings before a committee of Congress with a broad national policy responsibility.

Gradually, but much too slowly, the American people are beginning to perceive the nuclear energy problem as the moral and political issue Dr. Kneese said it was. Both the Ford Foundation Energy Policy Project's report, *A Time to Choose* (1974), and the second report to the Club of Rome, *Mankind at the Turning Point* (1974), highlighted the moral and survival aspects of large-scale nuclear reactors scattered over the globe. Clearly, there is no way in which any existing international control system—or any that is likely to be developed in the foreseeable future—can prevent the diversion of plutonium for terrorist activities. Contemplation of the prospect of spending a substantial part of the next half-century under the threat of wildcat use of radioactive poisons and bombs is profoundly disturbing, to put it mildly, and consequently, some of the most fervent political activity in opposition to nuclear energy is to be found on college campuses.

In the fall of 1975, the National Council of Churches took a major step toward opposition to the use of plutonium as a nuclear fuel. An eighteen-member committee of scientists headed by Dr. Margaret Mead and Dr. René Dubos recommended to the Council that they oppose both the further development of the breeder reactor and the recycling of plutonium as a means of enriching the fuel in conventional reactors. The committee included only two physicists—Dr. Hannes Alfven of the University of California at San Diego, a Nobel Prize-winner, and Dr. David Inglis of the University of Massachusetts—but it also had other distinguished scientists and Nobel laureates, including Dr. George Wald of Harvard and Dr. James D. Watson of the Cold Spring Harbor Laboratory. With alacrity, the

Atomic Industrial Forum wired the National Council of Churches, calling the statement biased. The committee had nobody on it who was paid by the nuclear-industrial complex.

As a consequence of this report, the National Council of Churches began considering whether to reverse its 15-year-old stand supporting the development of the peaceful uses of the atom. The churches are just beginning to wake up to the full ethical implications of a world in which plutonium and terrorism are being produced simultaneously at a rapid pace, with no dependable method of keeping them apart.

Zero Energy Growth

The Energy Policy Project was another hopeful sign that attitudes may be changing significantly. Established by the Ford Foundation to explore the nation's policy options in the energy field, the project conducted a technology assessment exercise and offered three choices. The first involved an attempt to increase energy consumption at past rates. The second envisaged a determined effort to reduce demand through the application of energy-saving technologies, which would require a rate of growth about half that of the past. And the third, wonder of wonders, is called the "zero energy growth scenario," which "represents a real break with our accustomed ways of doing things."

The ZEG scenario does not, according to the report, represent austerity:

It would give everyone in the United States more energy benefits in the year 2000 than he enjoys today, even enough to allow the less privileged to catch up to the comforts of the American way of life. It does not preclude economic growth.

It might come about if society became concerned enough about the social and environmental costs of energy growth, and if technology seemed unable to solve these problems. It might also reflect broader social concerns, like uneasiness about the dehumanizing aspects of big centralized institutions. *Zero energy growth* would emphasize durability, not disposability of goods. It would substitute for the idea that "more is better," the ethic that "enough is best."

Not surprisingly, industry representatives from Westinghouse, Commonwealth Edison, the Aluminum Company of America, and Mobil Oil Corporation entered demurrers to this scenario. Typical of the thoughts they expressed was this observation by the late J. Harris Ward, Director of Commonwealth Edison:

> The rising standard of living in the world and in the U.S. is related very directly to the substitution of other forms of energy for human sweat. Progress in this respect has increased geometrically as the ox and the mule have been replaced by wood, coal, oil, gas, and uranium in an ever-increasing supply of energy units. Fission is here and fusion is on the way. Neither the minds nor the data are available today to tell us the effects of additions to or changes in the energy mix, nor the growth rate of total energy use.

The Energy Policy Project may have been the first important step toward a meaningful national discussion of energy policy. Slowly, it seems to be stimulating increasing skepticism about the need for an indefinite further increase in the supply of energy and acceptance of the idea of zero energy growth.

As the national dialogue on energy warms up, we shall hear increasing claims of righteousness by partisans, especially those who have energy to sell or have invested their lives in developing the peaceful applications of nuclear energy. They will assert that restricting the production of energy in a world of scarcity, famine, and poverty would be morally indefensible. Dr. Weinberg has evoked the Judaeo-Christian ethic most forcefully to cloak the new age of nuclear energy in high moral principle. Here is his denunciation of the unrighteous advocates of zero energy growth:

> When people starve, do we have *any* alternative but to try to give them food? When people are sick, do we have any alternative but to try to restore them to health? The idea that misery imposed today, by those who claim to see man's future with a certainty that obviously evades mortal man, is necessary for the long-term good of man is scientific arrogance at its most outrageous.
>
> Yet this seems to be what we are being asked to do. We are

told that technology cannot possibly provide sustenance in time for two, let alone four, times as many people as we now have; hence we should not waste money on new technologies of abundance, but instead should spend the money on more extensive birth-control measures.

One cannot quarrel with trying to do everything one can to control population, provided the measures themselves do not add to present human misery, as, for example, would enforced starvation. But widespread birth control is a tedious, difficult feat of social engineering. There is at least as much chance (and probably much more) that it will not succeed as that it will. And if the population, despite all our attempts, does spiral up to 7 billion to 10 billion to 15 billion, will not the plight of these billions be infinitely worse if there is no technology to provide them with means of subsistence than if there is such a technology? The obvious and prudent course is to work both sides of the street: to develop new technologies of abundance at the same time one is developing social strategies that will limit population growth.

When he speaks of new technologies of abundance, Dr. Weinberg is employing a euphemism for nuclear breeder reactors. The end, we are told, justifies a Faustian bargain—his own metaphor. Has this mode of thought not plunged us recently into the gravest of difficulties?

Such an invocation of Old and New Testament moral principles in support of succoring all suffering members of the human race has strong appeal for those who have a highly developed sense of compassion for their starving fellow humans and those whose consciences speak single-mindedly and authoritatively. When the economists step forward with facts showing that the energy crisis had a more severely adverse effect on the Blacks than upon the white majority, and agreeing that the most important single way to improve the condition of the poor is to achieve higher economic growth, the believers in the abolition of national and world poverty would seem to have no choice but to support the continued expansion of energy production and consumption. When to these voices are added those of the far larger group that would in any event welcome the conversion of more energy for their own enjoyment or profit, but who are happy to have their ignoble motives sanctified, the result would appear to be an overwhelming majority in favor of maximizing our use of energy, from whatever source.

The dissident minority consists of a mixture of variously motivated people, the central core of whom are environmentalists who have become increasingly concerned about the effect of excessive energy use on the natural environment. Only a few have so far begun to have similar concern about the effects of excessive energy use on the structures and values of society. The concerns are mutually reinforcing, but many of the environmentalists have not yet made the leap of understanding from their desire to protect nature and provide all citizens with unpolluted water and air and streets to a realization of the ways in which excessive energy use may and does erode the cohesion and stability of basic social structures. It is the dissidents who have come forward in the Energy Policy Project and pointed directly at energy as the potential source of much trouble for society if consumption in the United States continues to rise exponentially. They have accurately identified zero energy growth as an ethical issue.

Two Basic Energy Options

The United States has two principal energy options. The first is to make a strong commitment to the further development of nuclear fission, including the breeder reactor, in spite of its hazards. This option is based on the premise—widely believed, but unproven—that the more energy we have at our disposal, the better off we will be. Thus the benefits of huge additional quantities of nuclear energy are judged to outweigh the risks of radioactive poisoning. The second option is to make a decision on moral and survival grounds that the dangers to ourselves, and especially to our children and grandchildren, are so great that almost any tolerable sacrifice should be accepted as a price to avoid the possible horrors of an overwhelmingly plutonium world. This option would mean a three-way commitment to energy conservation, substantial substitution of coal for nuclear energy in spite of its sulfur and fly-ash content, and a large government-financed effort to accelerate the development and maximize the use of various forms of solar energy, gradually substituting it wherever possible for other forms of energy. A variation of this second option would be to couple it with a continuing, well-financed research program to make fusion energy practical and economical, since the fusion process is expected to produce few radioactive poisons. Such a fusion-energy development program is unlikely to pay off before the 21st century, if ever, so it would not be wise to gamble heavily upon its success.

In starkest terms, therefore, our options are either to plunge ahead from our petroleum addiction to a plutonium addiction, or to recognize our energy binge for what it has been, turn over a new leaf, and seek to develop a new moderate-energy civilization, based ultimately upon living within the annual budget of energy that comes from the sun.

To any person with a deep concern about the future, the choice would not seem to be closely balanced. Yet pressures from the vested interests of the nuclear-utility-industrial complex toward a nuclear extension of high-energy technology are so overwhelming that it will be remarkable if the body politic is able to perceive the issue in its true terms. The nuclear industry has billions of dollars on its side and a well-organized lobby, while the articulate nuclear skeptics and opponents are still comparatively few, have little money, and are not well organized. Nevertheless, the opposition is clearly gaining ground, and the bright new dawn of a nuclear age is now turning cloudy.

THE DILEMMA OF EUROPE AND JAPAN

Europe and Japan are caught in a cruel dilemma. Compared to North America, their oil and coal reserves are small, their population is large, and their agricultural land is insufficient for the nutritional support of their people, assuming continuation of their current diets. They have far less opportunity to adjust to the new age of scarcity of fossil fuels through conservation of energy than do we in the United States, since they have never been so profligate in energy use. Their positions in northerly latitudes diminish the amount of solar energy to which they have access, and the extreme seasonal variation compounds the problem still further. Even when the costs of solar cells and collectors and wind generators are reduced to their feasible minimum through automated high-volume production, Europe and Japan will not be able to supply a large share of their energy needs through the conversion of solar radiation and windpower. It is entirely understandable, therefore, that many of the policy-makers of these nations feel that they have no acceptable alternative but to affix their signatures to the Faustian contracts proferred by the peddlers of plutonium. Where else will they get the energy to meet their needs when the age of petroleum approaches total eclipse, as it will in a matter of decades? Disturbed as some of them may be by the dangers of radioactive products in huge quantities, it seems extremely likely that they will continue down the plutonium road.

If there is any hope for the human race to avoid nuclear terrorism, it will almost certainly lie in the direction of the tightest possible national and international control over the lethal radioactive materials used in reactors, and the maximum feasible substitution of other forms of energy. Up to now, nuclear technology has been confined to relatively stable, high-energy, technological societies, but national policies of the United States and other nations are moving toward the exportation of reactors to nations whose social and political institutions are more mercurial and susceptible to perversion. This is particularly unfortunate, since their geographical location and climatic conditions make them ideally suited for rapid development and extensive use of solar energy. If ever there was a clear case for the United States to invest multiple billions in the development of a new peacetime technology and make it available to the heavily populated, sun-drenched world, as well as making maximum use of it within our own borders and sharing it with the other industrialized nations, it is surely a "Manhattan Project" for solar energy.

SOLAR ENERGY: THE ORIGINAL AND ULTIMATE POWER SOURCE

The more one examines the subject of energy, the more compelling becomes the evidence that humankind, if it is to survive, has little choice but to learn to live from the continuous flow of energy from the sun. As the era of fossil fuels nears and passes its zenith, and as the dangers of substituting nuclear fission for fossil fuels become more widely and deeply understood, the absolute necessity of devising technologies for converting, storing, and retrieving the energy of the sun's rays to meet the reasonable needs of the human race becomes correspondingly apparent.

During the current era of maximum exploitation of petroleum and gas, their cost has been too low to enable solar energy to become competitive. As we reach the maximum feasible extraction rate for fossil fuels (as we have already done in this country in respect to oil and gas) and as the price of fossil fuels mounts, the economics of solar energy will gradually become more attractive. A central problem is whether solar energy can be developed and mass-produced rapidly enough and made cheap enough to reduce the compulsion to use nuclear energy to fill the breach. That depends on how much we in the United States are prepared to invest in its development. No other nation has the combination of resources and opportunity to undertake a major effort to bring down the costs of solar energy to the point where the rest of the world will seek to buy its solar technological products, rather than its nuclear reactors.

Solar technologies fall into two basic categories: those that are now feasible and need to be converted from the stage of high-cost, limited production to low-cost, automated, high-volume production, and those that are not yet developed to the point of demonstrated practicality for wide use. In the first category, the heating and cooling of homes and other buildings is the foremost example; photovoltaic cells similar to those used to generate electricity in space satellites are a second; and various ways of making wind energy more useful are a third. In the second category, the collection of solar radiation and its conversion to thermal energy for the propulsion of generators is perhaps the leading candidate for a large R&D effort, with the conversion of organic wastes and other products to useful heat energy (or to recycling back to the land for fertilization) being a second. The conversion of the ocean's surface heat for the operation of turbogenerators is a third and more remote possibility. All of these combined received only about $75 million in support from the Federal Government in 1975-76.

In a report prepared for the Federal Energy Administration's November 1974, Project Independence Study, an Interagency Panel on Solar Energy, under the direction of the National Science Foundation, estimated that with an accelerated implementation plan, the combined contribution of the six major technologies could reach a maximum of 0.4 percent of the nation's total energy demand by 1980, 3.4 percent by 1990, and 21.6 percent by 2000. A more conservative projection was made by the Energy Research and Development Administration in July, 1975: 0.8 percent of the nation's energy demand by 1985, 7 percent by 2000, and 25 percent by 2020. Both of these estimates assumed a steady and substantial increase in the nation's energy demand. If total demand were to level off because of further price increases and conservation, the importance of solar energy could increase significantly.

Large governmental expenditures are standard practice to achieve the rapid development of a new technology when the central purpose is military or a part of a Federally financed effort like the space program. The nuclear utility industry could never have developed without the government's investment of tens of billions of dollars in research and development before the first reactor-generator started producing electricity for civilian use. The computer industry was a similar beneficiary of NASA's large expenditures for research into miniaturization and large purchases of resultant products, which led to the automated production of transistors, diodes, and printed circuits, and the reduction in size and cost of computers to the point where many schoolchildren now have their own pocket computers. But when the purpose is to speed up the cost reduction that will come from the high-volume, automated production of solar energy units for the heating and cooling of homes and other low buildings, and the manufacture of solar cells, direct subsidy is treated as improper, except on a demonstration basis. Modest tax incentives are considered acceptable, but by themselves they are hardly enough.

Since more than 20 percent of the nation's energy consumption goes for the heating and cooling of homes and other buildings, the maximum feasible substitution of solar energy for oil and gas at the earliest possible date would be a conspicuous benefit from almost every point of view. We have never before had a comparable situation—a situation in which we have found it to be in the clear national interest to give a direct subsidy to consumers to help them buy something that is more expensive than a competitive product. The obstacle is a strong ideological prejudice against such a subsidy. In traditional economic terms, it runs directly contrary to accepted principles, yet it would now be a far-sighted and sound move. *Accelerating the exploration and exploitation of our remaining and diminishing domestic oil reserves without sharply diminishing our demand for oil will have the ultimate effect of increasing our dependence on foreign oil, whereas the substitution of solar energy for oil will have exactly the opposite effect.*

The contribution to the reduction of unemployment that would come from retrofitting millions of houses and low buildings with solar heating panels and related equipment would be of major importance.

It would be an industry which could benefit every section of the country and contribute to the recovery of the economy in an increasingly useful way. This would be feasible with known and currently available technology if only the strong ideological bias against substantial and direct consumer subsidies could be overcome for this exceptional and compelling case.

For the generation of electric current through solar collectors and thermal generators, much more research and development work is needed on alternative methods to minimize costs. This is one area on which a "Manhattan Project" with a new name seems most likely to have a high payoff. Such a large R&D effort has been advocated by several members of Congress, Ralph Nader, Harlan Cleveland (in a paper published by the Atlantic Council), and others. The idea is picking up strength. Less than $15 million was budgeted for this purpose in 1975-76, as compared with well over a half a billion dollars for the further development of the breeder reactor. If the funds spent on the breeder were to be switched to a concentrated attempt to accelerate the development of solar radiation collection systems and low-temperature thermal generators, and related solar energy technologies, it would signify an awakening by American policymakers and the public. It would demonstrate the capacity of alert and sensitive citizens to realize that we are at a crucial fork in the road, and that more energy does not necessarily mean a better life. One fork is labeled, "The Plutonium Superhighway, Speed Limit 90 mph." The other is labeled, "The Sunshine Parkway, Slow Down and Enjoy the Scenery."

THE RELATIONSHIP BETWEEN ENERGY SOURCES AND DEMOCRATIC VALUES

The more centralized the operation of our society, the more difficult it becomes to sustain the democratic values upon which the nation was founded. This applies to centralized government, gigantic business and industrial corporations, and the public utility companies that generate and distribute electric power. The adverse effect of centralization is much more frequently observed in respect to government than in respect to energy sources, but they are closely related.

When systems of converting fossil and nuclear fuels to electric power, for example, are progressively enlarged into enormous utility combines and distributional grids, with huge generating plants, the governmental structure that is required to regulate so vast a utility complex must inevitably become ever larger, more intricate and specialized, and more centralized in its planning and control. A large expansion of nuclear power plants would rapidly increase the degree of centralization of planning and regulation, not to mention financing, by the Federal Government. Studies have indicated that if we continue to move down the nuclear road, it would be highly desirable to create huge nuclear enclaves, euphemistically called "energy parks," in which would be concentrated enough nuclear generating capacity to provide for the needs of many millions of people in a number of different states. These would contain reprocessing plants for nuclear fuel so that it would not have to be transported long distances over public rights of way, with the danger of having radioactive poisons spread over the landscape by accident or having nuclear fuels hijacked. These energy parks would have to be planned by the Federal Government in collaboration with states and utility combines, and when built would have to be carefully regulated and supervised by the government. It would be another large step in the direction of Federal concentration and centralization of control, with an infinitesimal degree of influence by local communities and consumer groups.

Such a form of organization would further imperil democratic institutions in the event that some extraordinary event or accident forced the shutdown of an energy park and the blackout of a large area for any significant length of time. To avert chaos, the likelihood is substantial that martial law would have to be invoked. Even on a temporary basis, this suspension of normal civil rights could seriously undermine the foundations of civil government. Complexity and centralization greatly compound the potential adverse effects of error and accident, and reduce the capacity of any system to heal itself through the adaptive processes and redundancies that are common in simpler systems.

Solar energy would move us in precisely the opposite direction. Since it is so widely dispersed, its maximum feasible use would reduce vulnerability to regional blackouts and greatly increase the degree of individual and community control over energy use and policies. It would in fact help us to preserve and enhance democratic values.

It is worth noting that the same principle applies to generating plants fired by fossil fuels, where the concept of total energy use is embodied in community and architectural planning. Under this concept, much smaller generating plants are built than has been the general practice in recent years, and a large proportion of the heat which is now wasted in mammoth plants is used for space heating within the surrounding community. The economy of this type of total energy use has been demonstrated in Sweden and elsewhere; the heat savings more than compensate for the higher cost of generating electricity in smaller power plants. From the standpoint of the structure of society, it harmonizes far better with democratic values.

The more one examines the energy problems of this country, the more evident it becomes that energy as a commodity has a unique status to which the normal laws of supply and demand will have declining applicability and on which social attitudes and politics will have increasing effect. Social and political factors will thus establish more proximate limits to energy growth, and therefore economic growth, than the exhaustion of physical resources or environmental pollution and destruction. If and when physical growth, as roughly measured by energy consumption, is no longer considered by the body politic as a self-evident good, it may come to an end sooner than most technologists and economists have forecast.

IX. Human Procreation: A "Right" Without Social Responsibility

As the future of energy—its sources and quantities—seems likely to be the single most important factor influencing the future of modernized societies, so the dynamics of population seem overwhelmingly likely to be the prime determinant of the future of the low-energy societies, where the majority of the human race live. The demographer Ansley Coale has distilled the essence of population arithmetic:

> The present rate of world population increase—20 per thousand—is almost certainly without precedent, and is hundreds of times greater than the rate that has been the norm for most of man's history. Without doubt this period will be a transitory episode in the history of the population. If the present rate were to be maintained, the population would double approximately every 35 years, it would be multiplied by a thousand every 350 years and by a million every 700 years. . . .
>
> Arithmetic makes a return to a growth rate near zero inevitable before many generations have passed. What is uncertain is not that the future rate of growth will be about zero but how large the future population will be and what combination of fertility and mortality will sustain it.

During the first 2-3 million years after homo sapiens emerged as a species, population grew at no more than 0.002 percent annually. Ten thousand years ago, when man converted his life-style from hunting and gathering to the agricultural mode and began to build villages and cities, population growth jumped to something on the order of twenty-five times: Human population grew from an estimated 5-10 million in 8000 B.C. to 200-400 million in A.D. 1. This was a population explosion in itself, but not overwhelming in relation to the rest of the natural kingdom, and small in comparison with what was to come in the 19th and 20th centuries. And the rate of increase in the third quarter of this century—2 percent per year—reached a thousand times what it had been during the first 2 million years of man's life on earth. Obviously, such a rate of increase cannot continue much longer. The crucial question is whether it will end by an extraordinarily rapid decrease in birth rates, by a tragic increase in death rates, or by some combination of the two.

THE DYNAMICS OF POPULATION GROWTH

The more closely one examines the dynamics of population growth in the densely populated, low-energy societies, the poorer the prospects of such nations appear. Their population problem has the unusual characteristic of becoming more serious each year, *even when the per capita food supply in these nations is increasing*. To understand why this is so, and why severe famines are highly likely to be the primary force for reducing the world population growth rate during the balance of this century, it is necessary to examine four basic concepts: (1) parental motivation as the primary determinant of fertility rates and family size; (2) the ease and cheapness of transferring death control from the high-energy societies to the nonmodernized societies, in contrast to the enormous difficulty of creating conditions in agrarian societies that are conducive to low birth rates; (3) the meaning of population momentum and demographic supersaturation; and (4) the foreseeable voluntary decline in the population of high-energy societies, in contrast to the implacable population crunch in the low-energy societies.

1. Parental motivation: the primary determinant of family size. To a greater degree than is generally realized, families in widely varying cultures have approximately as many children as they want. It is often assumed that until modern contraceptive technology was developed, families always had many more children than they wanted and that it was only such technology that enabled parents to

TOTAL FERTILITY RATE

Average U.S. Family Size Implied By Current Fertility Patterns

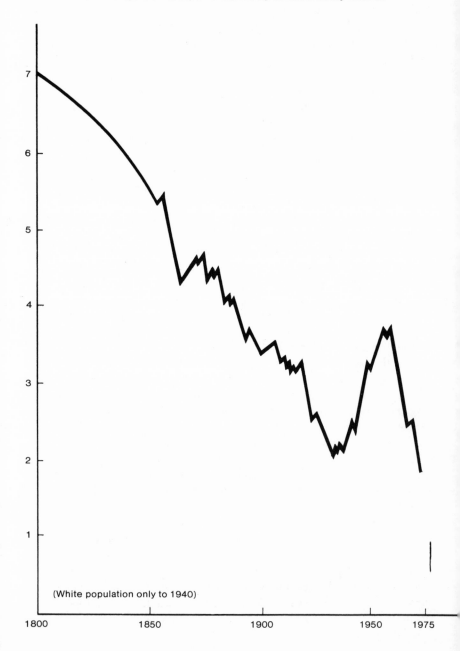

(White population only to 1940)

1974 total fertility rate was 1.86; the replacement level is 2.11.
See *Notes* for information as to sources.

control family size as they desired. Similarly, until recently, it has been rather widely believed that if the poor farmers in agrarian societies were given access to the contraceptive knowledge and methods available to modernized societies, the birth rate would fall rapidly. It now appears that neither belief was well grounded. It is instructive to compare the experience of the United States and India as case studies that throw light on the dominant force of motivation in determining family size, no matter what means of birth control may or may not be available.

In 1800, when the United States was 94 percent rural and children were frequently the main source of farm labor, American women bore an average of seven children. By 1935, when the nation had become 56 percent urban, the average had declined drastically to only two children per mother. (See graph on facing page.) Farm machinery, gasoline, and diesel oil had made farm labor surplus; and children, even on farms, were no longer the economic assets they once were. In the cities, they were conspicuous liabilities, or, to express it a bit less harshly, they were expensive outlets for the love and self-fulfillment of parents. The 135-year decline in the fertility of American women occurred because families wanted fewer children, not primarily because of any radical improvement in contraceptive technology. The means were ancient: abstinence, coitus interruptus, condoms, douches, diaphragms, the rhythm method (the "safe" period), self-induced abortion, and therapeutic and illegal abortions. The pill and the IUD did not become widely used for three more decades. The will was demonstrably far more important than the pill.

The shift from high to low birth and death rates, with a much longer life expectancy—the "demographic transition"—occurred only in societies where the per capita consumption of energy increased rapidly and that energy was used to mechanize and urbanize the society, substitute cheap energy for labor, and elimi- nate child labor, thus making children expensive to support and educate. Cheap energy, and the society it created, offered adults all sorts of alternatives to children: larger and more luxurious homes or apartments, automobiles, television sets, air conditioners, jet travel, and scores of other energy consuming means of enjoyment. All the high-energy societies developed wage economies in which families could choose to dispose of their income either to produce many children and live at a low material standard, or to produce few or no children and live at a higher standard. The incentives were clear, and the long-term decline in fertility was a logical result.

Even the post-World War II baby boom was understandable in these terms, since it came at a time when parents suddenly wanted and thought they could afford more children. The Great Depression had caused a substantial number of parents to limit family size or at least to defer having more children until better times; World War II had separated young men and women from normal relationships and sentimentalized family life; the war also put large savings in the hands of young people, and the postwar change in economic mores put more credit at their disposal; and finally, most young parents had steady employment at wages that enabled them to marry and begin their families at early ages. All these factors gave young parents the false impression that they would be able to raise a good-sized family and still have enough money for the other things they wanted. It took a decade after the war was over before they learned otherwise, and when they did learn, the long-term downward trend in the fertility rate resumed its former course (again, before the pill or the IUD were widely used)—dropping from an average of 3.7 children in 1957 to 1.86 in 1974, a 50 percent reduction.

In India, the dominant economic motivation had the opposite effect because of totally different conditions. As an overwhelmingly agricultural society (three-quarters of its population live in the half a million agricultural villages), where human and animal labor is the principal source of energy for producing food and income, Indian families have many children for the same reason that rural American families had many children in 1800—because it is in their self-interest to do so. Children not only till the land and harvest the crops, but when they grow up, they become the principal "social security" for Indians in their old age. (There is no governmental old-age insurance.) Under such conditions, the creation of numerous family-planning clinics throughout the country, with free or low-cost contraceptives and special inducements for sterilizations, has understandably had only limited effect in reducing birth rates. The program makes it easier for couples who have already achieved their desired family size to avoid unwanted pregnancies, but it does little to persuade farm families to have fewer children.

The examples of the United States and India show that economic self-interest can have exactly opposite effects in respect to the production of children—producing small families in high-energy, urban, wage societies, and large families in low-energy, largely non-wage agricultural societies. The rich nations thus have a set of demographic incentives that tend to make them richer, while the poor societies are afflicted with incentives that push them further and further into the Malthusian quagmire. A greater perversity in the operation of human institutions would be hard to imagine.

2. The ease of deferring deaths and the difficulty of reducing births. The population explosion in the poor nations resulted primarily from a dramatic drop in the death rate without a corresponding decline in the birth rate. Instant death control was a product of the knowledge revolution that took place in the high-energy societies, and it became extraordinarily easy and cheap to export such a seeming boon to humanity to the agrarian societies. Beginning with basic public-health systems of sanitation, pasteurization of milk, and vaccination and innoculation against communicable diseases, death control became easier and easier to apply on a massive scale, until finally the use of DDT and other insecticides and the availability of the so-called "miracle drugs" made it possible to reduce death rates drastically in the least modernized areas of the tropics and subtropics at little expense.

But what began as a humane act to "save" lives was carried out with little realization of the enormous difficulties the nations would face in trying to create conditions in which the people saved could live healthy lives. And the West had no way of transferring the conditions that had enabled industrial societies to cut their fertility rates down to the replacement level. The result was the population explosion that is now heading toward disaster.

India has, in 1976, some 600 million people in a land that is only a little more than a third the size of the United States (not including Alaska and Hawaii), and each year it is adding about 13-15 million more people. Its birth rate is about 39 per thousand per year, its death rate about 15, and its growth rate 2.4 percent per year. Fully half of all Indians are either undernourished, malnourished, or at the bare minimum of adequate food intake. At the very least, therefore, India must increase its food supplies by enough to take care of 13-15 million more people each year. Over the past two decades, it has managed, on the average, to increase its food production by a little more than enough to keep up with the ever-mounting number of mouths to be fed, but such a rate can probably not be kept up for long enough to sustain another doubling of the Indian population. At its present growth rate, the population would double in 28 years, and would, if sustained, quadruple in 56 years. By just after the beginning of the 21st century, India would have 1.2 billion and would be adding about 29 million a year. Obviously, such rates of increase cannot long be sustained. Either birth rates must come down dramatically in the not distant future, or death rates will certainly rise. Neither the Green Revolution—the new seeds developed by the Nobel laureate Norman Borlaug, plus the improved fertilization, irrigation, and cultivation demonstrated in the Punjab—nor industrial modernization has the prospect of aiding India sufficiently to extricate itself from the population trap. The situation is, in fact, worse than it appears from raw statistics. India, Bangladesh, and other nations are becoming demographically supersaturated.

3. The meaning and tragedy of demographic supersaturation. Human supersaturation of a poor land—when a nation unwittingly acquires a substantially larger population than it has the long-range capacity to sustain while its population is still growing rapidly—is a tragic condition from which there is no known escape but famine. Agrarian nations can become supersaturated in two principal ways. The first is to become excessively dependent on one or two crops as a source of food and income—crops that may be vulnerable to blight, drought, or other failure. That is what happened to Ireland during the first half of the 19th century, ending in the potato famines of 1845-48, from which some 20 percent of Ireland's people perished; in the ensuing decades, Ireland's population dropped to less than half of what it had been before the great famines, mostly through emigration and patterns of primogeniture, extremely late marriage, and nonmarriage.

The second way in which a heavily populated agrarian nation can become supersaturated without realizing what is happening is exactly what is occurring in India and Bangladesh: a prolonged period in which death rates plummet, but birth rates stay high. Under such conditions, the number of children skyrockets, creating a massive procreation potential, a time bomb that ticks away until those children reach the age of reproduction. This procreative momentum is evident from the accompanying graph that shows the enormous size of the lower age groups of the Indian population. By 1970, the five-year age group had reached nearly 100 million, and each succeeding cohort will be still larger. The number of Indian children in the youngest age group is thus about seven times that of the United States, the young-child density some twenty times as great and still rising rapidly. This mammoth child population casts a long, dark shadow ahead for India.

Assuming India's practical limit of food production will eventually turn out to be sufficient to sustain no more than a billion people—nearly fifteen times America's current density—(a not unreasonable assumption), India already has so many children that the population momentum cannot be stopped at a billion by suddenly reducing its fertility to the replacement level when the population reaches a billion. Even if Indian women were to reduce their childbearing to two by 1990 (an extraordinarily optimistic assumption), the population would eventually exceed a billion unless limited by famine or provided with food from external sources. The population momentum is evident from the accompanying age-sex pyramid showing more than 40 percent of India's population to be under 15 years of age. Visualize more than a hundred million children aged 0-5 living out their lives (the current life expectancy is a little over 50 years), while each succeeding cohort is equally large. The pyramid then becomes rectangular, and the volume of the rectangle with an average of over a hundred million children added every five years would exceed a billion people. When a tremendous population momentum has been created, it takes from 50 to 70 years (the life expectancy of the population) *after* its family size has been reduced to the replacement level of just over two before natural increase comes to an end. If the nation is to be self-sufficient in food, it must therefore bring its average family size down to the replacement level fifty or more years before it reaches the practical limit of its food production.

The information-feedback mechanism by which adaptive adjustments are made in ecological and economic systems is simply not working in some of the poor agrarian societies. Economists are used to thinking in terms of automatically self-correcting tendencies of the market system. If the automobile industry produces more cars than it can sell, it learns of that situation with little delay, whereupon it cuts back on production and lays off workers. When it comes to producing

INDIA: 1970 POPULATION BY AGE AND SEX

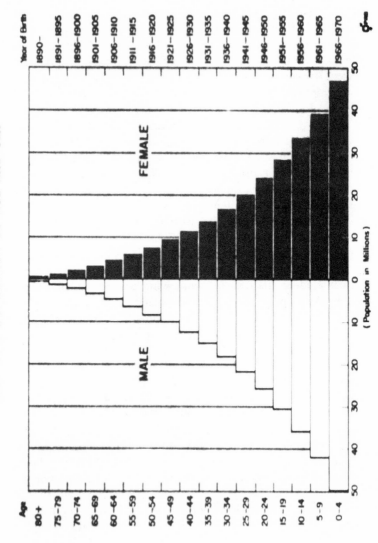

babies in poor agrarian societies, however, the feedback mechanism is a very inefficient means of informing parents that the point of supersaturation has been reached. As long as large families are advantageous, as they surely appear to be to most poor farmers, parents will continue to have many children regardless of how many contraceptives they are offered and urged to use. Tragically, by the time a powerful enough message reaches them, it is too late by half a century. It is hard to imagine a more inefficient and cruel feedback information system.

4. The profound gulf between the two demographic worlds. The chasm between the two demographic worlds is growing wider all the time. One world, overwhelmingly Caucasian, is well-fed, meat-eating, highly industralized and urbanized, literate, consumes vast quantities of energy, lives in temperate zones, and seems now to be approaching an era of population decline. The other, a much larger proportion of humanity, overwhelmingly nonwhite, is poorly fed (more than half of its members are seriously undernourished, malnourished, or both), gains most of its sustenance from plant foods, is predominantly nonindustrial and agrarian, has low literacy, lives mostly in the subtropical or tropical zones, uses small amounts of energy per capita, and has moderate to low death rates and generally high birth rates. In between these two extremes are a number of nations in rapid movement toward modernization. With one or two exceptions (for example, Brazil), these either are oil-rich nations or are very small, such as Taiwan, Singapore, and Hongkong.

The affluent Caucasian minority is declining in relative numbers and soon may begin to shrivel in absolute numbers, while the majority of the human race continues to move, seemingly inexorably, toward supersaturation. Some of the poor nations may already have more people than they can sustain over the long range, but even those that may be able to double their food production have small prospect of bringing their population growth to zero by nontraumatic means before another doubling of their population occurs. It is instructive to take a closer look at the divergence of these trends.

THE FORESEEABLE POPULATION DECLINE IN THE
INDUSTRIALIZED WORLD

Almost every industrialized nation has shown a marked decline in its total fertility in recent years, and this decline is consistent with, and an extension of, a long-term trend. Charles F. Westoff, who served as Executive Director of the Commission on Population Growth and the American Future, summarized the key findings of a study he made in 1974 of fertility in 31 developed nations:

> The variety of patterns in these 31 countries should not obscure the central and most important fact that fertility in most of the developed world has virtually collapsed. Only New Zealand (in which fertility has been declining), Ireland, Spain, Portual, and the Jews of Israel still have relatively high rates, ranging between 2.8 births per woman and 3.9. In 20 of the 31 countries the total fertility rate is not far from, and in some cases is below, the replacement level of 2.1 births per woman; it appears headed in that direction or hovering around 2.3 births in most of the remaining 11 countries. The average fertility rate for all 31 countries is currently 2.3 births per woman. If the figure is weighted for population, the average drops to 2.2 for the total population of the developed world. The population growth rate in all but a few countries is now less than 1 percent.

The countries whose fertility rate had dropped below the replacement level by 1973 were Austria, Switzerland, East Germany, West Germany, Denmark, Sweden, Finland, the Netherlands, Bulgaria, Hungary, the United States, and Canada. Belgium, England and Wales, and Scotland seem headed for subreplacement fertility in the very near future, if they have not already reached it. Japan's fertility rate which underwent the most dramatic decline in history when it dropped from 4.5 births per woman in 1947 to 2.0 a decade later, is now only slightly above the replacement level.

It seems apparent that the entire industrialized world is heading toward subreplacement fertility, and that this is probably not a transient phenomenon. The general recession precipitated by the quadrupling of oil prices was not the cause, although it undoubtedly compounded an already existing tendency. If, as earlier theorized, the United States and the rest of the high-energy, urbanized world are in for a long-term decline in living standards or, at best, very slow growth, it seems probable that economic pressures will tend to have a continuing negative effect on the fertility rate. Once people have reached a standard of living to which they would like to continue to be accustomed, they try very hard to hang on to it, even if it means foregoing their idealized family size. Subreplacement fertility is likely to become normal throughout the industrialized world.

What we are likely to see, therefore, in the industrialized world is a general population decline, starting in some countries in the 1970s and 1980s, and somewhat later in those countries that had a large post-World War II baby boom. The number of young women in the latter countries now reaching their prime reproductive years is so great that, even at subreplacement fertility rates, the number of babies they produce will substantially exceed the number of deaths in the general population for a good many years to come. Thus, for Canada, the United States, Australia, and New Zealand—the nations with the largest baby booms—it seems likely to be several decades before deaths exceed births. But once the decline sets in, it will have accumulated a downward momentum in the same way the baby boom generated an upward momentum. Population stabilization, an increasingly discussed objective, seems a very unlikely condition. A rather extended population decline seems far more probable.

At the 1974 World Population Conference in Bucharest, much was made of the fact that even with their modest increases in population, Western societies were placing a greater strain on the world's resource base than are the agrarian societies. In consequence, said many delegates, the affluent nations had an even greater responsibility to bring birth and death rates into prompt balance than the low-consumption countries. This raised the question as to whether a nation like the United States should develop policies that would create further discouragements to childbearing than the negative incentives that already exist. The answer, under current circumstances, would seem rather clearly to be no; the results would be startling and counterintuitive.

Earlier, it was indicated that the total fertility rate—the average number of children born to each woman—had declined from 3.7 in 1957 to an implied level of 1.86 in 1974, a 50 percent drop, and by 1974 some 12 percent below the level needed for replacement. Immigration aside, if the fertility rate were to continue at 1.86 for the indefinite future, the population would begin to decline in about half a century. But for several decades, the momentum of the baby boom will cause the population to continue to increase. If the nation were to try to offset totally the effects of the baby boom and stabilize the population in the near future, the effects would be astounding.

Because of the distortion of the age structure by the baby boom, if one were to set a goal of bringing births and deaths into balance by 1985, as some have advocated, it would mean that the total fertility of American women would have to drop to 1.2 children per woman. As calculated by the Population Council demographer Tomas Frejka, if the nation then wished to stabilize population at the 1985 level (setting immigration aside), the very small baby crop that emerged in 1985 and immediately subsequent years would have to more than double its fertility when these girls grew to womanhood—up to 2.8 children per woman. A generation later, the offspring of these women would have to drop their fertility back down to about 1.4, and such wild oscillations would have to continue, with diminishing amplitude, for some two centuries. When the age structure becomes as grossly distorted as it was by the post-World War II baby boom, there is no way of bringing births and deaths into balance in the near-term future and keeping them there, except by incredible gyrations in which each generation must offset the excessively high and then the excessively low fertility rates of previous generations.

Under the circumstances, now that fertility is appreciably below the replacement level and shows no signs of bouncing back above it in the near future, the wise approach would appear to be to let nature take its course rather than trying to accelerate its downward trend or reverse it. It is now within a range that seems to be in the long-run interest of the nation—no longer so high as to warrant concern about excessive growth, but not so low as to suggest that the nation needs to consider policies to save itself from extinction. So long as fertility remains in the range of 1.6 to 2.1, no governmental action or non-governmental hortatory advice to influence women to increase or decrease their family size would appear necessary or desirable. Reducing the wasteful consumption of the overdeveloped nations, especially the United States, is a problem that should be addressed directly and not through efforts to reduce fertility so abruptly and drastically as to bring about further serious distortion of the age structure.

This is not to suggest that the United States and other Western nations have totally solved their problems of population and procreation. Far too high a percentage of the babies now born are the unintentional result of premarital and extramarital intercourse. The national percentage of children born out of wedlock rose from 3.9 percent in 1950 to 13 percent in 1973, with teenage pregnancies accounting for a significant proportion of the total. It is clear that the vast majority of the resulting children are less likely than wanted children to grow up under conditions that will give them the opportunity to become contributing members of society. Procreation as a right without corresponding social responsibility plagues over-developed societies as well as the less developed.

THE PAINFUL PROSPECT FOR THE AGRARIAN NATIONS

The decline in fertility to levels that seem to presage an end to population growth in Europe and North America took place in the two-century period when fossil fuels—nature's richest legacy—were extracted and burned at an ever-increasing rate, enabling the consuming nations to change their life-style from an agricultural non-wage economy to an urban wage economy and thus reverse the economic incentives of procreation. Now, suddenly, the poor agrarian nations are confronted with the need to reverse these incentives in a much shorter time, and without massive amounts of cheap energy. It is an almost impossible challenge.

Drs. John and Carol Steinhart—one a geologist, the other a biologist—have carefully studied and documented a comparison between American high-energy agriculture and Indian low-energy agriculture, and assert that such countries as India simply do not have access to energy in quantities required for the rapid mechanization and intensive fertilization of large segments of their lands. They calculate that to feed the people of India at a level of 3,000 calories a day would require more energy for food production alone than India now uses for all purposes. And the enormous price increase for energy can have no other effect than to put a heavy damper on the hopes of those who had counted on the Green Revolution to keep agricultural output ahead of the baby crop.

Even if India could earn enough foreign exchange to buy the enormous quantities of oil and equipment needed for the mechanization, fertilization, and irrigation of Indian agriculture, the dislocation of the scores of millions of farmers rendered surplus by the process would put a burden on the society that would create chaos. Under such circumstances, Kingsley Davis's speculative forecast of incredibly bloated cities—of 20, 40, or even 60 million people—might become a reality, with vast numbers of the people unemployed and barely existing, under subhuman conditions.

What India needs, it seems—looking at the situation with an open rather than a Western technological perspective—or one that has been Westernized by envious imitation—is a labor-intensive agricultural system that will produce much more per man-hour of labor without rendering the labor surplus and banishing it from the villages, coupled with small industries that can be operated in modest-sized communities.* Seeking to follow the development paths of the high-energy technological societies can only end up in dismal frustration for the Indian people.

But even such a plan has small hope of genuine success as long as the Indians believe it to be in their self-interest to have large families. Unless they rapidly reduce their families to an average of two or less, they are headed for an Irish-type disaster. Conceivably, an intensive educational program, beamed via satellite to the half-million Indian villages, with multiple sound tracks for the numerous language groups, coupled with a renewed and enlarged campaign for voluntary contraception, sterilization, and abortion, might have a major impact. As this is being written, India is experimenting with telecasts via a satellite that the United States has temporarily positioned over West Africa and made available to the Indian government for programming. A mixture of entertainment and genuine education about the problems of India, especially its population problems and the reasons why delayed marriage and small families would be in the interests of both parents and their children, plus a continuing discussion of the best methods of improving agricultural production and conserving the land, just might have a chance of changing the perceptions of Indian villagers about their individual and collective self-interest.

The most crucial concept Indians and others must begin to understand—either through education or the experience of famine—is that *any nation which hopes to be reasonably self-sufficient in food must achieve the small-family pattern, averaging about two children per*

*An exposition of this concept is cogently set forth by a British development economist and businessman, E. F. Schumacher, in his excellent book *Small is Beautiful: Economics as if People Mattered* (1973).

woman, about two generations before the upper limit of food-growing capacity is reached. Otherwise, the nation will be faced with increasing food shortages and famine until the population is brought into line with its long-range food-carrying capacity.

China, after many years of dogged adherence to the Marxian, anti-Malthusian doctrine that population pressure in a totally socialist nation is a figment of reactionary imagination and propaganda, finally faced the reality of human arithmetic forthrightly and concluded that drastic action was necessary. Since the late 1960s, Mao has made it a patriotic duty for young people to delay marriage until their late twenties and to have smaller families. Since emigration is not now generally available as an outlet to the Chinese, the Indians, or most other agrarian nations, late marriage and nonmarriage are the most hopeful means by which the small-family pattern can be achieved in such nations. China's traditions and social institutions make the rapid adoption of such a change in mores far more feasible than would be the case in India, Bangladesh, Indonesia, or the Philippines. But it remains to be seen whether China has taken action in time. Whether China will be able to continue to increase its food production in coming decades sufficiently to feed another half-billion people—a rough estimate of the number who may be added by the current population momentum—is rather doubtful. It seems unlikely that many of the other large agrarian nations that are not endowed with great storehouses of natural resources can or will arrest their population momentum in time to prevent catastrophe.

X. The Ethics and Politics of Food

The current distribution of the world's people in relation to the productive capacity of the land over which they have control is extremely disparate and becoming more so all the time. Theoretically, it would be possible to bring about a much higher level of equity either by redistributing people or by redistributing the products of their labor in relation to the basic needs of each person. The fossil fuels and minerals of the earth would require similar redistribution; they would have to be treated as world resources to be divided up among the entire human family. Nothing could be more evident than that none of these changes has the remotest possibility of coming about in the foreseeable future. And even if they could be brought about, the results would not benefit the human race. Equal distribution of the earth's food might enable the world to sustain more people, but it would rapidly depress all mankind to the near-poverty level and leave the problem of excessive procreation unsolved.

Georg Borgstrom has pointed out: "If all the food in the world were equally distributed and each human being received identical quantities, we would all be malnourished. If the entire world's food supply were parcelled out at the U.S. dietary level, it would feed only about one-third of the human race. The world as a global household knows of no surpluses, merely enormous deficits. Yet in the well-fed nations there is a great deal of nonsensical talk about abundance and self-sufficiency."

There is no escape from the logic that humankind must learn to restrict its numbers so as to live within its growing but limited food supply. We have already seen that the outlook is gloomy in India, as it is in various parts of the Third World. We now come to the question as to how the rest of the world will treat Third World hunger and possible famine—an ethical and political issue of great magnitude. For the purposes of our analysis, we shall concentrate on the way this problem seems likely to be dealt with in the United States.

The American delegates to the U.N. World Conference on Population in Bucharest in August 1974 assumed that most of the 136 nations represented there shared their deep concern about the high rate of population growth—75 to 80 million additional people every year— creating an especially heavy burden on the less developed countries. But they were to learn that many of the LDCs resented the efforts of the United States to tell them how serious their population problem was. A large anti-American bloc engaged in a largely successful effort to shift the main subject from population to economic development.

Prior to the conference, Lester Brown, the "Worldwatcher" and food expert, produced a book, *In the Human Interest: A Strategy to Stabilize World Population,* in the hope of communicating to the conferees his sense of urgency about the need for a crash program to bring world birth and death rates into balance sooner than had ever been seriously discussed. He suggested that all the LDCs set a goal of reduction in their birth rates to 25 per thousand by 1985, and that the more developed countries strive for population stability by 1985 (by which he meant bringing birth rates down to the level of death rates). If the LDCs were able to meet such a goal, Brown believed it would be possible to continue the downward momentum thus achieved and bring world population to a figure of just under 6 billion by the year 2015. It was a call to action by one of the world's foremost food experts whose head and intuition told him the earth probably could not support many more than 6 billion people in health and dignity and peace and hope. But Brown's idealistic plea enlisted little support, though it may have given pause to many delegates. The conference wound up with what amounted to a conclusion that population was not an international matter, but should be left to national responsibility and self-judgment. Those countries that thought they had a problem and needed international assistance were invited to seek such aid, but the international "community," it was made clear, should put no pressure on others who were not concerned about population.

The position of the LDCs had been apparent earlier in the growing attitude of resentment toward the "overdeveloped" nations. A not uncommon viewpoint was that additional development, Western-style, must occur before the less developed nations should seek to cut back sharply on population growth. Any effort to reverse the order and stabilize population before achieving a decent standard of living was said to be racially inspired. No counterargument, however logical, put forward by Western analysts, had a chance of convincing representatives of LDCs who approached the subject with such convictions.

THE ROOTS OF ANTI-MALTHUSIANISM

Disbelief in the validity of the theory that population has an inherent tendency to outrun food supply—the proposition with which Malthus has been associated ever since his first essay on population in 1798—is shared by people with very different philosophical orientations, but particularly by all Marxists on ideological grounds. Marx despised Malthus, and the disciples of Marx remain no less contemptuous of 20th-century believers in the impending spectre of Malthusian scarcity. In their view, the Third World's poverty would gradually recede if all nations were wise enough to organize themselves according to Marxist principles. Evidence to the contrary is ignored or brushed off; the fact that the Soviet Union's record in the production of food has not been spectacular and that it sank below the self-sufficiency level in 1972 and 1975, necessitating huge purchases of American wheat, is said to have no meaning. India, it is asserted, is a continuing victim of economic exploitation by the imperialist nations, and it is now the duty of the United States and the other economic imperialists to lower their excessively high prices for the capital goods the Third World nations need to industrialize, as a means of reparation for the centuries of exploitation. The argument is thus shifted from its original Marxist doctrinal position that socialism can solve all problems of scarcity to the assertion that the rich capitalist nations, on moral grounds, owe the poor exploited nations reparations in the form of capital goods to industrialize and food to make up deficits from crop failures. No empirical evidence is ever adduced to show the Marxist principles will make scarcity obsolete. Yet the doctrine persists.

The Western liberal idealist shares the Marxist's faith that humankind has not come close to the physical limits of the earth in its efforts
to produce food and goods sufficient to assure all people everywhere
a decent standard of living. Having grown up amid burgeoning
technology, powered by unlimited quantities of cheap energy, and
having watched the so-called "free-enterprise system" turn out mammoth quantities of food and goods, the 20th-century humanitarian is
hardly less convinced than the Marxist that scarcities represent
human failures which we should be able to overcome by appropriate
problem-solving and reform. It is deeply ingrained in the American
liberal's ideology that there must be some way of solving every
problem if it is approached with reason and good will by the parties
involved, and if science and technology are imaginatively and diligently applied.

Ever since the marriage of science and technology in the 19th
century, and especially as a result of the phenomenal fertility of that
marriage in the three decades during and after World War II, the
feasibility of abolishing poverty, both at home and abroad, has
seemed increasingly to be coming within our grasp. Few were star-
tled when, in 1960, John F. Kennedy proclaimed in his inaugural
address that "man holds in his mortal hands the power to abolish all
forms of human poverty and all forms of human life." Even the
disheartening events of 1965-75 could not shake the faith of ardent
believers that the Malthusian trap of the Third World nations could
be loosened and the world population problem substantially solved
before devastating famines descended, if only appropriate economic
aid were provided by the United States and other high-energy
societies to hasten the industrial development of the low-energy
societies.

As the final quarter of the 20th century begins, this optimism is
under severe strain, but faith that severe famine can be avoided is an
ethical imperative for many people. Such an imperative leads them
to two hopeful answers to the population problem of the Third
World, both of which would require large amounts of foreign aid.
The first is the optimistic thesis that economic development actually
can bring the birth rate down within some kind of sensible time
frame. The second is that improved nutrition and health, also with
aid from abroad, could have a rapid effect in diminishing birth rates.
It is important to look closely at each of these.

1. Economic development: solution or mirage? By an odd reversal of roles, economic development experts and those concerned with reducing rapid rates of population growth (there are no genuine experts in this field) now seem to be moving in opposite directions. Most of the development economists who went to the LDCs, rolled up their sleeves, and did their best to find ways of improving the per capita output and income of the poor agrarian societies have become increasingly discouraged about the prospect of indefinitely keeping ahead of a 2-3 percent increase in population each year (sometimes even above 3 percent). Some way, they feel, has to be found of decreasing that rate of population growth in a shorter period of time than would occur as a by-product of economic development. At the same time, some members of the population "establishment" that invested so much of its faith in making contraceptives available to all who might wish them, have become increasingly discouraged about relying so heavily on this method of bringing down the birth rate, and feel that since economic development is a proven means for reducing fertility, it should receive primary emphasis, with family planning made an integral component of such development. No other alternative seems now to exist, they feel, but to push hard for economic development. Such a conclusion would also seem to put the population establishment in a more defensible moral position vis-à-vis the late comers to the world economic smorgasbord.

At Bucharest, where these late comers rebelled against the emphasis on birth control and successfully turned the conference in the direction of economic development, John D. Rockefeller III, spiritual godfather of the population movement in the United States, threw his intellectual and moral weight behind this revised emphasis by asserting to the Population Tribune—a parallel conference—that: "The only viable course is to place population policy squarely in the context of economic development." The implication was that Western-style economic development—that is, the kind the Third World nations want—was essential to the lowering of birth rates, and that high-energy societies had an obligation to aid the LDCs in achieving such development. Moral as the position may be, there is unfortunately little evidence that this avenue can lead to the solution of the population problem within any realistic time frame.

Curiously, though, this position acquired a certain standing in professional demographic circles at the same time it was losing ground among discouraged development economists. In an essay entitled "A New Demographic Transition" (1971), Stanford University's respected demographer Dudley Kirk undertook to demonstrate that demographic transitions from high to low birth and death rates used to take a very long time, but that there is now evidence that the time required to achieve the economic development and the related conditions that underlie demographic transitions has been greatly shortened. But when one examines his data, one finds that the countries that have recently made rapid progress in bringing down both death and birth rates, thus moving toward a new demographic transition, are atypical of the Third World nations. They are Albania, Sri Lanka (Ceylon), Hong Kong, Malaysia (West), Puerto Rico, the Ryukyu Islands, Singapore, Taiwan, and Trinidad and Tobago. All are small, and most of them have had large amounts of American (or other Western) money poured into them in one way or another. Just consider the amount of U.S. military expenditures and aid allotted to Korea, Taiwan, and the Ryukyu Islands; the American industrial investment in Puerto Rico and Taiwan; the global corporations' investment in Singapore, Taiwan, and Hong Kong. These small nations began with the head start of much higher literacy than the large agrarian LDCs, and were plunged rapidly into becoming industrial (and tourism) wage economies in which children increasingly became conspicuous financial liabilities rather than assets. How can one infer from such cases that countries like Bangladesh, India, Pakistan, and Indonesia have a similar opportunity to move rapidly through even so partial a demographic transition?

2. Can improved wealth and nutrition rapidly reduce fertility? A related doctrine has also become widely accepted: that further improvement in the health and nutrition of the people of the less developed countries will reduce fertility and help stimulate a rapid demographic transition, thus overcoming the population problem. A further reduction in infant and child mortality is strongly urged as a means of persuading parents that it is not necessary to have as many children as formerly in order to achieve their desired family size. It is an appealing idea; the wish is undoubtedly father to the thought. But there is little evidence to support the thesis and more to rebut it.

The case of Sri Lanka—one of the nations cited as having shown a substantial decline in birth rate and thus a high promise of passing through the demographic transition rather quickly in contrast to the two centuries and more that has been required (and still will be required) for the United States to bring birth and death rates into balance at low levels and high longevity. Ceylon's birth rate in 1945 was about 37 per thousand, the death rate 22 per thousand, the natural increase 1.5 percent, and the life expectancy 42 years. In the following six years, various public health measures—especially DDT to eradicate malaria—were instituted, with the result that the death rate was cut in half, and continued to drop thereafter until by 1973 it had reached 6.4 per thousand, even lower than that of the United States. Meanwhile, the birth rate began to come down rather sharply, reaching 32 by the early 1960s and remaining at approximately that level for most of the decade, when it again declined slightly; by 1973 it had reached 28.6 and life expectancy at birth had reached 68 years. By 1973, therefore, Sri Lanka had a death rate that was 22 points lower than its birth rate, resulting in a natural population increase of 2.2 percent per year, appreciably higher than the rate some three decades earlier.

Thus, although birth rates have indeed come down very significantly in the last 30 years, Sri Lanka's rate of increase has not and its prospect of completing the demographic transition by bringing birth and death rates into balance with a population that it can sustain on a long-term basis are poor. Some 39 percent of the population are under 15 years of age, with each age cohort much larger than the previous one. In 1945 its population was some 6.5 million; by 1970, it had doubled to 13.5 million; the 1985 population is estimated at 17 million, and it may approach 20 million by the year 2000. This is a nation with an area of 25,000 square miles, a little over half the size of the state of Louisiana. And when the year 2000 is reached, population growth will be very far from over unless something very extraordinary and possibly calamitous happens. It seems very hard, indeed, to find any ground for believing that improved public health measures can have a significant effect in the major LDCs in the critical next quarter-century in lowering birth rates considerably faster than death rates so that the natural increase is sharply reduced. Without such a sharp reduction, it is even harder to see where the food is coming from to meet the basic nutritional needs of the added billions that will be born in the poorest nations in less than three decades.

Similar wishful thinking seems to lie behind the notion, sometimes advanced as a theory, that improving the nutrition of the Third World's poorest agricultural workers can, by itself, significantly assist in bringing down the birth rate. This idea was given wide currency in the early 1950s through a book by a Brazilian scientist, Josue De Castro, entitled *The Geography of Hunger* (1952), in which he claimed that there was a direct and causal connection between low protein intake and high fertility. De Castro attempted to demonstrate this theory statistically, arraying figures that seemed to show a definite inverse correlation between the daily consumption of animal protein and the birth rates in a list of nations. He also asserted that this tendency could be demonstrated physiologically—that "protein deficiency leads to deficiency in the functions of the liver; this results in a reduction or loss of the liver's ability to inactivate estrogens; the excess of estrogens increases the woman's fertility."

The theory was discredited by various critics, but it seems to be having a revival as the population problem becomes more severe. In 1960, Karl Sax showed that De Castro's neat inverse correlation was achieved by careful selection of countries, and that a different selection showed wide variations and no correlation at all. He pointed out that: "The Eskimos consume more protein than any other ethnic group, 45 percent of their food being in the form of animal proteins; yet their birth rate of 47 is among the highest in the world." Various other data were adduced to invalidate the De Castro thesis. Yet its influence persists in writings on population today. There seems no ground for the belief that either moderate increase in protein intake or moderate increase in total caloric intake by the 2 billion members of the human race who are poor and who have large families will appreciably reduce their fertility and thus narrow the current wide gap between birth and death rates, especially not in the crucial final quarter of the 20th century.

Thus, we arrive at the dismal conclusion that none of the methods so far advanced for coping with the worsening population problem has a realistic possibility of significantly alleviating it in the next quarter-century or even the quarter-century after that—not economic development, or additional public health measures to bring death rates down further, or a slow improvement in the food supply of the world's hungry, (and nothing faster than that is in prospect, even on the most optimistic assumptions), or the widespread distribution of contraceptives to all who will accept and use them. Logic seems to tell us that the problem will not be solved until each national society arrives at an internal consensus (or is persuaded by its leaders) that it must learn to live within its means and that when its population is outrunning its food supply (or its means for obtaining food from a reliable source), the society must shift very rapidly to a small-family pattern.

Obviously, no international body and especially no rich nation can tell poor nations that they must raise the age of marriage or adopt any other form of fertility control. This was strongly evident at Bucharest, where, unfortunately, the emphasis was much more on sovereign prerogatives than upon the responsibilities implied in sovereignty. In consequence, there was little evidence that any of the poor agrarian nations that are pressing against their own food supply and do not have adequate foreign exchange with which to buy food in the international markets regard their population problem as being serious enough to warrant strong action to change their traditional mores.

WHAT HAPPENS WHEN THE FAMINES COME?

Predictions of massive famine in the poor agrarian nations have burgeoned in recent years, especially since the droughts and actual famines of the rather sparsely populated Sahel region of sub-Sahara Africa. In 1967, William and Paul Paddock—the former an experienced agronomist, the latter a retired foreign-service officer—wrote a gloomy forecast in their book *Famine 1975! America's Decision: Who Will Survive?* They predicted that the hungry nations of 1965 would be converted into starving nations by 1975, and that nothing the United States or any combination of nations could do would stave off famine. So massive and inevitable did they believe the famines would become that they asserted that choices would have to be made by American policy-makers as to which nations should be given major aid. They analogized this condition to the triage system used in World War I by doctors who sorted the wounded into three survival categories and then concentrated their limited medical resources on those who could benefit from them most. Thus, the Paddocks proposed using the triage system in allocating the exportable food resources of the United States in time of massive famine—in effect helping those most susceptible of being saved and writing off the hopelessly needy nations.

At the time the Paddocks wrote, the prevailing liberal temper in the United States was so optimistic about extricating the world from poverty and overcoming the population explosion by massive birth control and propaganda techniques, that the world regarded their book as sensational doomsaying, and paid it little heed. The triage concept as applied to starving people was so revolting in terms of traditional ethical values that it was dismissed out of hand. But the book proved to be uncannily prophetic in estimating that famines would occur and begin to become an extremely vexing public policy issue in 1975.

When hunger and famine reached serious proportions in 1974-75, discussion of the triage concept was revived and the idea of the "lifeboat ethic" was introduced. The metaphor of the lifeboat was publicized by the biologist Garrett Hardin. The "lifeboat ethic" is intended to convey the idea that the whole world is approaching the desperate situation of lifeboat occupants, where the number of persons cast adrift in the sea exceeds the capacity of the boat; if all try to share the limited space in the boat, all will perish. Hardin, William Paddock, and others formed a new organization to urge that the U.S. Government create within the Department of State a special policy-analysis unit to study the implications of world hunger and the probabilities that famines would increase for the balance of the century. While the creation of such a unit is entirely rational, the lifeboat analogy is far-fetched. The prospect that the American lifeboat will sink if we give away too much grain (allow too many starving people in our boat) is not a serious danger. Just why the United States needs to take on the role and bear the onus of deciding that some nations should be "written off" is far from clear. The authors had a penchant for the cataclysmic.

In sharp contrast to the Hardin-Paddock line was the approach of Lester Brown, Frances Moore Lappé, and various others, which was to urge Americans to eat less animal protein foods—especially beef and pork—since these are very inefficient converters of agricultural products to human energy. If Americans would reduce their meat consumption by only 15 percent, said Brown in 1974, it should free enough grain to aid the starving citizens of Bangladesh and India markedly in 1975. Just how the grain that would be saved by not feeding it to cattle would get to the Indians who needed it was not made clear, but it was the start of an informal campaign to prick

Americans' consciences about their protein-rich diets at a time when millions in the Third World were starving. How much effect this humanitarian effort may produce remains to be seen. At the moment it does not look very auspicious.

The U.S. record of international aid in recent decades may, on the surface, seem to reflect a generous spirit, but on closer examination much of it appears to be motivated as much by self-interest as by any genuine desire to share food with the hungry people of other nations. Under the terms of the Agricultural Trade and Development Act of 1954 (P.L. 480), the United States has provided India with some $4.8 billion worth of foodstuffs, mostly surplus grains from the highly productive farms of the nation's heartland. The U.S. Government, which had committed itself to buy these surpluses at stipulated rates from farmers who could not sell them at those rates in the open market, had inadequate storage facilities for such enormous surpluses and sought appropriate ways of disposing of them. Conceivably, it could have sold them in the international market, but this would have depressed the price farmers were receiving for their exports and would have vitiated the purpose of the agricultural price-support law. So the P.L. 480 program was conceived, under which these surpluses would be made available to nations in urgent need of them, particularly the underdeveloped nations like India, to be paid for mostly with foreign currencies that could only be spent within the aided countries. While these shipments helped India and other nations tide themselves over periods of bad weather and low agricultural production, they could not be said to have tested the American capacity for sacrifice on behalf of starving millions.

More relevant tests of American (and world) capacity for sharing food with starving nations came in 1972 in Bangladesh and in 1972-74 in Africa. The Bangladesh crisis was brought on more by war and social chaos than by weather, but the food shortage and consequent starvation were just as real as if caused by crop failure. Moderate help from the United States was forthcoming, but the amount was small and slow in relation to the need. Some help was also given to the starving nomads of the Sahel region extending across Africa just below the Sahara, but despite dramatic reporting of conditions in the *New York Times* and a few other newspapers and journals, the aid furnished was very late in coming, even though the quantities required were not large. The same was true of the aid contributed by other nations through the Food and Agriculture Organization of the United Nations—too little and too late. If these experiences are indicative of the capacity of the United States and the international community to come to the rescue of starving people, they should not be a bit reassuring to the citizens of Bangladesh, India, and other Third World nations.

A BREADBASKET FOR THE WORLD?

The United States and Canada are increasingly regarded as the potential breadbasket for the world, and in one sense they are just that, as more and more of the nations of the world are becoming partially dependent on U.S. and Canadian grain. Lester Brown estimates that in 1976 the United States and Canada will export 94 million metric tons of grain (between 7 and 8 percent of world production), and that no other major area of the world will be net exporters of grain except Australia and New Zealand, which will export about 8 million tons. Japan imports from North America nearly 20 million tons of grain—more than is grown in Japan—but does so on a steady and dependable basis, while the Soviet Union's purchases are extremely unpredictable, badly unsettling international markets and prices. The OPEC nations, with more than a quarter of a billion people, now have far more money to spend on food and are purchasing increasing amounts of American grain.

"Literally scores of countries," Brown points out, "have become important food importers, but not one new country has emerged as a major cereal exporter during [the last quarter-century]." This trend cannot long continue. From 1970 to 1974, world reserve stocks of grain dropped from 188 million tons to 108 million—equal to a 33-day supply. Reserve stocks should be replenished as a hedge against bad crop weather, but increasing demands will probably make that infeasible. The United States has now put all of its so-called idle cropland back into production, including some that is too fragile to be put to the plow. American farmers are doing their best to make up the world's grain deficits, but their capability for further expansion is now low, and demand continues to rise at a rate that cannot be met.

World population is increasing by some 75 million each year—just under 2 percent—and the demand for food is increasing faster than 2 percent. As the huge numbers of young children move toward their fast-growing years, they will need more food per person; nutritional deficiencies are so great among the developing nations that any increase in foreign exchange is likely to be reflected in a disproportionately high expenditure on food; and the modernized nations have shown an increasing appetite for animal proteins—an appetite that can no longer be supplied from the oceans because the world fish catch has come to the end of its long years of steady increase. It is obvious what another billion people—only a little more than a decade's growth at current rates—will do to this situation. And then another billion, and another. Not even a low meat diet, as Frances Moore Lappé recommends to us, will solve the problem. Her central point, however, has much validity. It is that Americans eat far too much meat proteins and fats for their own good and that if they ate more sensible diets, a great deal more grain would be freed for export to nations now not adequately nourished. Lester Brown asserts that the United States feeds more grain to its livestock, mostly in feed lots, than the entire 600 million people of India consume—a staggering disparity. And it is indisputably true that Americans would be healthier if they ate less meat, especially beef marbled with fat that makes it tender but increases their intake of cholesterol. But how would it be possible to get Americans to eat less meat, and then get the grain that would be freed shipped to hungry people in Third World nations? On one level, it is a very simple question; on another, a complex and difficult one.

The simplest way of dealing with the problem would be for all Americans who are persuaded to eat less meat in the interest of starving or underfed people abroad to send the money they save to CARE and let the money be used for the purchase and shipment of grains to whoever needs it most. This could be a simple and effective approach; if large numbers of people participated, large shipments of grain could be made. Yet cash donations for food shipments abroad at present aggregate less than $25 million annually. There seems to be a widespread assumption that if such aid is to be given, the government ought to do it.

When the government confronts the problem, it begins to get complicated. Government officials begin to ask themselves how much grain the government should buy at market prices and sell at reduced prices (or for long-term, low-interest loans that may never be paid back), and to whom? What are the criteria by which to judge the comparative needs of competitive claimants for such food?

Should nations that are friendly be given preference over those that are unfriendly? On what basis should determinations be made as to how much a nation can afford to pay? What if a nation should keep asking for more and more grain each year, falling further and further behind in its ability to feed its own people while its population continues to grow rapidly? Should consideration be given to the amount of effort a nation is exerting to bring its population and food production into balance? What would happen if another nation became increasingly dependent on U.S. grain with little or no ability to earn foreign exchange to pay for it? Since the cost of the grain comes out of the general budget and would reduce the foreign exchange with which the United States pays for imported oil, how serious a balance-of-payments problem does this present? How much grain could the government buy and ship abroad without significantly raising domestic prices, as in the Russian grain deal? These are some of the complications created by converting the issue from a private to a public question.

The United States seems unlikely to spend large sums to buy food to send to Third World nations, donating it or selling it on credit terms with little prospect of repayment, if it finds itself in continuing economic difficulty at home, if the stability of its currency is in jeopardy in international markets, and especially if it should begin to appear that such a policy may be but the beginning of an escalating and never-ending expectation. Much more likely is a policy of limited aid to the Third World countries through the international arrangements established by the World Food Conference in Rome in November 1974. Americans with a sense of moral obligation to aid starving people abroad will have their moral sense tested by their private contributions to CARE or another organization performing similar work.

When the point comes that a steadily growing disparity occurs between population and food in many low-energy societies, as seems almost inescapable during the last quarter of the 20th century, the United States will not be able to serve as an international breadbasket. A world growing at the rate of 70-80 million people each year adds the equivalent of the total population of the United States in three years. It surely behooves us to discontinue our grossly wasteful ways, and our excessive and unhealthy high-meat, high-fat diets, for the benefit of both our bodies and our moral position vis-à-vis the rest of the world, but it would be a grave error to conclude that it can go very far in solving the world's food problems.

CAN A WORLD FOOD BANK PREVENT FAMINE?

The United Nations World Food Conference, held in Rome in November 1974, exacerbated the growing tensions between the Third World nations and the developed nations, with the United States becoming the principal target of criticism. Part of the conflict concerned the purpose of the conference, with many of the nonaligned nations seeking to use it as a means of dealing immediately with the conspicuous and growing agony of Southeast Asia, and the United States seeking to keep to the agenda of trying to create long-range mechanisms to cope with growing world food problems. In the end, the United States informally committed itself to increase its food shipments to Bangladesh and India, and the Conference agreed to establish a new organization, to be called the World Food Council, which would have a secretariat in Rome associated with the FAO. The Council would channel to the needy nations both food aid and investment funds for the development of agriculture. The conferees also agreed to set up an international grain reserve, with the grain stocks held by the food-exporting nations. An "early warning system" was agreed upon to provide much-needed information about the state of the world harvests and the degree of hunger. The food-donor nations agreed to try to meet a target of transferring 10 million tons of grain annually for several years.

Can such an arrangement prevent famine? If the logic of the foregoing analyses means anything, then a world food bank could alleviate small famines and increase the number of people who can be kept alive in those nations where millions are hanging on to existence with incredibly small rations, but when the famines grow larger, and especially if there should be a major crop failure or series of failures, such a food bank could do little. From the standpoint of the United States, channeling aid through an international organization such as the World Food Council might relieve the onus that would come from the kind of unilateral decisions that Paddock, Hardin, *et al.* would put in the lap of the State Department and the President. To those who hold hopes that the World Food Council can significantly improve the long-range prospects of the Third World nations to solve their food-population crunch, little encouragement can be offered.

THE EFFECTS OF FAMINE ON HIGH-ENERGY SOCIETIES

It is commonly believed that massive famine conditions not adequately relieved by food shipments from the developed world will
bring on large-scale international wars between the "have-not"
nations and the "haves"—in other words, starving people will do
anything as a last resort to stay alive, including organized attack upon
those who have food. This assertion, upon examination, seems to
have little or no evidence or logic to support it.

The poor nations have very little military capability. They are
separated from the modernized and wealthy nations by thousands of
miles. They have no navies worthy of the name, no means of transporting armies over great distances, and generally limited air power.
There is no conceivable way they could use conventional military
means to obtain more food than they could obtain through diploma-
cy—an amount that will almost surely be insufficient. There remains
only one other way starving nations might possibly apply sufficient
leverage on the well-to-do nations—especially the United States
since it is the richest of all and has the most food—and that is nuclear
blackmail. Conceivably, an activist group within a nation suffering
from severe famine might threaten to blow up a large segment of
New York or Washington by detonating a smuggled atomic bomb if
the United States did not agree to ship large amounts of food.

Richard Falk, Robert Heilbroner, and others have discussed nuclear blackmail against the United States as more than a long-shot
possibility during the remainder of the 20th century, not merely to
obtain food, but to achieve a transfer of wealth. It seems difficult to
imagine how such blackmail could achieve its intended purpose.
Much more likely, it seems, would be nuclear explosions of "suitcase
bombs" by terrorists as acts of overwhelming frustration and hostility
with no necessary expectation that a compensating benefit would
result for any nation. It is for this very reason, as I discussed in
Chapter VIII, that such a strong alarm has been sounded concerning
the prospect of proliferating nuclear reactors—especially breeder
reactors—around the globe from which plutonium could readily be
extracted to make such bombs.

If nuclear blackmail were to be attempted, or if one or more
nuclear devices were to be detonated in a large city, it would have
enormous psychological effect on the people of the United States. It
seems predictable that it would simultaneously fan the smoldering

embers of xenophobia into a substantial bonfire and greatly accelerate the movement of people away from dense urban centers, especially New York City. The public would be likely to support unprecedented measures of search and seizure, inspection, and punishment. International travel would be sharply curtailed, both voluntarily and by increasing restrictions, and American air carriers might
well discontinue flights to countries where security was not
extremely tight. Foreign trade would predictably be diminished.
The real per capita income of Americans would receive an additional
setback. Illegal aliens would be rounded up and deported, and the
influx of additional aliens would be sharply reduced. The general
psychological atmosphere would be one of pulling up the Atlantic,
Pacific, and Caribbean gangplanks.

Such, it seems to me, would be the very probable reaction to the
terrorist use of nuclear bombs. More imminent, though, is a rapid
increase in the use of nonnuclear devices—in London department
stores and pubs, in Wall Street, in the State Department in Washington, just to name a few that have occurred at the time of writing.
These cannot be tied to famine in the Third World nations, but they
are manifestations of the type of intense alienation of people who feel
socially and economically deprived, and acutely antagonistic toward
those whom they see as the conspirators and exploiters. More of the
same could very well happen—in fact, it seems likely to happen—if
famine, poverty, and psychotic frustration overwhelm the nations
now nearing Malthusian population disaster.

It is hard for us to face the realities of a world in which the gulf
between the rich minority and the poor majority is widening and
apparently cannot be overcome by any benign and feasible means.
Demands for redistribution of wealth are becoming louder, shriller,
and more frequent. Jealousy and animosity toward the wealthy—
particularly the United States as the wealthiest of all nations and the
controller of the world's largest granary—are every day more evident. It is self-delusion of the first order to expect that relations
between the haves and the have-nots of this world will not result in
increasing terrorism, no matter how nonproductive it may be to the
cause of the terrorists. Hard as it may be for us to realize, the
population supersaturation of a large part of the poor agrarian world
will be one of the major determinants of the social and political
atmosphere within which we live out our lives. The more random

violence, the more our cherished freedoms will yield to tightened political surveillance and control. Added to the growing indigenous violence, terrorism from foreign sources could touch off a demand for much tighter police controls than anything we have ever known. This is one of the most disheartening factors in any honest appraisal of the probable future of our society.

XI. The Political Limits to Human Interdependence

For some, the thesis that the era of cheap energy is over may be unacceptable. There dangles a tantalizing hope that a major breakthrough may enable scientists and engineers to present us with "clean" (nonpolluting), "safe" (free from plutonium), and cheap fusion energy in vast quantities before massive famines overtake us. The assumption that such a breakthrough would be a great boon to the human race is almost universal. Yet, if we consider it quite carefully, we may conclude that, in fact, it would be one of the worst things that could happen to us.

My thesis, in this chapter and the next, is that there are limits to the human capacity to design and manage, by the political process, huge, complex, interdependent human and ecologic systems, and that we are now pressing against those limits. Scientists and engineers may offer technical solutions to all sorts of problems, but politicians and the bodies politic are the ultimate deciders as to how the largest human systems will be designed and managed. That the current level of complexity is putting a heavy strain on man's political capacity is self-evident. The availability of much larger quantities of energy could generate still further complexity and interdependence and bring on severe systems breakdowns caused by political and management failures.

The conventional wisdom of the mid-1970s is that the world has become irreversibly and massively interdependent. The only way to cope with the problems brought on by such interdependence, it is asserted, is to move forward confidently on this road, but learn to manage our increasing interdependence better. Yet the trend, as we shall shortly seek to show, has probably reached its zenith and has now begun to decline. Individuals and nations struggle to reduce their vulnerability by becoming less interdependent. Improving the management of existing and unavoidable levels of interdependence will continue to be one of our most important tasks, even as we draw back from the hazards of excessive, unnecessary, and undependable involvements. Social management is now being strained close to the breaking point.

It is useful to ask ourselves: How much interdependence is it reasonable to expect that humankind can manage effectively? Leaving aside, for the moment, the issue as to whether the people of the United States and the rest of the world are becoming more interdependent, is greater interdependence a feasible and intelligent goal toward which to set our sights, or are we approaching the limits now? To grapple with this question, we must examine the nature and meaning of interdependence.

The American economic system of production and exchange is, of course, so interrelated with the systems of other nations that it is fair to characterize it as a subsystem of a not too coherent international system, which in turn is a subsystem of larger organic and inorganic systems. The earth in its entirety is a subsystem of still larger systems. In the next chapter, we shall be examining the relationship of humankind to the larger natural systems of the earth, but first we must explore the question as to whether high energy technology is pushing us to design and manage economic and political systems that are so complex as to be beyond the comprehension of human beings, and therefore unmanageable by them.

To the extent that the free-enterprise system worked as Adam Smith expounded its theory, it was an extension of a natural system that existed without the necessity of human master planning. If labor and capital were paid in proportion to their respective contributions to production, and if the products of their labor, saving, risk-taking, and managerial expertise were then exchanged in a free market economy, according to Smith, the wealth of nations and the welfare of their citizens would steadily increase as if the system were guided by an invisible hand. The self-interest of workers and capitalists would work in the larger interest of the whole society, according to a convenient natural law. It was a system of competition and cooperation that bore certain resemblances to the behavior of lower organisms.

Although Smith antedated Darwin by nearly three-quarters of a century, his theory of free enterprise was based on a form of natural selection. The survival of each entrepreneur depended on his capacity for adaptation to his environment. Not a hunter and gatherer, as had been his ancestors, he was nevertheless engaged in a similar competitive and cooperative race for survival. He sought to produce or acquire those items others needed or highly prized; he could then exchange his wares or products for other products he needed or wanted; the more he produced of what others wanted, the more assured he was of survival; the less he produced, the nearer he came to the margin of existence. The survival of the fittest was at work in Smith's *The Wealth of Nations* as surely as in Darwin's *Origin of Species*.

If the economic system had worked according to this theory, and continued to do so, the invisible hand of nature might have guided it indefinitely. The reciprocal effect of competition and cooperation would have weeded out those who did not produce, or produced what nobody else wanted, as ill-adapted to their environment, while those who produced what was in great demand would have thrived. The result would theoretically have been a generally prosperous economy, with a range of wealth among its members not so great as to undermine the stability of the society. But it did not work as Adam Smith had envisioned it.

Several factors intervened to prevent the system from working smoothly. Nowhere did the participants have a fair start. At the start of the Industrial Revolution, land ownership was already concentrated in the hands of a few, especially in England, where the Industrial Revolution had its start, and the accumulation of capital needed for factory production also became rapidly concentrated. The rewards of production were not allocated in proportion to the contribution of labor and capital, and competition was stifled in various ways, all of which was spelled out by Karl Marx and Friedrich Engels, when they became convinced that the free-enterprise system could never be made to work in the general interest. Income was so heavily concentrated in the hands of entrepreneurs that the laborers could not afford to buy back the products of factories and periodic depressions produced destitution and threatened the stability of the state, not to mention disturbing the consciences of those who professed compassion for their fellow man. Governmental intervention to redress the most obvious malfunctions of free enterprise became inevitable.

In the two centuries since Adam Smith's laissez-faire doctrine was propounded, there has been a marked increase—at first slow, but very rapid during the middle of this century—in the degree of governmental intervention into what had been believed to be a "natural system." Generally speaking, the citizens of Western societies had originally sought to have their governments intervene only to the minimum degree considered necessary to cope with the system's obvious malfunctions. They did not want to substitute human master planning for free enterprise except when crisis situations arose. Unfortunately, crises came upon them at an ever increasing rate. In the United States, where major national intervention came much later than in Europe, governmental intervention took on major proportions during Franklin Roosevelt's New Deal and has increased in each decade since, reaching a point in the 1970s where one of the prime qualifications of governmental officials is competency in crisis management. Crisis and consequent governmental intervention is now a way of life.

At some point in this transition from a natural to a planned system, there is a crossing of a kind of threshold or divide, which we seem now to have crossed. The natural system is no longer dominant and the human system exercises so many controls that the natural system can no longer function as it formerly did. At this point, the mix can function only if the people who plan and manage it treat it as a total system. This is what Marx wanted to do at a time when industrial societies were vastly simpler. But where Marxian socialism has been tried in the 20th century, the evidence is that even in a situation where governments need not pay close attention to the consent of the governed and can plan to their hearts' content, master planning to replace the natural market system appears to be beyond the full comprehension and managerial capacity of the responsible political leaders to operate effectively.

In a democracy such as the United States, where the political planners must present themselves and their ideas periodically to a plebiscite of the people, and where the mixed economy is in a constant state of flux, the difficulties of master planning and management are greatly compounded. When things go badly with the economy, as they have recently, most economists and politicians are reluctant to go much beyond the use of the levers of fiscal and monetary policy as the means of setting things straight. John Kenneth Galbraith is the leading advocate of stronger action, including governmental controls over the prices and wages of that portion of the economy which Galbraith calls the "planning system"—the nation's several thousand largest corporations. Without such controls, he says, unacceptable inflation cannot be avoided. Conceivably, this is the least objectionable of the unpleasant alternatives, yet the management burdens it would place on an already overstrained government might well push the bureaucracy beyond its limits. The problem is symptomatic of the excessive burden upon political management that has been generated by extreme technological, economic, and social complexity and interdependence.

The Role of Energy in Causing Increased Interdependence

What has been little observed about this astonishing increase in the degree of interdependence and consequent governmental intervention in the economy is the central role of energy. Insidiously, energy rapidly increases interdependence when used in great quantities, eventually to the point of creating an unmanageable society—and then the very conditions and values energy was thought to preserve and promote are undermined and destroyed. Beyond some undetermined point, the use of large quantities of energy seems to be strongly adverse to the capacity of any society to govern itself effectively and to provide its citizens with the social and psychological satisfactions societies are created to assure. Let us state this in five propositions, followed by an elaboration of each:

(1) The more energy a society uses, the more interdependent it tends to become, both within itself and in relation to other societies.

(2) The more interdependent a society becomes, the more complex it becomes, and the more man-designed and man-controlled its

economic, ecologic, and political systems and subsystems become.

(3) The more complex and interdependent the systems and subsystems, the more vulnerable they become to design failures, since:

   (a) No human designers, and this applies especially to the politicians who are responsible for designing the largest human systems, can know or comprehend all the factors that need to be taken into account, and their interrelation, sufficiently to make the current set of systems work well. If complexity and interdependence increase further, the problems will be further compounded and the stability of the systems further jeopardized:

   (b) Those responsible for selecting the designers—the voting public in a society like the United States—are even less informed about the intricacies of the systems than the politicians who represent them. They cannot judge, therefore, which programs or social designers (politicians) to support, and in consequence they are highly likely to vote for the representatives who promise to support programs that benefit them directly and immediately—a fatal flaw in designing workable complex systems for interrelating enormous numbers of human beings with each other and their environments.

(4) The United States is probably nearing the point (it could even be beyond it) where the complexity of the systems of interdependence exceeds the human capacity to manage them, causing system breakdowns to occur as fast as or faster than any combination of problem-solvers can overcome them.

(5) World systems of interdependence are more remote, inefficient, and precarious than national systems, and may have exceeded their sustainable level of complexity.

1. The more energy, the more interdependence. Substantial levels of interdependence occurred in various civilizations before the Industrial Revolution, but thereafter an explosive increase in the consumption of coal, oil, and gas went hand in hand with the development of larger and larger cities, complex technology, transportation of raw material and goods over great distances, and ever larger business corporations and government bureaucracies. These are signs and measures of interdependence.

Historically, moderately high levels of interdependence were developed without fossil fuels by using human organization as the means of concentrating energy. The construction of cities was made possible by the development of mankind's capacity to organize human and animal power and apply the principle of leverage to construct fortresses, buildings, aqueducts, roads, coliseums, and later cathedrals. The ability to organize technical skills and compel slaves to perform these feats showed organizational skill of an extremely high order. To have built and operated the city of Rome, for example, and to have managed the provinces needed to support the city with its million people without fossil fuels was one of the most remarkable feats of human management in history. But the management genius that built the Roman Empire could not be sustained indefinitely. The high levels of interdependence produced complexities and strains that eventually became unmanageable. When the end came and Rome fell and was sacked, its population collapsed to a mere 30,000, 3 percent of its size at the peak of its glory. The concentration of human and animal energy, and wood fuel, had greatly exceeded the capacity of the Romans to sustain it. Interdependence had exceeded human capacity.

During the last two centuries, fossil fuels have enormously magnified man's capacity to build large cities, the epitome of interdependence, but there has not been a corresponding increase in his capacity to manage them. The steam locomotive, steam-powered generators, electric motors, electric lights, elevators, high-rise buildings, the telegraph, the telephone, the internal combustion engine, the automobile, the airplane, radio and TV, and the computer came in bewildering succession, each increasing the degree of interdependence. And each placed greater strains upon human capacities to manage that interdependence.

Most Americans are likely to resist strongly the idea that it is in large measure their consumption of vast quantities of energy that has made government so expensive. To think that it might be the energy converted by their marvelous machines that is, in major degree, responsible for creating huge government bureaucracies seems at first hard to believe. But the more one examines the evidence, the more evident it becomes. Every doubling in the consumption of energy creates more problems that require man-designed and man-controlled systems and subsystems, managed by bureaucracies, to minimize the human and vehicular collisions and accidents that would otherwise become intolerable. A fire in a skyscraper in São Paolo, Brazil, in 1974 that killed some 250 people made abundantly clear to the citizens of that city the lack of a proper building code with adequate safety standards. So the Brazilians immediately set to work to increase their bureaucracy to try to assure that such a fire would never happen again.

High-energy war machines also generate intricate interdependence. Each B-52 bomber requires a large industrial organization to produce it and a large governmental bureaucracy to sustain it. The complexity of the web of interdependence that surrounds the construction and operation of a billion-dollar aircraft carrier is hard for most people to imagine. The military-industrial complex becomes steadily more complex and interdependent the more energy it uses.

Each time we try to trace the causes of increased interdependence back to their sources, we find one source that seems to overshadow all others in magnitude and importance—the increase in the consumption of energy.

2. The greater the interdependence, the more man-designed and man-controlled are the economic, ecologic, and political systems and subsystems. Adam Smith recognized that free trade would increase interdependence among nations, but did not shy away from the idea on that account. Each nation, he thought, should specialize in mining those resources it had in abundance, in growing those crops that were best suited to its land and climate, and in manufacturing those products that its capitalists, its entrepreneurs, technologists, and workers could most economically turn out. They would then exchange these various outputs among themselves and achieve the maximum benefit to all. Smith seemed confident that a system of free enterprise and free trade would be self-adjusting and would not require the development and intervention of large government bureaucracies to attempt to regulate the operation of large corporate bureaucracies. There was an implicit belief in the efficacy of the invisible hand that would mesh the increasingly complex strands of international commerce. But two centuries later, we live in a world of bureaucracy that began at the urban level, then spread to the national level, and since World War II has moved extensively into the international arena.

By charter and inclination, bureaucracies design and create systems. More precisely, they create subsystems of larger systems, which are either national or worldwide in scope. For example, the Federal Aviation Agency was needed to assure that there would be a nationwide set of airports with proper safety equipment, air traffic controllers, and a communication system to facilitate an efficient air-transport system. The Civil Aeronautics Board was needed to regulate the pattern of airline routes among competing airlines, to establish passenger and freight rates, and perform other regulating functions. When international air travel developed, it became necessary to set up the International Civil Aviation Organization to serve somewhat the same purposes on an international level as those performed on a national level by the CAB. And still another international organization—the International Communications Union—has jurisdiction over establishing the frequencies used by the various international airlines for their communications.

The rate-setting mechanism of the Civil Aeronautics Board is a subsystem of the nation's total transportation system and the still larger economic system. The members of the CAB must take into account the relationship of the airline industry to the railroads (regulated by the Interstate Commerce Commission), the interstate highway system (designed by the Federal Highway Administration), the bus and trucking industries (regulated by the Interstate Commerce Commission), and the subsystem of water transportation (regulated by the Federal Maritime Commission). They must take account of the operating costs of the airlines, advise the Office of Management and Budget and the President about such matters as the need for operating subsidies for airlines and the economic sanity of supersonic transports, and at the same time keep in close touch with the kinds of issues being monitored by the Council of Economic Advisors. And on the international level, they must serve as the experts to back up the negotiators who come together in Montreal at the headquarters of the International Civil Aeronautics Organization to hammer out international aviation agreements.

Each added technological development that uses large amounts of energy or increases human interdependence requires a further increase in bureaucracy, since the problems proliferate in complexity. As noise pollution becomes a problem and communities complain, the bureaucracy is called upon to develop noise standards for aircraft engines, add inspectors to enforce the standards, requiring new experts and new superiors of the experts to conduct negotiations with the cities and community groups. When the supersonic transport was under consideration, it was necessary to have a greater range of expertise than ever before, including scientists and technicians to study the potential effects of the sonic boom and, even more complex, the potential effects of a possible reduction in the amount of ozone in the upper atmosphere. Eventually, the problems become so complex—as they did in the case of ozone destruction—that neither the bureaucracy nor anybody else can come up with dependable answers.

This is just one example of the reason for the enlargement of man-designed and man-controlled systems, managed inescapably by bureaucracies. The wonder is not that they are so large, but that they manage as well as they do. With the growth in the consumption of energy, and the corresponding increase in interdependence, it is hardly surprising that Federal, state, and local bureaucracies have reached unprecedented proportions.

3. The more complex and interdependent the systems and subsystems, the more vulnerable they become to design and operational failures. No person who works in any of these systems and subsystems can begin to imagine the interrelationship of the decisions he makes for his particular subsystem with the larger systems of which it is a part. Roberto Vacca, an Italian systems expert and computer wizard, wrote a book—*The Coming Dark Age*—on the incapacity of men to comprehend and manage effectively the systems they design. As its title implies, the book predicts massive systems breakdowns resulting from design mistakes and excessive stresses. His gloomy forecast may underestimate the capacity of man to adapt to systems breakdowns, but there appears to be much validity to his central thesis—that the more complex the systems and subsystems become, the more susceptible they become to domino-like collapses.

Vacca concentrated on the design failure of technical systems. The

famous power blackout of November 9, 1965, in the Northeastern
United States and Canada was a keenly felt example of such a design
failure; New Yorkers will always remember where they were "when
the lights went out." Some, such as those caught in dark subway
tunnels, had terrifying experiences. The steady stream of shutdowns
of atomic-powered generating plants because of unanticipated
stresses and accidents further illustrates the vulnerability of high-
energy systems to design failures. But an even greater degree of
vulnerability lies in the design and operational weaknesses of
economic, political, and social systems.

In human-systems terms, how does one design and operate a
system to cope with crime in our major cities, the hijacking of
airplanes, terrorist kidnapings and murders, 20 million people on
welfare, the pollution of air, land, rivers, lakes, and the oceans, the
degradation of housing in central cities, rampant vandalism, political
corruption, inflation, and public cynicism? Few have much faith left
that these are discreet and separable problems, soluble by known
techniques. To ask this question is to make one realize that hardly
anyone thinks of these as related to some overall humanly designed
system. Which is precisely the problem! If all we have are subsystems —or, more precisely, haphazard attempts to create new subsystems to respond to particular crises as they arise—with no thoughtful
relationship to the larger system of interdependence that high-
energy technology has drawn us into, is it a wonder that society is
becoming unmanageable?

We are caught between two powerful forces. One is high-energy
technology, alternately enticing and driving us toward more interdependence at the national and international levels. The other is the
strong desire to avoid too great interdependence with people whose
values and purposes we do not share, or who are so geographically
remote that we share no sense of place. People with high standards of
living do not wish to be called upon to feel more than limited and
sometimes token responsibility for those with low standards of living.
Each of us wants to huddle with people of our own kind and behave as
if we would all be better off if others would do the same. That is what
we want if we have a high standard of living. It is even what a great
many people want whose standard of living is well below the national
average, just so long as there are other groups below them on the
social and economic scale.

We are schizophrenics. We want the benefits of high-energy technology without its responsibilities. We want its automobiles and superhighways and jet aircraft and snowmobiles and riding mowers and a thousand power tools and gadgets, but we do not want to recognize that to have them, and to have a reasonably stable society within which to use them, we would need an even more complex set of politically designed and bureaucratically managed systems and subsystems than we now have. We would have to develop national plans of an extraordinarily expensive and complicated nature to overcome the deterioration of American cities and bring into the mainstream of our society the 20-40 million people who are now largely excluded from membership and participation. Few people claim they know how to do it, and these are mainly Marxists. In any event, there is little evidence that the American people would be willing to pay the cost.

The attraction of Marxist socialism to a tiny proportion of Americans is that they believe they have faced the dilemma inherent in high-energy technological society and consciously opted for the man-designed, centrally controlled system to bring order and equity out of an unplanned, incoherent system. They have faith that somewhere within our society there are men and women with the brilliant minds, the selfless public spirit, the motivation and energy, and the commitment to preserve the best elements of American democracy (including its Bill of Rights?) that would be needed to make a centralized, man-designed system work. They also have faith that it would be possible in some manner to identify these superhumans and vest them with the power necessary to develop and operate such a system, all within the "consent of the governed," and with no grave danger that so much concentration of power would result in an unacceptable reduction in human freedom.

Merely to state such a proposition is to make it seem absurdly unrealistic. In the first place, there are almost certainly no such people. In the second place, even if there were, the nature of the political process—any political process ever invented by man—would not bring them to the top. And thirdly, if there were such people, and if, by some miracle, the political selection process did bring them briefly to power, the kinds of things they would have to do to make a highly interdependent system work in the broad,

general interest of this and the next generation would make them so
unpopular that they could not long stay in control.

The probability is, therefore, that we shall continue to do what we
have been doing—that is, to allow and encourage the forces of
high-energy technology to make us more interdependent than we
now are, in the face of the fact that we cannot manage the degree of
interdependence we already have. And thus the more vulnerable we
will become to systems breakdowns.

The exclusion of millions of people from genuine membership in
American society is a "systems failure" of the first order, and one that
has spawned alienation on a massive scale. Up to now we have been
fortunate that the alienated have shown so little talent for organization. When they learn to organize, the possibilities for social disrup-
tion could be enormous. If the Symbionese Liberation Army with a
handful of kidnapers, murderers, and saboteurs could create so much
havoc—the FBI interviewed, shadowed, or spot-checked nearly
30,000 Americans in its coast-to-coast search for Patty Hearst and the
Harrises—imagine what a larger group could do on a nationwide
basis. An American equivalent of the Palestine Liberation Organization could deal devastating blows to American technological society.
What we think of as rational behavior becomes involuted when
people are excluded from membership in and the benefits of the
society around them. A person who has no stake in the preservation
of society feels that he has nothing to lose by aiding in its destruction,
and just possibly something to gain. Violent sabotage may become
uncannily rational from the standpoint of a person who places no
value on his life, and who hates the society that has made him a
nonperson.

*4. The complexity of human interdependence has reached the
point within the United States where systems breakdowns occur as
fast or faster than any combination of problem-solvers can overcome
them.* The cities of the United States, as in all civilizations, are the
focuses of its technological systems, and ultimately the test as to
whether the complexity of interdependence of our society has
reached the point of unmanageability. Without doubt, many American cities are in deep trouble largely because the degree of their
interdependence with other political and economic jurisdictions over
which they have no control makes effective management almost

impossible. The largest American cities have a greater concentration of factors pushing them toward decay than those of any other nation. Consider the following factors:

- A heavy influx of persons of low skill, low economic status, and of different racial origin from the city's basic middle-class and blue-collar groups.
- The subsequent exodus of the middle class.
- Deterioration of housing and other structures, increase in the use of narcotics and violent crime beyond the capacity of the city to control.
- Business recognition of the plight of the central city, with a resultant departure of manufacturing and commercial enterprises, and a corresponding failure of the city to attract new businesses.
- A low level of willingness on the part of most businesses to invest much corporate income or leadership talent in revitalizing a decaying city when they can perceive little or no corporate gain in doing so.
- Continuously improving communications techniques that make it unnecessary or even disadvantageous for many commercial operations to be conducted within central cities.
- Federal transportation policies—especially the Federal Highway Trust Fund—that have encouraged the development of suburbia at the expense of central cities.
- The consequent steady decline in the number of central-city jobs.
- Marked erosion of the tax base, with no politically feasible way of making suburban commuters and residents bear their share of the city's fiscal burden.
- Escalation of the costs of operating the city, even as its population declines, to support more welfare recipients, increased requirements for fire and police protection, and larger sanitation and health programs, all directly attributable to the foregoing causes.
- Further cost escalation arising from the power of public employee unions to exact extremely high wage and pension settlements.
- Expectations on the part of the central-city residents for the

provision of free services beyond the fiscal capacity of the city to provide (for example, the free higher education system of New York City).

- Reluctance of the residents of small cities and rural areas— where public services are fewer, costs are lower, and income levels are lower—to vote to have their tax dollars used to under-write the higher costs of central cities. This applies both on a state and a national level. (Often, as in the case of New York City, the actual flow of Federal income tax dollars has been in the reverse direction, but much of the rest of the nation does not perceive this.)
- The extraordinary difficulty in finding and electing politicians who are able to lead the nation or its subdivisions toward durable solutions to these overwhelming problems, solutions that will enlist broad and continuing support.
- The virtual impossibility, in the absence of such leaders, of educating the public to understand the level of interdependence the nation has developed, and the imperative need for mutual support. Willingness to make sacrifices would depend heavily upon a belief that citizens were being asked to bear an equitable share of the sacrifices so demanded.

No other industrialized nation has so long a list of factors contribut-ing to the decay of its major cities. The centrifugal forces operating on New York City are especially acute, but New York should not be thought of as unique. One may use these factors as measuring rods for the condition of other American cities and conclude that a sub-stantial number are in deeper trouble than their residents or the nation are prepared to admit. Prior to 1975, one would not have picked New York to head the list of cities headed for bankruptcy. The nation has no early warning system to inform us reliably on the condition of other cities, nor would it know what to do if it had the information.

New York is, of course, extraordinary in a variety of ways, one of which should be consoling to the municipal officials of London, Paris, Rome, Tokyo, and many of the other great cultural and commercial centers of the world, which are also the capitals of their nations. Those cities are the political power centers of their countries, as well as being their major cultural centers, which makes it unthinkable that

England could treat London or France Paris as the United States has treated New York in its time of fiscal extremity. Animosity toward New York has long been smouldering, and its financial problems offered politicians the opportunity to fan it into flames. It is inconceivable that the government could treat Washington, D.C., in the same manner or that it would have treated New York as it did if it were the capital of the nation.

No matter how charitable or cynical one might be in explaining President Ford's repeated castigation of New York City's financial profligacy, it seems evident that the origins of the problems and the issues regarding default were so complex that he almost certainly did not understand their implications. He was right that the cities cannot be run from Washington, but he did not comprehend the degree of economic, psychological, and political interdependence between New York and the rest of the nation. If the President, surrounded by a galaxy of advisers to counsel him on such matters, cannot comprehend the implications of our extreme interdependence, it may not be so much a reflection on any particular President who happens to hold office at the time; the more important lesson may be that the level of complexity is now such that few, if any, people can really understand the many factors involved and their ramifications. And if such a person existed and were to become President, the odds would be strongly against his or her being able to persuade the Congress and the public to take the painful decisions that would almost certainly be necessary.

The plight of New York, viewed dispassionately, offers extraordinarily abundant evidence of the social and political limits to growth. Economic growth depends to a much greater degree than we have yet realized upon the effective operation of the components of the political structure that support the technostructure. No economy can continue to make headway if its political system and leadership are not equal to the demands placed upon them by such growth and change. When interdependence reaches such levels of complexity that elected officials cannot fathom the intricacies and manage the governmental components of the economic system in a manner that inspires confidence, the end to growth may be near. Sustained economic growth depends heavily upon confidence in the reliability of political institutions and contracts. If that confidence is deeply undermined, economic growth models have little predictive value. It behooves the economists, therefore, to reunite themselves with the political scientists from whom they separated nearly a century ago, and resume the study and profession of political economy. If and when they do, they seem likely to find that the social and political limits to growth are both more proximate and more intractable than the physical limits. Some have already reached this conclusion, but few have illuminated it well.

5. *World systems of interdependence are more remote, precarious, and inefficient than national (or subnational) systems, and have probably exceeded their sustainable level of complexity and dependability.* What better illustration could there be of the precarious level of international interdependence than the 1973 energy crisis? The rapidity with which some of the high-energy societies, dependent primarily on oil, came to the end of their reserves and then had to slam on the brakes of their industrial empires was a clear warning that technological societies had become too dependent on undependable oil sources. Immediately, the heads of the affected nations began to seek means by which they could reduce their overdependence on imported oil.

The Arabs had the oil and therefore the upper hand, and at a crucial moment they used it. Nothing that the oil-dependent nations could do in economic retaliation could be nearly as damaging. Suddenly the oil importing nations realized that they were more dependent than mutually interdependent, and that their dependence placed them in continuing jeopardy. In such a case, where the interdependence is so out of balance, it is clear that more dependable substitutes must be sought. Those alternatives will, in most instances, take the form of seeking more independence and less interdependence, as is occurring in the United States.

Nor can international bodies overcome the growing difficulties of managing interdependence. The prestige of the United Nations as a means of mediating conflicts between nations is now on the decline. The U.N. has even less capacity to make a system out of nonsystems than the Mayor of New York has, which is very little. The European Common Market seemed slowly headed toward greater viability for a time, but the problems of oil and inflation caused severe strains. France insisted on going her own way in dealing with the Arab nations, and the treatment of the Dutch by their European neighbors at the time of the Arab oil embargo exhibited the fragility of the European Community. The instability of the NATO alliance is likewise becoming increasingly evident as American taxpayers and their representatives show resentment over the size and cost of the U.S. military commitment to Europe. The Soviet threat was what held it together, and ironically, as détente grows stronger between the United States and the Soviet Union, the more uncooperative the nations of the NATO alliance become.

Attempts to develop international cooperative systems have proceeded at a rapid pace since the formation of the United Nations at the end of World War II. Not only the general, diplomatic components of the U.N., but its numerous specialized agencies, have grown rapidly in responsibility and size. (In the quarter-century from 1947 to 1972, their administrative budgets increased from less than $50 million to more than $750 million.) Without them, the world's mixed economy could not have functioned nearly as well as it has. But the management difficulties under which they work are extremely onerous. They are hardly models for a world government.

The bleak future of the United Nations was underscored by a speech given to the U.N. General Assembly on December 5, 1974, by the U.S. Ambassador to the U.N., John Scali. In it, Mr. Scali, with the obvious approval of Secretary Kissinger and President Ford, warned the member nations against a trend toward the tyranny of the majority—meaning the numerical majority of nations in the Assembly, where each nation, large or small, has one vote—and the erosion of support for the United Nations among the people of the United States. His stern and foreboding lecture was precipitated by the admission of the Palestine Liberation Organization to the councils of the United Nations, the substantial exclusion of Israel from the United Nations Educational, Scientific, and Cultural Organization (UNESCO), and other actions that seemed to the United States representatives to be converting the United Nations into a politically short-sighted and increasingly irrelevant forum for emotional reactions to grievances. Innocent bystanders such as UNICEF became victims of lost sympathy and support by the American public, and UNESCO was in grave peril of losing not only American financial support but the cooperation of scientists and scholars without which this body would be but a hollow shell.

Sooner or later, the "one nation, one vote" structure of the U.N. General Assembly was bound to produce a serious schism between one or more of the large nations and the numerous small countries that nurture an understandable desire to demonstrate in some manner their unhappiness with a world system so dominated by the economic and military strength of a few nations. Obviously, the problem would not be solved but exacerbated by reshaping the U.N. General Assembly on the principle that each delegate should represent a constituency of approximately the same size—the "one man, one vote" system by which the U.S. House of Representatives is chosen. In that event, Asia would have more than half of the votes in the Assembly, an obviously unacceptable arrangement from the standpoint of both the European and North American nations and the small nations from all continents. It is a problem without a solution—emphasizing the inadequacy of humankind to conceive, create, design, and manage systems of human interdependence at their current levels of complexity. Any world model or system that could conceivably work would be unacceptable to a substantial proportion of those whose cooperation would be essential to its success.

The effective functioning of international agencies depends entirely upon comity among the nation-state participants. The less important the issues under discussion, the more assured is the cooperative spirit; the more important, the less able the organizations are to cope with the issues. Since none has enforcement power, decisions that seem wise to even a large majority of the participating nations cannot become binding upon those who disagree. International interdependence is thus far less manageable than national interdependence.

Unfortunate as may be the effect of the nation-state in encouraging the divisiveness of nationalism, nations are the largest aggregations of human beings that have sufficient commonality of traditions, culture, and purpose to be held together under common government and enforceable law. When internationalists insist that the only way the world can work its way out of the threat of mutual annihilation is to develop a world without national borders—meaning, presumably, the rapid development of world government—one must wonder, in the face of the difficulties of getting the citizens of nation-states to show concern for the disadvantaged and poor within their own borders, how a world outlook can suddenly be brought into being among the masses of the world's people.

This is not to say that war is the only means of resolving international tensions. What it does mean is that faith in the "one world" idea has reached its high point and is receding. More and more nations are looking for ways of becoming more independent, rather than more interdependent, even if to do so they will have to be satisfied with a lower standard of living. Those social analysts who have asserted that we will inexorably continue to move toward higher levels of technology, higher levels of energy consumption, greater volume of international exchange of raw materials, goods, information, culture, and tourists may be in for a surprise. Humanly designed and operated systems have upper limits of complexity, and when they reach those limits of complexity, they simply break down.

THE FUTURE OF AMERICAN INTERDEPENDENCE

From this line of analysis, we can only conclude that the United States and perhaps other high-energy societies are approaching, and some may even have reached, the upper limits of human interdependence. We shall be seeing in the future, if this hypothesis is correct, two seemingly opposite trends proceeding simultaneously: a retreat from interdependence by private individuals, private businesses, and nation-states, each seeking to reduce the degree of their vulnerability that derives from undependable interdependence, while at the same time, additional bureaucracies, national and international, will be established to cope with system breakdowns as they occur, thus conveying the impression that we are becoming more interdependent, rather than less. An example should make this point clearer.

In the case of oil, the United States has set itself a course that is intended to increase its independence. A considerably enlarged bureaucracy in the Federal Government is necessary to cope with this effort to reduce its dependence on imported oil. If rationing should become necessary, a still larger bureaucracy will be required. This will give the appearance of moving toward greater interdependence when the purpose is quite the opposite.

Regarding the management of national monetary systems, a high degree of interdependence has emerged as the levels of international trade have mounted. We have not yet learned how to manage our international monetary relationships well enough to cope effectively with current levels of international trade, and a great deal more effort will be required. As this goes forward, it will appear that the nations involved are becoming more interdependent at the very time they are seeking to reduce their reliance on other nations for raw materials or products that their money could buy. Canada, for example, has decided to reduce its imports of oil from OPEC countries to eastern Canada and to reduce its exports of oil from western Canada to the United States. Canada is thus in the process, just as the United States is, of seeking to reduce its interdependence. It will continue to participate in efforts to improve the stability of international currency relationships at the same time it is trying to reduce its vulnerability to system breakdowns arising from causes outside its own boundaries.

Within the United States, the flight from interdependence seems very likely to be reflected in a further decline of the nation's central cities (although there will be some countertendency as the limitations on gasoline make suburban living less attractive), and a consequent slower growth and then a slow dispersion of the nation's major megalopolises. If bombing and other forms of sabotage and violent crime should continue to rise because of deteriorating world and national conditions, the centrifugal effect will be accelerated. There is more than an even chance that this will occur.

The American people seem increasingly disposed to downvalue monetary income beyond some level that they regard as sufficient to meet their basic requirements in comparison with an increased sense of security and community. This dovetails with a general disinclination to travel further down the hazardous road of international interdependence.

XII. The Limits to the Political Management of Nature

If interdependent economic and political systems are becoming so complex as to exceed man's management capabilities, designing and managing ecological systems by the political process is vastly more complicated. Only because nature has evolved an incredible resilience has it withstood the recent aggravated assault to which it has been subjected. How much more such abuse and human mismanagement the ecosphere can withstand without reverting to much earlier stages of the evolutionary process would seem to be a crucially important question for mankind, but one which, it is fervently to be hoped, will never be demonstrably answered. If empirical proof is possible only when the biosphere is so overstrained as to reach the point of no return, it is prudent not to seek a scientifically satisfactory reply to the question. It is equally prudent to ponder the implications.

That man has for thousands of years been consciously intervening in natural systems, seeking to squeeze sustenance and wealth from them and to nurture those species of fauna and flora that sustained or delighted him, is self-evident. But the degree and character of his intervention in the 20th century are of a magnitude so unprecedented that he can no longer rely on the comfortable assumption that he is operating *within* the recoverable limits of the natural systems. In all previous millenia of history, he was fascinated and puzzled tinkerer with natural forces. Now there is no limit to his self-confidence as a manager of such forces.

To put it baldly, man now seeks to become the political manager of his own evolution and to manage, by the political process, whatever proportion of the totality of nature may be necessary to fulfill his needs and purposes. If that should turn out to be the whole biosphere, so be it. Some time ago, man promoted himself from a comparatively modest assistant to the Creator, without his name or title on the door, to Assistant Creator and General Manager of Human and Ecologic Systems. More recently, he has promoted himself again, this time to Deputy Creator and Acting Creator, justifying his action by the prolonged and unexplained absence of the Creator, possibly on account of His or Her demise. He is just beginning to feel occasional twinges of humility and even, now and then, an unsuppressed desire to have the Creator back in charge. But so far, at least, he has managed to turn aside such weak and unmanly thoughts as unworthy of his greatness. The outcome of such hubris was forecast by Aeschylus some 2,400 years ago in a few words so wise that they are quoted at the beginning of this book and are here repeated:

> All arrogance will reap a harvest rich in tears,
> God calls men to a heavy reckoning
> For overweening pride

That the political management of nature is the direction in which we are headed, if recent trends continue, is well illustrated in an essay by McGeorge Bundy, entitled "After the Deluge, the Covenant," in which he imagines the history of the next 50 years from the perspective of a historian and critic reflecting upon the difficulties surmounted by humanity in the half-century leading up to 2024. Bundy recounts the effects of the "Great Famines" in 1979-81, in which at least 65 million people died. After a period of political pulling and hauling, like the years 1783-89 in the United States, a "Great Covenant" was signed in 1989 creating three instruments of international control: the Nuclear Control Authority, the Food Commission, and the Population Court. Of the Food Commission, Bundy explains:

> The constraint on liberty required by the Food Commission is less direct [than that of the Nuclear Control Authority] and we are used to it, but it would have been surprising to our

grandfathers. In effect it has meant that the sowing of crops and the uses of the harvests—for export, for chickens, for cattle, or for bread—have been regulated not by national but by international authority, and this regulation has extended into other fields that affect the productivity of the world's land. Fertilizer has a priority even now, which is a source of jealousy to other claimants on the raw materials it uses and on the energy for its plants.

An international bureaucracy, operating through national bureaucracies, would have to decide what each farmer should plant, how many acres should be plowed and cultivated, what proportion of the rain forests of the Amazon—and how great a proportion of the forests of all other nations—should be cut and converted to crops, and which crops. The pair of bureaucracies would decide how extensively hybrid grains should be used, and which hybrids should be used where, whether and to what extent long-lasting chlorinated hydrocarbons like DDT should be used as pesticides, whether and under what conditions herbicides could be used, how much agricultural produce should be shipped from nations with low population density but good crop yields to nations with high population density, and how it should be paid for. They would decide where and how much fertilizer was to be manufactured, where the oil, gas, and other materials for the production of the fertilizer would come from, who was to pay for it, and a thousand other questions.

Bundy does not explain the political process by which the Food Commission would be chosen and supervised, or the sanctions that would be applied to nations or citizens that failed to comply with its decisions. By 1989, and increasingly thereafter, mankind will presumably have made a leap of monumental proportions toward cooperation and mutual accord, a kind of instant mutation toward a one-world disposition and mentality.

Bundy has performed a useful service in providing us a glimpse of the political mechanisms that would be needed to change a global ecology. But he provides us with no sense of the vast amount of information that would be required about the unimaginable intricacies and interdependencies that keep the world's local ecologies and the global system in reasonable balance. Nor does he reveal the manner in which politicians and bureaucrats of more than a hundred nations would assimilate, digest, and act upon that information in a manner that would be acceptable to the farmers and the bodies politic of their respective nations *and acceptable to nature*. When it comes to nature, the "consent of the governed" is either taken for granted or else it is assumed that the international bureaucracies and their political superiors that make the crucial political decisions about the governance of nature will by then have total understanding of nature's laws and behavior. In fact, it is necessary to make a further assumption—that the bodies politic and the farmers of all the affected nations will have sufficiently broad understanding of all the factors involved and sufficient commitment to the common as well as the *long-range interests* of the whole human race that they will comply with the freedom-limiting directives of the World Food Commission.

Let us hypothesize one of many problems that would be likely to come before such a World Food Commission. In order to feed at reasonable nutritional levels the nearly 7 billion people projected by Bundy, the World Food Commission would be forced to decide early in its existence that most of the world's crop land suitable for the growing of grain would have to be sown with high-yielding hybrids. But such hybrids, as many geneticists caution us, are more susceptible to blights and pests than are some of the lower-yielding, more durable strains. In the year 2010, a sudden and widespread pest infests the hybrid wheat crops of Southeast Asia, threatening to destroy half or more of the total wheat crop unless it is promptly treated with a new synthetic spray, more powerful than DDT and reserved "for emergency use only," since its effects if used continuously would be even more adverse than DDT upon both humans and the entire food chain. The world stockpile of food is first drawn down to the danger point and then the Food Commission orders that the emergency insecticide be used. It is successful in arresting, but not stamping out the pest; only a quarter of the wheat crop is destroyed. Ten major nations, especially the United States and Canada, are directed to divert an even larger proportion of their total grain crop than the 50 percent they have been exporting to the areas of potential and actual famine in Asia. Since Americans have for some time been limited to eating range-fed meat (and for only three days a week), the additional export of grains necessitates a further reduction in their consumption of milk and cheese, poultry and eggs. If the pests cannot be eliminated in a second year, these foods will have to be carefully rationed for as long as the famines or threat of famines continue. Americans and the citizens of other nations still consuming significant amounts of animal protein would then have to get most of their protein requirements from vegetable sources, as do the Asians.

The impact of the pest is somewhat reduced in the second year, but still far from controlled. Without continued use of the potent spray (the effects of which would harm the next generation of humans and a variety of fauna more than it would the people suffering from malnutrition), the famine will grow to major proportions, causing tens of millions of people to die. The Food Commission is faced with hard questions: How long is an emergency? How long should use of this spray be authorized? (It was intended for use for a maximum of two years, but if we do not continue to use it, millions of people will die.) Some members of the Commission argue that the time had come to reopen the "Population Protocols," reducing the levels originally agreed upon when the covenant was signed in 1989. These were unrealistically high target figures, they argue, allowing a totally inadequate margin of safety for just such unforeseen calamities. But others, and they are in the majority, assert that this is a selfish ploy on the part of the nations with large amounts of food-growing capacity per person. "How," they ask, "can anyone talk about stopping the use of this life-saving pesticide at a time when millions are facing death from starvation? Besides, the population problem is under the jurisdiction of the Population Court. You should not confuse our deliberation with an issue outside our jurisdiction." To which a few of the representatives of the animal-protein nations respond, "But what about the next generation? Think about what we will be doing to them if we continue to use this spray. Furthermore, the people of the high-density, largely vegetarian nations would be better off in the long run to reduce their maximum allowable population to provide a margin of food that would provide both better nutrition in normal times and a reserve to be drawn upon in times of unforeseen natural calamities."

Needless to say, since the next generation is not well represented, no revision of the population protocols is recommended and use of the pesticide is continued. But the unhappiness of the people of several of the animal-protein countries, already acute over a long series of difficult downward adjustments in their standard of living, flares to the point of refusal to accept further decisions of the World Food Commission unless they are put to national referendum. The first such national referendum—on the question of whether to abide by the directives of the Food Commission that would force them to continue rationing grain for the feeding of milk cattle and poultry—is roundly defeated. This marks the end of the remarkably long honeymoon period of the World Food Commission. Thereafter, it becomes increasingly difficult to gain compliance with its decisions.

Such a scenario gives far greater credence than seems warranted to the plausibility of the notion that a World Food Commission with such powers might come into existence in the current century, or have its decisions followed for twenty-one years after it was brought into being. It also ignores the complexity of the millions of factors that would have to be taken into account, the hundreds of millions of farmers who would become the puppets of computer printouts, and the trillions of plants, insects, rusts, and plant viruses in which lurk the desire to express their own creativity and frustrate any bureaucratic attempt to know their inner secrets and program their destiny. It ignores the problems that will certainly be generated by long-range shifts in weather patterns, causing droughts of long duration. It ignores the question of where the supermen will come from to manage such a global ecology. And, most of all, it ignores the quantum jump in human understanding and compassion that would be required of the ordinary citizens—and the extraordinary citizens—of the affluent societies toward their billions of brethren in the less developed nations.

This is only the beginning of the problems of managing a global ecology. Bundy gives us no notion as to how the large problems that lie outside of the areas of nuclear technology, food, and population would be dealt with. Let us briefly examine two of these: the preservation of the oceans and the vulnerability of the ozone layer.

THE PRESERVATION OF THE OCEANS

Life began in the oceans, and their deeps and shallows still nourish more organisms that does the land of the six continents. Yet man remains astoundingly ignorant of the ecosystem of the seas. Because they are so vast and perhaps because man has observed that nature herself uses the oceans as an ultimate dumping ground for silt and organic wastes from the land masses, he has assumed that he can do the same with all sorts of man-made wastes. He has assumed, too, until quite recently, that he can harvest the fish to his heart's content and never worry about depleting them and imperiling scores of species of sea life. Only in recent years have the warnings of marine biologists and ecologists begun to be heard and heeded. But it will be a long, hard struggle until the oceans are made safe for marine life. The peril of dead oceans is the ultimate of all perils. We may or may not be close to that point; we are not really sure just where we are.

In the summer of 1974, a United Nations Conference on the Law of the Seas was convened in Caracas, Venezuela, to try to reach agreement on a whole host of issues. Some 3,000 delegates and their advisors from 140 nations struggled for weeks, but not even the limitation of the agenda was achieved, and eventually it was agreed to resume discussions in Geneva in March 1975. Some of the subjects discussed at these marathon sessions were: the extension of territorial waters to 12 miles; the establishment of a 200-mile economic resource zone (covering fishing and mining); jurisdiction over seabed mining in deep-sea waters (increasingly important because of the large supply of manganese nodules on the seabed which also contain copper and nickel); international standards for pollution and conservation; special treatment for migratory fish such as tuna and salmon; revenue-sharing for land-locked nations; the rights of other nations if a nation cannot fully utilize the fish, mineral, and petroleum resources in its zone; and whether to establish an international seabed authority. The major preoccupation of each of the 140 nations was to maximize its share of the oceans' bounty. Preserving the biotic life of the oceans did not figure prominently.

The purpose of an international seabed authority would be to take charge of the exploitation of the minerals in the deep oceans that are presumed to be the common property of all nations. The technology for such deep-sea mining, now possessed only by the United States, is gradually being developed by a few other nations. The issue as to how the mining would be done, under whose auspices, and how the revenue from such mining would be distributed is most complicated. If an international seabed authority is established, it will presumably set its own safety standards, but the general ecological health of the seas will not be a primary concern of the new authority, if and when it is set up.

The initial steps toward the exploitation of the deep-ocean floors is reminiscent of the basic error that was made in the creation of the Atomic Energy Commission. When established shortly after the end of World War II, the AEC was charged with multiple functions including the production of fissionable material for military purposes, the development of nuclear energy for peaceful purposes, and the establishment and monitoring of safety standards applicable to its own operations and to nuclear power plants licensed by it. Its developmental responsibilities were thus in direct conflict with its charge to assure the safety of all workers and the public as the huge new nuclear power industry developed. Eventually, this built-in conflict of interest was bound to become so conspicuous and such obviously bad public policy that the safety monitoring function would have to be separated from the others. This separation occurred in 1974, when the AEC was abolished and its functions more logically and properly distributed. A new Nuclear Regulatory Commission was established to oversee nuclear safety. The same problem is now developing in respect to the exploitation of the oceans—that is, disproportionate degree of emphasis is being placed on exploitation, and an almost minuscule amount of attention is being given to the preservation of their ecological health. The oceans could become chronically ill before the "law of the sea" evolves to the point where as much attention is paid to their preservation as to their exploitation.

Individual nations can now decide to establish offshore nuclear-powered electric-generating plants without knowing enough about the effect the enormous heat transfer into ocean water will have upon the marine life in surrounding waters—and they probably will do so. They can bury atomic wastes in the ocean with no "law of the sea" to stop them. For every 100 things modern man can do to the ecology of the oceans, 99 of them will have a bad effect. Yet the oceans have no strong national or international voice speaking up to defend them against despoliation. The Environmental Program of the United Nations issues warnings occasionally, but it has no power and too little influence. The oceans have no constituency as the land masses do, and are therefore in far greater ecological peril than the terra firma over which men are prepared to fight to the death and even, when they are at peace, show some signs of understanding the imperative principle of conserving the land and much of its fauna and flora.

International management of the oceans for the purpose of maximum food yield is envisioned by some as an ultimate necessity if we are to feed the multiple billions of people that will be seeking essential nutrients, especially proteins, in the next century. If this were to occur, it would represent an almost insuperable hazard to the oceans. It would be the largest conceivable project in the political management of nature. Man's ecological knowledge does not yet come close to adequate understanding of the oceans for such a gigantic undertaking, but that shortcoming is nothing beside the political incapacity of man to carry out so complex and difficult an enterprise. The long-range ecological welfare of the oceans would be outvoted every time.

The hope of preserving the oceans from accelerating deterioration lies in three directions. One is to keep pursuing diligently the effort to establish international treaties on the law of the sea in the hope that before exploitation has gone too far, the pendulum will shift, as it seems now to be shifting in the atomic energy field, from preoccupation with development (an embarrassing euphemism for what is actually happening in the case of the oceans) to conservation and safety. The second is for the overdeveloped world to reduce and reverse its emphasis on material consumption, and stop increasing its already excessive demands for energy and minerals. As long as that demand curve spirals upward, the graver the danger to the oceans and to the quality of life in general. The third is the development of a worldwide, nongovernmental constituency for the oceans, able to do for them what the Sierra Club and other environmental groups have done for land ecology. Such a transnational movement could dramatize, educate, and bring political pressure to bear on governments and international bodies. The basic idea is growing. It is being pursued in respect to the preservation of whales and has been partially successful. It needs to be broadened to cover the preservation of the basic ecological health of the oceans. Professor Richard Falk of Princeton would like to see it broadened still further to apply to all large matters of common concern to humanity, expressing itself through a worldwide political party. Such a proposal seems visionary and impractical, but when applied to the more limited purpose of saving the oceans from irreversible degradation, it could become influential. If some combination of these three lines of action cannot succeed in halting the sickness of the seas, man could suddenly discover that it is too late.

THE VULNERABILITY OF THE OZONE LAYER

"For sheer size and perfection of function," says the scientist-poet Lewis Thomas, "the sky is far and away the grandest product of collaboration in all of nature." And one of its most remarkable aspects is the security blanket and ozone overlaying the biosphere 30 miles above the earth's plants and animals. Though it keeps most forms of life secure, we know very little about it. Until recently, we have not had to, but now the ozone layer is in jeopardy—just how serious we do not know, but enough to warrant the attention of a rapidly increasing number of scientists. Without that protective layer reflecting most of the ultraviolet rays from the sun, all complex forms of life would shrivel and die. At the time the supersonic transport was under discussion, most Americans became aware for the first time of the importance and the possible fragility of this ozone blanket. Oxides of nitrogen from already existing high-flying jet aircraft may be causing noticeable amounts of ozone destruction; it was argued that the large increase in these oxides that would be produced by the SST posed too great a hazard to be acceptable. The rejection of the SST was an unusual political act, one that offered more hope for future generations than most of our treatment of the environment.

Reports (in 1974) from the Australian Commonwealth Scientific and Industrial Organization of a continuous downward trend in atmospheric ozone concentrations, not yet serious enough for alarm, present new reason for concern. The American scientist F. S. Rowland advanced the hypothesis that the main cause of this decline might be the propellants used in aerosols; he theorized that these inert compounds escape into the stratosphere, where they are broken down by ultraviolet light, releasing chlorine atoms which react with atmospheric ozone, causing ozone destruction.

By early 1975, more sources of potential or actual ozone destruction were being identified. Dr. Michael B. McElroy of Harvard reported that bromine (now coming into increasing use in manufacturing plastics and fumigating crops) was so effective in depleting ozone that it could be used as a military weapon. If injected into the stratosphere over enemy territory in sufficient quantities, according to Dr. McElroy, it would purge the ozone, permitting the ultraviolet radiation from the sun to reach the earth with enough intensity to destroy crops and incapacitate the inhabitants.

It is increasingly clear that there may be numerous culprits, none of which alone might be threatening, but all of which in combination could become extremely hazardous. The chlorination of water supplies, sewage and power-plant effluent requires vastly greater quantities of chlorine than that contained in aerosol sprays. These, conceivably, could be sources of ozone destruction. We simply do not know what technology is doing to our precious reflective blanket. The stratosphere, said Dr. McElroy, has become "the chemical garbage dump of industrial civilization."

The massive intervention of man in natural systems without understanding what he is doing has now reached the point where some observers are beginning to realize how extraordinarily hazardous it is to the future of the whole biosphere. Dr. Barry Commoner has alerted us to the complex, humanly constructed molecules that are strung together to make nonbiodegradable synthetics, plastics, long-lasting chlorinated hydrocarbons, and numerous other products that are supposed to represent "progress." Chemicals dumped into the stratosphere are even harder to monitor, understand, and regulate politically than those dumped onto the land or into the air we breathe, since they are less conspicuous. Like the deep oceans, the stratosphere has no strong, organized constituency. Its future depends on a few scientists who are unorganized, a few national and international bureaucrats in environmental protection agencies that are comparatively uninfluential, and a somewhat inchoate but increasingly influential group of ecologically concerned citizens. Yet we need not be totally pessimistic. Five years ago, the ozone blanket could not carry a single precinct; five years hence, the increase in its political support just might be surprising.

THE BURDEN AND HUMILITY OF ECOLOGISTS

If the world's agriculture, its oceans and aquaculture, its atmosphere, its weather, and its ozone layer are to be managed increasingly by politicians and bureaucracies, one must be concerned about where the managers are to come from and what their training, perspective, and philosophy will be. To oversee the land and the oceans, one may assume, persons trained and skilled in the relatively new science of ecology will be called upon to put their pandisciplinary knowledge to the service of mankind. Ecology is a kind of super-science, drawing upon the storehouses of data of other sciences and integrating them in a variety of ways, including extensive use of computer technology, to understand how ecosystems work. As Leontief has used computer technology to make input-output studies of the flow of materials, goods, services, and money in human economies, ecologists use similar techniques to study the flow of energy within ecosystems. Energy flow is the most basic but only the beginning of the numerous dynamic factors that have to be understood in order to intervene intelligently and on a large scale in ecosystems.

To perform their role well, ecologists need to have considerable understanding of a wide variety of specialized disciplines which occupy the full lives of other scientists—such as plant and animal biology, physiology, genetics, physics, chemistry, geology, meteorology, mathematics, statistics, economics, anthropology, and sociology. Even this is not a full list. Some traditional scientists think that ecologists spread themselves so thin over so many disciplines that they do not understand any of them adequately. Until quite recently, ecologists were denied the respect accorded to their associates in the hard sciences. One would suppose, then, that the strong trend toward creating environmental protection agencies and the invitation to ecologists to accept high posts in them as advisors and problem solvers would be welcomed by ecologists as opportunities to demonstrate their newly developed knowledge, skills, and insights. But the more knowledgeable ecologists become, the more modest they tend to be.

The elevation of ecologists to positions of prestige within the U.S. Government began in 1970 with the creation of the Council on Environmental Quality, paralleling the Council of Economic Advisers in the Executive Office of the President. Later in the same year the Environmental Protection Agency was established, with the power to promulgate and enforce a variety of standards concerning the pollution of the environment, and ecologists were promptly recruited for key posts. They would thereafter be involved in advising the President and the EPA Administrator on what to do and what not to do about environmental systems, and would advise Congress on legislation.

Ecology had suddenly come of age. One might suppose that ecologists would regard this as a major step forward. But here is what two ecologists—William Murdoch and Joseph Connell—have said about their new role:

> Tinkering with technology is essentially equivalent to oiling its wheels. The very act of making minor alterations, in order to placate the public, actually allows the general development of technology to proceed unhindered, only increasing the environmental problems it causes. This is what sociologists have called a "pseudo event." That is, activities go on which give the appearance of tackling the problem; they will not, of course, solve it, but only remove public pressure for a solution. . . .
>
> In short, the ecologist must convince the population that the only solution to the problem of growth is not to grow. This applies to population and, unless the population is declining, to its standard of living. It should be clear by now that "standard of living" is beginning to have an inverse relationship to quality of life. An increase in the gross national product must be construed, from the ecological point of view, as disastrous. (The case of underdeveloped countries, of course, is different.)

Not all ecologists feel as strongly as Murdoch and Connell about the hazards of continued growth of the GNP. (It is theoretically possible to have a growing GNP without increasing consumption of energy or growing human intervention in ecological systems, but rather unlikely in the near-term future.) Few ecologists, however, regard themselves as competent ecological engineers, able to prescribe with confidence what kinds of untested, large-scale interventions in ecosystems will have a nonpathological effect. They can raise cautionary flags, express warnings, and explain the reasons for their serious doubts, but none is so bold or arrogant as to offer to become nature's manager. The very essence of the ecological viewpoint is an attitude of humility toward man's place within the awesome forces of the natural world.

It is not surprising, then, that ecologically minded appointees to such agencies as the Environmental Quality Council and the Environmental Protection Agency should feel as though they have been thrown into the trenches of political guerilla warfare, with shooting coming from all sides. Business, labor, the economists, politicians, and the public all are committed to a steadily rising GNP and the rising consumption of energy that goes with it. How else, they ask, can the nation provide jobs and a decent standard of living for its people? The environmentalists are therefore given a limited assignment by the power structure. They are, in effect, told to find feasible ways of improving the quality of the environment as much as feasible without impeding its physical growth. As Murdoch and Connell assert, this makes them essentially tinkerers.

The burden placed on ecologists, if we expect them to tell us how to solve all the environmental problems generated by physical growth, is an impossible one. An ecologically minded anthropologist, Roy A. Rappaport, after making a study of energy flow in a primitive agricultural society in New Guinea, concluded an essay on his findings with a number of profound observations concerning the efforts of civilized man to substitute his own simplified agricultural monocultures for the complex ecosystems evolved by nature. Here are three excerpts:

> As man forces the ecosystems he dominates to be increasingly simple, however, their already limited autonomy is further diminished. They are subject not only to local environmental stress but also to extraneous economic and political vicissitudes. They come to rely more and more on imported materials; the men who manipulate them become more and more subject to distant events, interests, and processes that they may not even grasp and certainly do not control. National and international concerns replace local considerations, and with the regulation of the local ecosystems coming from outside, the system's normal self-corrective capacity is diminished and eventually destroyed.
>
> ....
>
> It may not be improper to characterize as ecological imperialism the elaboration of a world organization that is centered in industrial societies and degrades the ecosystems of the agrarian societies it absorbs. Ecological imperialism is in some ways

similar to economic imperialism. In both there is a flow of energy and material from the less organized system to the more organized one, and both may simply be different aspects of the same relations. Both may also be masked by the same euphemisms, among which "progress" and "development" are prominent.

....

It seems to me that the trend toward decreasing ecosystem complexity and stability, rather than threats of pollution, overpopulation, or even energy famine, is the ultimate ecological problem immediately confronting man. It also may be the most difficult to solve, since the solution cannot easily be reconciled with the values, goals, interests, and political and economic institutions prevailing in industrialized and industrializing nations.

Those who have sought most diligently to understand the complex interactions of natural systems counsel us most strongly against trying to develop a politically and bureaucratically managed global ecosystem. Yet the momentum of national and world forces has been driving us in this direction. Whether that momentum can much longer be sustained seems dubious.

EVOLUTION AND ENTROPY

The most awesome paradox of the universe is the conflict between the general tendency of physical systems to run down, to move from organization to disorganization—the principle of entropy contained in the second law of thermodynamics—and that of the creative force which is manifest in organic evolution. Until the advent of homo sapiens—perhaps even until the modern era—this creative life force seemed to be leading steadily toward more numerous and more complex forms of life and more intricate webs of relationship among them. To paraphrase Barry Commoner, nature has had 2 billion years of R&D to achieve the current stage of organic life. Through the mutation process, nature tried one idea after another, and determined by trial and error which ideas had survival value and which did not. According to generally accepted Darwinian theory, this experimental process, guided by an organizing force that ran contrary to entropy, eventually produced man. But man, unwittingly, is now in the process of curtailing the operation of the creative life force and accelerating entropy.

The life force operates on the principle of survival through diversity. Not only does nature never put all her eggs in one basket, she always puts a vast number of different kinds of eggs in an even vaster number of baskets. Nature's variety has been increasing throughout the 2 billion years she has been experimenting, either randomly or by some incredibly beautiful design, or by an orchestration of the one with the other. Diversity has been nature's first line of defense against critical setback. When particular species failed to adapt to their changing surroundings, others succeeded. The principle of diversity operated in respect not only to species and subspecies, but to local and regional ecosystems. Barry Commoner's "first law of ecology" ("Everything is connected to everything else") to the contrary notwithstanding, everything is *not* connected to everything else in any crucial sense unless human beings are so foolish as to try to make it so. Local and regional ecosystems used to be numerous, widely diverse, and in substantial degree independent. Many could be wiped out by glaciation or other climatic change without critically affecting the viability of most of the earth's remaining ecosystems. The degree of interdependence among the various ecosystems remained comparatively low until three centuries ago, when man began moving toward merging local and regional ecosystems into a single global ecosystem, a trend that has been enormously accelerated during the age of high-energy technology. In this latest phase, man has been destroying the creative forces within the numerous and varied local ecosystems and gradually substituting huge, humanly designed monocultures which he is seeking to relate on a global basis. Nature's incredibly imaginative counterpoise to the force of entropy—creative diversity within local ecosystems—is vitiated by moving toward a single man-planned and man-managed ecosystem for the entire biosphere.

The massive destruction of creative diversity of semi-independent ecological systems is the counternatural direction in which we have been moving as we seek to support the maximum number of human beings, or something less than the maximum with the highest possible level of material consumption. The profligate dispersion of the sun's stored energy through the burning of fossil fuels, is, in itself, a blatant acceleration of the disintegrative force of entropy. The use of that energy to destroy the creative forces of local ecologies and build mass production and homogenized urban societies is not a manifestation of the unique force behind evolution; it is powerful and painful evidence of man's abandonment of the spirit of creative diversity for the degenerative and entropic practice of voracious energy consumption. That practice has resulted in the unbalanced procreation of huge numbers of one mammalian species—man—fed by converting a precariously large and increasing proportion of the earth's surface to the cultivation of unstable hybrids of high-yielding grains. Essential as they may seem to man at this point in history, these high-yielding hybrids are artificially induced crosses which are more than ordinarily vulnerable to destruction from causes we may least suspect. This egocentric behavior of humankind is a perversion and defiance of the principles inherent in the diversity and balance of nature. It is an invitation to disaster.

Insofar as man has concern for the long-run preservation and further development of the human species, logic would seem to lead to the conclusion that evolution would be best enhanced by the encouragement of diverse ecologies and cultures, aware of and tolerant of each other's individuality and experimentation, but not so interdependent that if one fails in its adaptive process, all others succumb with it. Nor is it sensible to assert that humanity has passed the point where it still has this option open to it. If a single world ecology and the equivalent of a single world government are beyond the capabilities of man as he is now constituted, and not even desirable if he had the capabilities, then it is a counsel of utter despair to assert that man has already passed the point of no return in his voyage toward an impossible goal. He still has open the opportunity to move toward greater diversity and more numerous, smaller, and less interdependent ecologies if he decides this is the right direction and applies his mind to it.

XIII. An Upheaval in Religion, Ethics, and Ideology

More than any other national group, Americans have been accustomed to thinking that all problems are potentially soluble if only we apply ourselves with sufficient imagination and diligence. However, both ordinary citizens and national leaders have suddenly lost their confidence that even the best and the brightest of problem-solvers can cope successfully with the overwhelming issues now confronting the United States and the world. Each nation is struggling within a tangle of interdependence, and the tangle binds tighter as the struggling becomes more frantic. Suddenly, the questions have become far too big for the people who must decide them. Scientists have adopted a new term for our super-problems: *problematique*. But the problems exceed even their definition of this new term. Let us illustrate and ponder.

Fossil fuels—the seemingly benign substitute for slave power—and the minerals needed to convert the sun's stored energy to human advantage are even more unevenly distributed under the crust of the earth than are the people on it. The sea of oil that lies beneath the Persian Gulf and its surrounding sands contains half of all the known petroleum reserves of the earth. Pumping it out costs less than a dollar a barrel. At what price should it be sold? At a price so low that it will be used profligately all over the world and exhausted in a few decades, as was being done until 1973? The sheiks and shahs thought not, as would almost any dispassionate observer. But how high, then? At a price that will force the petroleum guzzlers of the automobile world either to cut back sharply on their standard of living or to exchange their fixed assets for continued flow of the fuel? What obligation do the nation-states enthroned upon the vast oil pools owe to other nation-states or to the world community? Do the words "obligation" and "responsibility" have any useful and universal meaning in a world where each owner of a disproportionate share of the earth's natural resources can interpret the words in his own interest?

If the fortunate possessors of storehouses of natural resources owe some obligation to the world community, and are thereby not the sovereign controllers of their property, who is to decide what that obligation is? Some world body? Just how is the world body to make and enforce international law on so touchy a subject? Is the world body to act on the basis of one nation, one vote? Or on the basis of one human being, one vote? If such an obligation is owed by the oil-rich nations, is a similar obligation owed by nations like the United States and Canada in respect to their excess agricultural capacity? How would one determine the degree of such obligation? And how could it be enforced?

Does each national government have both a sovereign right and a corresponding responsibility to control its population growth so as to keep within its capacity to feed, clothe, house, and educate its people? If so, how is such a responsibility to be discharged? If this involves a clash between the presumed right of parents to have as many children as they wish and the responsibility of the nation to avoid extreme poverty and famines, how is it to be resolved? Is the personal right of procreation to give way to the larger interest of the society? If so, does this mean that ultimately the nation may properly determine how many children each woman may bear? How would such determinations be enforced? If, on the other hand, the greater responsibility of the society yields to the lesser right of the individual, and if famines then occur with increasing frequency, what is the responsibility of other societies to come to their aid?

In a world of extremes of wealth and poverty, what is the obligation of the rich toward the remote and powerless poor? What, in fact, is the responsibility of the upper and middle classes of the comparatively wealthy countries to provide for the poor of their own countries? Do the more fortunate have an obligation to deal with their own nation's problems of poverty before assuming the larger responsibilities for the poor of the Third World even though the latter are much worse off? How large a tax burden would be required to abolish poverty in the United States? How much redistribution of wealth and income would produce a society that would be genuinely beneficial to the poor, or to the majority? If too much redistribution would be counterproductive, how is it possible to arrive at a reasonable and sensible national consensus as to the right amount?

What can be the meaning of the assertion that each child born on this planet should have the "right" to sufficient food, clothing, shelter, medical care, and education, to assure a fair chance in life? Can the word "right" have any meaning if there is no means of guaranteeing that right, or any consensus that it should be guaranteed? If the only means of guaranteeing such rights is to create a world government, or a system of enforceable world convenants that we euphemistically refrain from labeling a world government, is it within the capacity of human beings, at their current stage of development, to design, build, manage, and submit to such an enforceable international system? Would the vulnerability of a world system to failures of design and management or to sabotage be so great as to create an unacceptable hazard, even if its creation were feasible?

Overwhelming as these questions may seem, there are even larger dilemmas. If, as ecologist George M. Woodwell asserts, the biological impoverishment of the earth is proceeding at a frightening rate, reflected by the soaring increase in the rate of loss of species, and if, as he also warns, further increase in flows of energy through technology will cause a significant reduction in the capacity of the earth to support mankind, how then do we weigh and value the lives of starving or badly undernourished people in the low-energy societies in the balance scale against the capacity of the earth to serve the next generation and the next after that? If feeding, housing, and educating an additional billion people each new decade depends on large new inputs of energy from fossil and nuclear fuels, and if these will damage the biosphere irreparably for the use of future generations, what obligation does this generation owe its children and its grandchildren? Does mankind have the "right" to accelerate the extermination of hundreds and hundreds of species of fauna and flora? Does man have any affirmative obligation to preserve and cherish the biotic diversity of nature? Are these ethical decisions, or esthetic preferences, or ecological issues relating to the capacity of the human species to survive physically in degraded ecosystems?

If the inhabitants of the high-energy technologies place 20 or 30 times as much stress on the environment per individual as do the poor agrarian farmers of the Third World, by what right do they do so? If it is the well-to-do, educated people of the earth who are primarily responsible for its ecological degradation, is not their crime against nature and against future generations vastly more culpable and potentially dangerous than the overbreeding of peasant farmers in low-energy countries? If so, what is to be done about such culpability?

No widely accepted ideology, system of ethics, or religion has a consistent and persuasive set of answers to such questions. If we ponder these and many other questions just as difficult, we may rather quickly conclude that they exceed our analytical and judgmental capacities and are therefore best left to others. Unfortunately, the others who will make the decisions on our behalf have no good answers either. Such questions are not susceptible of being answered by the methods of either problem-solvers or politicians. To cope with such issues, we must be prepared to recognize that our fundamental belief systems must be re-examined, a painful undertaking most of us would prefer to avoid.

THE SHAKE-UP OF THE JUDAEO-CHRISTIAN TRADITION

Of all the world's religions, Christianity and Judaism are confronted with the most upsetting challenges to their belief systems. The Judaeo-Christian tradition, especially since the period of the Enlightenment, has become increasingly identified with a faith in linear growth, development, and progress—a tradition that goes back to the first chapter of the first book of Moses, wherein God authorized man to be fruitful, multiply, and "have dominion over every living thing that moveth upon the earth." In a widely anthologized essay entitled "The Historical Roots of our Ecological Crisis" (1967), the historian Lynn White, Jr., traced the current environmental crises to this unusual perception of man's place in the universe:

> Like Aristotle, the intellectuals of the ancient West denied that the visible world had a beginning. Indeed, the idea of a beginning was impossible in the framework of their cyclical notion of

time. In sharp contrast, Christianity inherited from Judaism not only a concept of time as nonrepetitive and linear, but also a striking story of creation. . . . God planned all of this explicitly for man's benefit and rule: no item in physical creation had any purpose save to serve man's purposes. And although man's body was made of clay, he is not simply a part of nature: he is made in God's image.

In no other religious tradition is there the implied concept that man is the surrogate for God on earth, authorized to appropriate the entire biosphere to his sustenance, comfort, and diversion. Had he read his Bible with more care, Western man might have observed the admonition to "replenish the earth" tucked in the very same verse that gave him such vast dominion. Instead, he accepted the power that was conferred upon him without recognizing the magnitude of the responsibility, the noblesse oblige that should have matched so great an implied delegation.

One of the major purposes of any ethical system should be to create a code of conduct that will help human beings to preserve their life-support system without the requisite that each person will be all-wise. To preserve the biosphere for future generations of humans requires an ethic that treats most of the species of the earth, the oceans, and the ozone blanket with the same basic ethic of protection we believe should be applied to defenseless humans. This does not mean that human lives are not valued more highly than the fauna and flora, or that the latter should not be thoughtfully and restrainedly appropriated to man's use. But it does mean that most *species* of fauna and flora—and especially all of the complex, higher organisms—should be regarded as having a presumably valuable and perhaps essential place in the world's life-support systems. This is a very different ethical concept from one that has sanctioned the competitive and shortsighted use of nature as if its only purpose were to serve man's needs and desires. By whatever name one wishes to give it, the ecological ethic has suddenly become of almost overriding importance to human survival. Man's horrendous power of destruction, both intentional and unintentional, has created this imperative.

The contrast between the values placed on human and nonhuman life in the Judaeo-Christian tradition lies at the heart of the gulf between ecologically minded persons and Western religions. The doctrines of both Judaic and Christian theology emphasize the sanctity of each human *physical* life, assuming that within every living body able to draw breath there is a soul of equal value in the sight of God. Nowhere in such doctrines does one find any reference to the sanctity of the natural kingdom in its totality, or of its parts. In doctrinal terms, therefore, the saving of one human body, regardless of its condition, and the soul within it, is considered to outweigh any amount of destruction of the fauna and flora of the earth.

Despite their fall from grace, humans are regarded as infinitely closer to the angels than to the animal kingdom from which they sprang. Western religions concern themselves overwhelmingly with the relationship of human beings to God (both directly and through intermediaries), and the manner in which they should behave toward one another, almost totally ignoring the complete dependence of man on the other living things of the earth. The other species can live without man (better than with him if he keeps up his present behavior), but he cannot live without them. Why, then, should not the natural kingdom share the sanctity of life that humans claim for themselves? And when human rights, including the right to life itself, come into conflict with the rights of the natural kingdom, should the latter always yield to the former? This last question is crucial, and we are now at the point where it will be asked increasingly and must inescapably be answered.

To illustrate, let us revert to the issue of what we should do about the prospect of major famines in the Third World. The high-energy nations will be urged to make various efforts to save millions of starving people. One suggestion is that we should speed up our production of nuclear plants, settle on a standardized model, mass-produce them, and make them available to such countries as Bangladesh and India, where they could generate electricity needed for the production of fertilizer and for economic development. Many religious leaders might favor such a proposal since it would make possible an increase in the number of people who could, at least for the time being, be fed and kept alive. It would "save" human lives. Yet it might permanently poison man's life support system.

Another suggestion is that the wealthy nations should put up the capital for a large-scale increase in the amount of land under cultivation in equatorial regions of Latin America and Africa. As mentioned earlier, ecologists are gravely concerned about the fragility of the soil in these regions and the possibility of irreparable damage to its stability and fertility as a result of converting the forests to the cultivation of hybrid grains. Yet there are those who discount these dire predictions and argue that the risk is low and worth taking to help save the millions who will otherwise die of starvation. What are the ethics of this kind of decision?

A sterner ethical test for Americans has to do with our high levels of consumption of fossil and nuclear fuels and natural resources, which does far more environmental damage than the current low levels of consumption in the Third World. American officaldom tends to underestimate the potential long-range effect of this damage, whereas erring on the side of caution is the only wise course. Much of the damage, especially in the elimination of species, is irreversible. Government policy is primarily directed toward the identification of additional sources of energy and their exploitation. But if there is only a moderate margin of tolerance left for added energy use within the world's ecosystem, should not this consumption be allocated to the low-energy societies rather than the already overdeveloped nations? If energy consumption is to be leveled off or reduced within the United States, how is it to be distributed so as to assure everyone a fair share? These are political questions, but they have a large ethical content. Members of the clergy have occasionally dealt rather tentatively and unsystematically with distributional ethics, but they have almost never engaged the question as to whether the total consumption of energy and resources by Americans may have exceeded what is ethically "right" in relation to the Third World and the rest of the natural kingdom.

As the problem of population supersaturation becomes increasingly acute and if and when subhuman conditions become pandemic not only in Asia but in a number of countries of Latin America, self-induced and illegal abortions, performed by inexpert people under unsanitary conditions, are likely to become rife, resulting in numerous maternal deaths. Professionally supervised abortions were widely used in Japan in the 1950s and 1960s in its record-breaking reduction in births to avoid severe overpopulation. While contraception is surely to be preferred over abortion, abortion is to be preferred over starvation. Yet such is the doctrinal emphasis on the sin of abortion that millions of unwanted children will be born, especially in the barrios of Latin America, only to die without ever having known anything better than struggling to stay alive in a sea of cardboard hovels. Such a doctrine is a strange interpretation of the central truths of Judaeo-Christian ethics.

If some parts of Christendom have begun to come to terms with the problems inherent in abortion, few theologians and fewer still of the church hierarchies have been willing to face squarely the need to incorporate into their doctrines the imperatives and ethics of ecology. Basically, ethics deals with the preservation of the human race and improvement of the human condition. Since man is completely dependent on plants and animals, as well as air and water, one might suppose that one ethical imperative would be to nurture nature, to "replenish the earth." But this is not thought of as a necessary part of religious ethics, and even as secular ethics, it seems to be relatively low on the humanist scale of priorities.

The loss of interest among large numbers of intellectually informed and even spiritually thirsty people in traditional religious doctrines stems in no small part from their feeling that religion is not coming to grips with the crucial ethical issues of the times. The relation of man to nature is as crucial an ethical issue today as the relation of human beings to one another—perhaps even more crucial in the sense that unless it is understood as such and treated accordingly, the relationship of human beings to one another may become irrelevent or, in any event, secondary as a determinant of survival. The ethical concerns of many ecologically minded people might be cultivated within a religious setting if churches were able to reinterpret their doctrines to strike a new, creative synthesis with pantheism. But unless the imperative quality of the new ecological ethic is recognized by organized religion, its contribution to the improvement of the human condition will continue to deteriorate.

THE ONE-WORLD ETHICAL IDEAL

It is the common belief of the intelligentsia that greater interdependence is not only inevitable but can lead, if properly managed, toward higher levels of material well-being for all humankind, and therefore toward improved personal and social well-being. While there is wide variation in the degree to which people are prepared to yield national sovereignty to a larger system of world order, there is a general commitment on the part of most Americans who consider themselves liberals to support steps toward a more and more interdependent world, with appropriate mechanisms and covenants to achieve peaceful regulation of that interdependence. In other words, it is fairly widely assumed that we are unavoidably moving, despite such temporary setbacks as may occur, toward one humanly-managed world system.

The desire for world unity is ancient, but only since the Enlightenment has it been converted to an article of humanist faith. Although there is no necessary logic to the reasoning that says the brotherhood of man implies a high degree of dependence by nations upon one another, or the substitution for nation-states of a world government that would assume responsibility for all citizens equitably, such concepts are implicit in the minds and speech of many of those who seek the humanist goal of universal brotherhood. That men and women of all nations should be able to live together in greater harmony than they do today is both a noble and a necessary aspiration for humankind, but as we shall increasingly see, it may be a hindrance to that purpose to insist that such harmony requires more interdependence of men and nations, and powerful world institutions that would necessarily accompany an organic world system.

It is important to repeat here a point made earlier: that implicit within the one-world faith is a concept that is equally Western liberal and Marxist—namely, a strong belief that we have not come close to the limits of the earth in our efforts to produce sufficient food and goods and services to assure all people everywhere a decent standard of living. It is a belief that has developed rapidly during the explosive consumption of fossil fuels with no recognition of their exhaustibility or what might come after them. One half of the knowledge-energy revolution of the last two centuries—the knowledge component—is cumulative and non-exhaustible (although this is not at all true of wisdom), while the other half—energy—has come from exhaustible and otherwise undependable sources. All of a sudden, this undepend ability has become painfully evident, but it will take years, probably decades, for those with deep faith in the feasibility of creating a poverty-free world in the foreseeable future to see how heavily dependent their faith has been on the widespread availability of cheap energy. They will remain convinced that technology and science could solve our production problems and enable Third World nations to industrialize, urbanize, and bring their birth and death rates into balance at low levels if only we could learn better how to assure a more equitable distribution of nature's bounty.

Although the humanist liberal's answer to allegedly unnecessary scarcities may not be Marxist socialism for the world, it would be some system that would adopt the best features of central economic and political planning and preserve the enterprise and high productivity of mixed economic systems of the West and Japan, assuming this to be possible. Such a system, the one-world liberal believes, could surely extract and cultivate from the earth enough of what mankind needs to provide a good living for all people now alive and all who will be added in the next generation or two or three. The one-world ideal would be hard to hold onto without such a conviction. But what if Malthus was basically right in his understanding of scarcity and only temporarily wrong in respect to the capacity of a lucky segment of the world—the West—to produce food and goods much faster than its population grew during a two-century period when it had enormous quantities of cheap energy? When a Westerner speaks of Malthus as having been proven wrong, one might well suggest that he spend a year or two in Dacca or Calcutta and see whether he holds to the same opinion still. Malthusian scarcity has stalked all but the lucky minority of the human race ever since Malthus wrote the first version of his "Essay on Population" in 1798.

If we are much closer than liberals had assumed to the limited capacity of the world's ecosystem to respond to the needs and desires of 4 billion people—increasing at a rate that would double in about 40 years—profound questions about the one-world ideal are raised, like those discussed at the start of this chapter. These questions cannot be solved by saying, as did the Humanist Manifesto II in the fall of 1973: "We have reached a turning point in human history where the best option is to *transcend the limits of national sovereignty* and to move toward the building of a world community in which all sectors of the human family can participate. Thus, we look to the development of a system of world law and world order based upon transnational federal government." The humanists and other liberals assert that there is no intelligent or workable alternative to such a one-world community. We will either organize it within the next generation or perish together, they imply. But no such gloomy view of a multiple-world future is dictated by logic. Quite the reverse. An attempt at this stage of the evolution of man to create a world federal government with genuine authority would be far more likely to end in disaster than an effort to restrict interdependence to relationships that are essential and dependable, thus reducing points of friction, while simultaneously seeking to increase tolerance and comity among nations. As Michael Oakeshott said, "To try to do something that is inherently impossible is always a corrupting enterprise."

It is vital to make a clear distinction between interdependence and dependence: Properly used, interdependence means a mutuality of dependence. If one nation becomes so addicted to the resources or products of another nation that its economy would collapse without the continued flow of that resource—as occurred in the case of oil—while the reverse dependence is only slight, this is not interdependence, but dependence. If trading relationships cannot be made genuinely dependable, the dependence of one nation upon the resources of another can become a serious international hazard. It is no wonder that the United States immediately launched "Project Independence" when the Arab nations embargoed oil to this country. All other dependent nations also sought ways of ameliorating their dependence. Nations are now more willing than they were prior to 1973 to reduce their standard of living in order to reduce the level of their dependence on undependable trading partners. Such a reaction is not a retreat into isolationism, but a sensible reaction to overdependence.

In the long run, a reduction in American consumption patterns— and this applies to other nations as well—in respect to any and all resources and products for which we have become overdependent on other nations would contribute to international stability much more than would the attempt to establish an international regulatory mechanism each time trading relationships break down. The lower the levels of consumption of imported resources or products by any given nation, the easier it is to protect itself against the hazards of undependable trading partners. This is not to suggest that trade between dependable partners where there is a reasonably balanced mutuality of interest is unwise or undesirable; quite the contrary. But addictive dependence of any kind is a road to disaster.

It seems predictable that in the decades immediately ahead, there will be an increasing effort on the part of many of the overdeveloped and some of the underdeveloped nations to diminish their over-dependence on others, especially those that have heretofore earned most of their foreign exchange from one or two exports. The under-developed nations will have to diversify; the overdeveloped nations —and this applies particularly to the United States—will have to work off much of their obesity.

If we have entered or are nearing an era of unprecedented resource scarcity in a world that is adding a billion people in scarcely more than a decade, the tensions between the rich and poor nations will be mounting at the same time internal tensions of the comparatively rich nations will also be rising. The strains that will be generated over the issue of redistribution of income (and possibly wealth) in the United States during a long period of unacceptably high unemployment and continuing inflation will predictably foreclose any possibility of yielding national sovereignty to a world super-government that would have the power to redistribute income internationally. Whether the one-world ideal will then continue to have any significant appeal seems dubious. The ethical search for the means to a more peaceful world may subsequently center on reducing the sources of conflict—the two primary ones being man's insatiable desire for material affluence and unbridled procreation. Curbing the first is the basic responsibility of the overdeveloped world, and curbing the latter is a requisite for the underdeveloped world. Each involves profound changes in individual and social values. International bodies cannot generate such cultural revolutions.

It will be difficult for humanists and others with great faith in the essential nobility of humankind to consider seriously the possibility that a humanly designed and politically managed one-world system might be an arrogant ideal. Yet the idea that billions of under-nourished, illiterate (or barely literate), extremely poor people and a billion or so privileged people seeking to keep their privileges can suddenly acquire the understanding and the will to design, manage, and support a beneficent world system seems extremely unrealistic. To hold out hopes and expectations that a humanly managed planetary economic and ecological system could solve the world's problems of hunger, poverty, and racial and religious tension is a gross exaggeration of the political management capabilities—to say nothing of the intelligence, wisdom, foresight and unselfishness—of humankind.

THE OBSOLESCENCE OF THE LIBERAL-CONSERVATIVE DICHOTOMY

If religious and secular ethics seem certain to be faced with upheaval in a world of increasing resource scarcity and ecological jeopardy, the obsolescence of traditional liberal and conservative political ideologies and allegiances will become even more apparent. More and more liberals will seem to some of their associates to be turning conservative on various subjects, while these "conservative liberals"—moving toward classic liberalism—will criticize the radical liberals for moving toward authoritarianism. Many conservatives will find themselves in a quandary. To many people who have little or no stake in the system of mixed capitalism and others whose disenchantment with it exceeds their apprehensions about the potential hazards of Marxian socialism, it may well seem as though the end of the capitalist-free-enterprise era is at hand, and good riddance. The compound malfunctioning of a system that is dominated and typified by billion-dollar corporations and millionaire managers, unable to make adequate provision for either jobs or basic sustenance for millions of its would-be members, is bound to generate an upsurge of acute discontent with the system that produces such inequities. The respectability of Marxist doctrine is noticeably increasing, and the ranks of its advocates and dialecticians are swelling. The poorer the showing of mixed capitalism, the more intense becomes the desire for a better alternative.

In the United States, the size of the middle and working classes who are still employed and feel they have a considerable stake in the system, and the strength of anti-Communist sentiment that has pervaded the nation, especially for the last 30 years, make it unlikely that Marxian socialism, per se, will gain sufficient strength to become a serious threat in the foreseeable future. Even if increasing numbers of the world's nations should adopt some version of Communist ideology and political organization—as seems not unlikely—the United States would probably remain strongly resistant to its appeal, perhaps the more so because it would feel increasingly beleaguered by a world from which democracies seemed gradually to be disappearing.

And yet, for all its resistance, mixed capitalism may be forced to move further in the direction of a governmentally planned and controlled economy. If the recession should turn out to be long-lived or a long-term economic decline, no government could stay in office that failed to take whatever action was necessary to see that most of the unemployed and the economically disenfranchised were provided the essentials through public-service jobs, unemployment insurance, welfare, and similar measures. Nor could it stay in power if it were to allow its essential industries, such as the railroads, or its major cities to go bankrupt and start a domino-like collapse. More central planning of the economy, more governmental regulation of the technostructure, more control of prices, wages, and profits, and more use of the tax structure as a redistributive mechanism seem quite likely.

If anyone doubts the imperative quality of a social system within the United States that will assure the essentials of physical life to the vast majority of all people, he need only reflect upon the vulnerability of the country's intricate technology to sabotage by strongly alienated individuals. What saboteurs could do if the economic system were to malfunction so seriously and so continuously that its victims were enraged beyond reason almost staggers the imagination. Some may respond that such sabotage would lead to a repressive reaction by government. It would, indeed. But in a nation like the United States, with its Bill of Rights, its court system, and its currently widespread sophistication in the use of the courts to protect basic Constitutional rights, heavy-handed repression applied to large numbers of persons aggrieved by acute social inequities would be less likely to succeed in keeping the lid on than anywhere in the world. In the end, the nation's only recourse would be to ameliorate the sources of the intense disaffection. This means a more centrally planned and managed economic system.

Ironically, although conservatives, liberals, and Marxists often think of themselves as being widely separated in terms of economic and political philosophy, they have certain basic values that are remarkably similar. They agree on such basic propositions as: The most important avenue to the individual and social betterment of the human race is through the elevation of material standards of living; humankind has both a right and an obligation to make such use of renewable and nonrenewable natural resources as may be needed to achieve a continuing improvement in the material standards of living; nature has vast storehouses of resources that we have only begun to tap; the best way to bring about a general improvement in the condition of man is to continue to apply our ingenuity to the extraction and use of more of these resources so as to assure durable economic growth. In the last decade these propositions have all come under increasing question, and in the next quarter-century they are likely to become the most central issues of social controversey. The struggle between the ethics and ideology of materialism and the ethics and ideology of ecology will gradually replace the traditional controversy as to how best to supply man's unending demands for material goods and services. As this occurs, distributional equity will become, more than ever before, the central concern of American domestic politics.

It hardly need be said that moderating the society's material aspirations will be perceived by all those who have not supped well at the table of plenty as a means of permitting the well-fed to retain their favored position while denying any hope to those of meager means that they may someday share in the affluence they have only heard about or witnessed on television. Also, business, labor, and government will be extremely reluctant to forgo the effort to squeeze out another half-century of physical growth. In such a contest, growth has the upper hand. Ethics may not be the primary determinant of the future, but could be marginally influential. The limitations upon man's capacity to manage matters so as to keep physical growth spiraling upward toward the invisible barrier of the limits of the earth will be the underlying determinant. Odd as it may seem, man's political limitations may turn out to be his ecological salvation.

XIV. A Profound
Turning Point

The limits to physical growth in the overdeveloped world, the limits to population increase in the underdeveloped world, and the limits to human capacity in both worlds to design and manage extremely complex systems of interdependence through the political process— these three factors, in combination, are now beginning to bring about a profound alteration in the momentum and direction of history. It could be the most profound of all, since never before has humankind pressed against such intractable limits. And never before have people been able to see that they are straining the resources of the earth and the capacities of their psyches and nervous systems to such a degree that they cannot long continue on their present course. Either they must consciously shift direction away from continued obsession with material growth or their social vehicle will simply break down.

The two reports to the Club of Rome—*The Limits to Growth* and *Mankind at the Turning Point*—both of which used computer-modeling techniques, concluded that an extrapolation of various key trends of the recent past would lead to crash curves within some of our lifetimes. My analysis not only concurs that the limits to material growth are near, but concludes that the political limits are probably much closer at hand than any of the physical limits considered by those two reports.

It is useful, at this point, to summarize the key ideas covered in the foregoing chapters, which seem to fit together as something of a theory of the American future. They can be stated in thirteen propositions:

1. The extraordinary affluence of the United States has been produced by a set of fortuitous, nonreplicable, and nonsustainable factors.

2. High energy use, much more than science and technology, is the taproot of affluence. Petroleum has been the primary 20th-century nutrient of that taproot. Its limited supply has been used at a rate that can only be characterized as insanely profligate. Intensive efforts to find and exploit new sources of oil only bring closer the day of its exhaustion without accommodating the nation or the world to renewable rather than irreplaceable sources of energy.

3. High-energy, open societies, such as the United States, are increasingly vulnerable to social deterioration, sabotage, and break-down. High energy use has a powerful centrifugal effect on the most fundamental institutions of society—the family and the community. Excessive energy use causes a society to come apart at the seams. Affluence is then bought at the high price of increasing social instability. Such escalating instability and vulnerability become especially acute and hazardous when large numbers of people are rendered surplus to the production and service needs of the economy and are excluded from basic membership in the society, thereby causing them to become intensely alienated and often psychotic.

4. The more affluent and urbanized an open society becomes, the more remote becomes any linkage between citizen rights and citizen responsibilities. Expectations and claims to rights continue to grow, while responsibilities atrophy. The legal system is designed to enforce rights but has no way of enforcing upon citizens the accept-ance and performance of responsibilities that would be required to undergird and sustain those rights. Thus the affluent high-energy society carries within itself the seeds of its own dissolution unless it can find a way to balance rights and reponsibilities. In recent decades, the separation between rights and responsibilities has been widening until it has become a chasm.

5. Excessive energy consumption, once developed, is as unheal-thy and hazardous an addiction as a narcotics habit, and as difficult to "kick." It is widely assumed, therefore, that the United States, Europe, and Japan have no other option than to move from the age of petroleum, now rapidly approaching its decline, to the age of nuclear energy, even though doing so would greatly escalate the unhealthy effects and hazards of the addiction.

6. The United States has been moving toward the substitution of nuclear energy for fossil fuels with little realization on the part of most of the body politic of the many severe dangers of doing so. If the United States were to continue to place the high emphasis that it has placed in the recent past upon the development of nuclear energy, the rest of the world would certainly do likewise—it may anyway, but the behavior of the United States could be decisively influential— and if the world goes nuclear, the chances of avoiding a world of nuclear terrorism are slim, indeed.

7. It is not too late to back out of the tentative nuclear commitment before the nation and the world become as addicted to nuclear energy as we now are to petroleum. Careful and concerted energy conservation, changes in life-styles, and the development of other sources of energy could make unnecessary the extraordinarily dangerous resort to nuclear energy. This is one of the most crucial and fateful decisions that will ever be made by a body politic, but it is being made the wrong way, with the public paying little attention to it.

8. Just as excessive use of, and dependence upon, energy is the Achilles heel of American society, excessive procreation is overtaxing the weaker economies and newer democratic institutions of the Third World. Recurrent famines during the last quarter of the 20th century will exceed the political capacity of Third World governments or of the overdeveloped world to overcome them. The United States will live under the psychological strain of knowing that it cannot indefinitely make up the food deficits of the Third World, but realizing that its traditions call upon it to provide more aid than it is politically prepared to grant, since the famines are very likely to occur during a period of belt-tightening in the United States. Democratic institutions in the Third World are unlikely to survive severe and chronic famines, as is already evident. Nuclear blackmail may be attempted as a means of forcing world food redistribution, but it is unlikely to achieve that purpose. Far more likely is the nuclear terrorism of desperation, which would have the negative effect of escalating xenophobia and isolationism.

9. The ultimate limits to growth, in physical terms, are in energy, resources, technology, and the tolerance of the biosphere, but the more proximate limits are political—the limits to the human capacity to design, manage, and accommodate to complex social systems. The

United States and much of the rest of the world are much closer to the political limits than we realize.

10. In terms of the long-range ecological health of the biosphere and the survival of the human race and many of the higher organisms, the control of energy growth is even more crucial than the control of population growth in the Third World countries. Mass starvation is tragic for those who die and for their survivors, but it does not threaten the survival of the human race, as would a continued escalation in the production and consumption of energy, especially nuclear energy. Further doublings of energy consumption by the over-developed world, no matter what the source, could threaten the biosphere and the human race more than another doubling of population in the Third World countries. The effort to convert the energy of nuclear fusion to man's use should therefore be abandoned. Voracious consumption of such energy would be likely to exceed human management capacities, and would almost certainly mean the rapid extinction of vast numbers of species of fauna and flora, irreparably damaging man's life-support system. Only more moderate use of energy is consonant with the preservation of human and ecological values.

11. The trend toward steadily increasing worldwide interdependence has either reached its zenith or soon will. Further interdependence will be unmanageable by the human race at this stage of its evolution. We will continue to try to manage our essential interdependencies better—a crucial activity in any event—while we simultaneously seek to reduce our excessive dependence on undependable sources of supply. The humanist one-world vision has no chance of achievement, and would not even be desirable if it could be achieved. It would move toward extensive, bureaucratically managed uniformity of human activity and behavior, stultifying and progressively eliminating the creative diversity of numerous semi-independent economic, political, and ecological systems.

12. These factors will create an upheaval in ideologies, ethics, and belief systems. None currently extant can cope with them. Keynesian growth economics is now obsolete, although most economists are reluctant to face the fact. Further economic growth of the over-developed world, insofar as it depends on further increase in the consumption of energy, will be dysfunctional both from the most crucial standpoint of the preservation of the biosphere and from the

secondary standpoint of achieving a reasonably stable society, yielding the benefits that societies are supposed to produce. The Marxists with their panacea of abolishing private property and production for profit, and substituting government ownership of the means of production, continue to be wedded to the obsolescent liberal fallacy that the world's growth potential is virtually unlimited. Nor do most religious or other ethical doctrines come to grips with the physical, ecological, and political limits to growth. Until intellectual and ethical leaders are able to come to terms with these limits, they will be unable to make their theories relevant to the real world of the next century and beyond.

13. No new economic theory can adequately provide policy guidance to this nation or to the other high-energy societies that greatly prize the ideals of freedom and representative government. The prerequisite to the preservation of freedom and the creation of a more humane society is the recognition that economic policies cannot continue to be the central means for achieving them. Although the severe maldistribution of income can defeat them, the creation of more energy, goods, and money cannot buy them. The value system of Americans must either undergo a major change in the direction of living more rewarding lives with fewer material demands, or the nation is headed toward endless and escalating crises, accompanied by increasing social breakdown.

Gloomy as these thirteen propositions may sound, they do not stem from overwhelming pessimism. The purpose is genuine understanding of the implications of alternative courses of action. If we are to avoid becoming mired ever more deeply in the slough of unmanageable cities and countries, we have little option but to cast off our fantasies of a world without scarcities, awake from our dream of super-affluence, and shed our childlike faith that a steadily growing economy is the certain road to happiness. We are now face to face with adult realities and hard choices, and all attempts to duck them can only make things worse. The capacity of Americans to understand the stakes will be tested more by their behavior with respect to energy than by any other challenge they are likely to face during the remainder of the century.

AMERICA'S FATEFUL CHOICE
Future historians of Western culture (if any survive) will almost

surely look back on the 19th and 20th centuries and wonder how it could be that seemingly intelligent people could have been so shortsighted as to extract from the crust of the earth the fabulous riches of oil and gas stored there a half-billion years ago and drink them up in a century-long binge of frantic movement from one place to another. These scholars will, of course, hold up the United States as the foremost spendthrift of these precious fossil fuels. They will be even more astounded that we allowed our energy addiction to become so overwhelming that when nature's legacy of liquid gold ran out, we felt we had no choice but to enter an irrevocable compact with the nuclear priesthood and their plutonium-breeding reactors to keep feeding our compulsive energy consumption, even though to do so would create a world unsafe for human habitation overwhelmed by crime, sabotage, and fear.

But the last part of this all-important page of future history need not appear. It is conceivable that Americans may develop a sufficient interest in sheer survival—for themselves and their children, not to mention other species—to seize the steering wheel of history and swerve the nation and the world away from the plutonium minefield toward which they are speeding. But to do so, they will have to be far more alert than they were when they allowed themselves, with no questions asked, to be drawn and then driven into the 30-year war in Vietnam.

The analogy with Vietnam is uncommonly apt. Foreign policy and nuclear policy have shared two important characteristics that have made it uniquely difficult for their conduct to be subject to scrutiny, discussion, and public approval: Each has been conducted largely in secret, and each has been the special prerogative of a group of cognoscenti. Only a tiny handful of people are permitted to know all the essential facts on which foreign-policy decisions are based. The same has been true of nuclear weaponry, and there has been a large spillover effect into the field of nuclear energy. We must trust our experts, we are told; there is no other way to run a complex, technological civilization.

If there were some correlation between expertise and wisdom, this might be true, but none is evident. Just as trusting the experts was a costly error in the case of Vietnam, so it is extremely likely to be in the case of nuclear energy. We are now at about the same stage in our no-questions-asked, follow-the-leader march into the quagmire of nuclear energy as we were in 1965 at the time of the Gulf of Tonkin resolution. We are not so far committed that withdrawal would be unacceptably difficult, yet the general public has neither sufficient knowledge nor strength of conviction to oppose the so-called experts. There is no Gulf of Tonkin resolution to focus attention on; we are being drawn into the nuclear trap, step by step, by appropriations of ever more public subsidy and other forms of support for the nuclear industry.

U.S. citizens are now faced with the most fateful political choice ever made by any people, although we hardly seem aware that we have any choice. We must decide, through our representatives in Congress and the President, whether to allow our government to continue to subsidize and further promote the development of nuclear reactors, or to change course and back away from the limited nuclear commitment before it is too late. Canceling the Faustian nuclear contract would require us to live within the energy budget that is available from other sources, and would mean either a leveling off of energy consumption or, more likely, a decline in per capita energy use.

Wrapped up in this one decision is a fundamental test of our values—a test of whether we can, through both personal behavior and the political process, perceive and act in the long-range interest of ourselves, our children, and the biosphere. It is partly a test as to how much we cherish the human values that American society was created to foster more than we prize those forms of economic growth that require continued expansion of energy consumption. It is even more a test of our capacity to understand the crucial issues of sheer survival.

Congress, Presidents, and the public have trusted the assurances of nuclear experts as to the safety of nuclear reactors. But nuclear experts are self-selected for their unquenchable faith that nuclear energy can be made safe and useful for society. They are unavoidably biased toward a belief that their lives have not been based on false premises. They are therefore undependable judges and protectors of the safety of American society and the human race. Intelligent citizens should be in a far better position to judge whether it will be safe for the nation and the world to produce vast amounts of plutonium through "peaceful" nuclear reactors, from which plutonium can be extracted, and after extraction converted into bombs with comparative ease. The possibility of large-scale nuclear accidents is not to be discounted, but the statistical probability is low compared to the hazards of terrorists with the capability of illicit construction of "suitcase" nuclear bombs and other horrible uses of plutonium. No less than the future of civilization is at stake. Those who would profit from nuclear energy have the advantage of a long head-start. But the outcome is by no means a foregone conclusion if the American people should wake up to the stakes involved.

The outcome of this choice will not determine, but could greatly influence, what the rest of the world does in respect to nuclear energy. If the United States were to shift the thrust of its research and development toward the most rapid possible promotion of the technology of solar energy collection, distribution, and merchandising, it would undoubtedly have a profound effect on the rest of the world.

Solar energy, when its technology is more fully developed, will become a boon to all and particularly to Third World nations, which combine both heavy concentrations of population and enormous amounts of accessible solar radiation. Solar energy will probably not become so cheap and plentiful as to permit continued escalation of energy consumption by the high-energy societies, but could aid the low-energy societies to meet their essential needs and move the world in the general direction of less disparity in energy consumption.

A political victory over nuclear energy would not, of course, suddenly create a good society. It would, however, be the most important single condition necessary for the reversal of the decay of our society. It is a necessary prerequisite, but by no means a sufficient condition. Nevertheless, its symbolism would be extraordinarily significant. Such a political victory is likely to occur only if we the American people become sufficiently informed, concerned, and aroused to readjust our value systems and priorities and realize that we must make painful choices. The price we will have to pay for zero energy growth, and possibly energy decline, will be voluntary reductions in waste and increasing penalities for it, the concerted beginning of the era of recycling, personal commitments to life-styles and attitudes that de-emphasize conspicuous consumption and luxurious mobility and stress greater simplicity, more durable goods, and, not least, the support of public policy-makers who will lead, not resist, this major shift of direction.

The United States uses approximately twice as much energy per capita as England, France, or West Germany, four times as much as Japan, and perhaps 20 times as much as China. By no imaginable standard can the psychological rewards—the sense of joy and satisfaction the American people display with their lot—be adjudged to have a direct correlation with the amount of energy consumed. Beyond some point, in fact, more energy almost certainly has negative value. No one has more clearly perceived or better expressed this crucially important concept than America's distinguished and durable social critic Lewis Mumford:

> What law of nature has singled out the increased application of energy as the law of organic existence? The answer is: No such law exists. In the complex interactions that made life possible on earth, energy in all its forms is of course an indispensable component, but not the sole factor. Organisms may also be defined as so many diverse inventions for regulating energy, reversing its tendency to dissipation, and keeping it within favorable limits to the organism's own needs and purposes. This screening process began, before organisms could make their appearance, in the atmospheric layer that tempers the direct heat of the sun and filters out lethal rays. Too much energy is as fatal as too little; hence the regulation of energy input and output, not its unlimited expansion, is in fact one of the main laws of life. In contrast, any excessive concentration of energy, even for seemingly valid purposes, must be closely scrutinized, and often rejected as a threat to ecological equilibrium.

THE SEARCH FOR A DIFFERENT KIND OF SOCIETY

As the United States embarks upon its third century, Americans are deeply troubled and confused about the future. Few have confidence that any political leader now on the horizon has sound and durable answers to the overwhelming problems that seem to mount steadily. More and more find themselves questioning the capacity of the economic system to allocate jobs, products, and services in a manner they would regard as satisfactory. Many, in fact, find themselves wondering whether a $2-trillion GNP will solve any problems that were not solved by a $1-trillion GNP. In recent years, increments to the national income have seemed to be accompanied by more, not fewer, social problems.

Such shattered confidence in the efficacy of economic growth as a social emollient or in its validity as the central goal of our society was no doubt a motivating impulse of the economist Robert L. Heilbroner when he wrote his provocative book *An Inquiry into the Human Prospect* (1974). A year later, in a review of his own book, Heilbroner re-emphasized the point, observing: "The malaise, I have come more and more to believe, lies in the industrial foundation on which our civilization is based. Economic growth and technical achievement, the greatest triumphs of our epoch of history, have shown themselves to be inadequate sources for collective contentment and hope. Material advance, the most profoundly distinguishing attribute of industrial capitalism and socialism alike, has proved unable to satisfy the human spirit."

The evidence mounts that materialism may have had its day and must now yield to other driving forces that shape each succeeding civilization. If it be so, we are in for harder times than most of us are prepared for. For what we shall be witnesses to, and participants in, will be the slow disintegration of our super-high-energy, super-materialistic civilization and its gradual displacement by something else. That "something else" is struggling to emerge.

One can sense it in the air. To understand what is happening to our society we must turn to our poets, dissenters, and counter-culturists. Around the edges of our social maelstrom are thousands, perhaps millions of people, many of them young, who seek desperately for some meaning to life that has eluded them. It is not a lunatic fringe. Hundreds of thousands grew up in middle- and upper-middle-class families, with no exposure to privation or hardship. Normally, one would expect them to follow their parents into the mainstream of business, the professions, academia, and government. But many have assumed a life-style that seems to say to their elders and to their upwardly mobile classmates: "Your road is leading to a dead end; we may not be quite sure where we're headed, but we're looking for something beyond your world of materialism, something closer to the true meaning of life."

Many of these young protesters are unquestionably easy marks for purveyors of meretricious spiritual nostrums. Their number may be some measure of the unslaked thirst that exists among young people for some kind of elevation above the banalities of most middle-class suburban living. Some, however—and their number seems to be growing—are neither easy marks for crypto-messiahs nor irresponsible dropouts from a society that claims to have given them much and expects much in return. They are earnest and responsible searchers for new life-styles, for fulfillment of their longing for a shared sense of community with their fellow men and women and a strong linkage to the natural kingdom, with its mysterious and ever-changing diversity. Intuitively, they realize that our high-speed, high-rise, high-energy civilization is rapidly destroying all opportunity to create and hold onto genuine communities.

A related motivation spurs many members of the younger generation and some of their elders. It is the deep human urge to see and feel good about the results of one's labors, something that is not usually possible when one becomes enmeshed in a large bureaucratic maze. It is the desire to relate one's work to the pattern of personal and group survival, or to the elevation of the human spirit. Huge organizations stultify that normal human craving. Many young people with the intellectual capacity to make their way in government and multinational bureaucracies are opting for other occupations where they are more in control of their own work and can gain greater satisfaction from the work process, the environment, and the more visible fruits of their labors, even though the monetary rewards may be far less.

Despite the obvious malaise of our society, the major effort of traditionalists—both traditional liberals and traditional conservatives—for the next decade and more will be to put the megamachine (Mumford's indispensable addition to the language) back on the growth track from which it has been derailed. Although the traditionalists are in the overwhelming majority, they are likely to fail. As energy becomes increasingly scarce in relation to demand, recriminations and tensions will rise and social order will be harder to maintain. As these conditions lead to increasing government controls, and as it becomes more and more apparent that the megamachine is never again likely to gain its previous momentum, a gradually larger group of people will begin to seek other ways of improving the human condition—and their personal condition—than the never-ending pursuit of more goods and services.

It is heartening to see a trend within the scientific establishment toward a more holistic view of the natural world. If modesty about their capacity to lead humankind to ever greater heights is not conspicuous among most scientists, at least there is a growing realization that narrow specialization may blind the specialist to an understanding of relevant and important influences outside his or her own field. The reductionist trend toward knowing more and more about less and less seems to have run its course and is now beginning to bend back upon itself. The microbiologist-philosopher René Dubos exemplifies the holistic movement within the natural sciences, an important augury of the possibility that increasing numbers of scientists may team up with the nonscientist seekers after new ways of improving the human condition. And, as mentioned earlier, many of the physical scientists are leading the way in realizing, discussing, and writing about the crucial implications of the physical limits of the earth.

The shift from a nation of spendthrifts to a country of conservators will come hard for a great many Americans. But it is evident that many others take to it with enthusiasm, if not with impeccable consistency. The emergence of widespread ecological consciousness and the strength of the environmental movement have demonstrated a pent-up emotional drive toward shifting from practices of heedless exploitation to an ethic of preserving and nurturing the diversity of nature in all its manifold and fascinating forms as well as the cultural heritage of Americans. These movements, when gradually broadened to encompass a wider range of people, families, and communities, and especially when they mature enough to include intense concern for the endangered portions of the human species, may become the seedbed from which there could emerge a new form of American—and Western—civilization.

The American public may be better prepared for the changes that loom ahead than political leaders realize. A release by the Harris Survey on December 4, 1975, began with this sentence: "If faced with a choice between a more modest lifestyle—buying fewer products, not raising their standard of living, working fewer hours, receiving lower pay— and the prospect of continued inflation, shortages and repeated recessions, a 77.8 percent majority of the American people would opt for a very different style of life in this country." In answer to a variety of questions, respondents revealed that frequent style and model changes, wasteful use of energy and materials, and numerous other features of our affluent society could be eliminated with no great sense of loss.

The arteriosclerosis and approaching demise of super-materialism will, like the deaths of plants, lower animals, and humans, make way for new life. Death is necessary to the creative development of new life, a hard fact for humans to accept. But the idea that is hardest of all to comprehend and accept is the paradox inherent in the counsel of philosophic and religious leaders at least since Socrates: that human life can be lived most abundantly in moderation. The exercise of moderation in the external world makes room for a more abundant life in the internal world of the human spirit.

For psychological and spiritual nourishment, both individuals and societies need the vision of a purpose larger than themselves toward which they can strive. Individuals need such a vision for personal fulfillment; societies need one or several such visions to achieve the cohesion and stability essential to their basic operation and survival. American society has lost its unifying vision and has begun a disorganized and desperate search for a new one. The combination of anger at those who are perceived to be killers of the dream and the strong thirst of the public for a new faith affords demagogues the opportunity for which they impatiently wait. To be successful, a demagogue must offer outlets for the public's anger and simultaneously prescribe some credible substitute for its lost faith. No period in American history, with the possible exception of the Great Depression of the 1930s, has produced so many susceptible minds, ready and even eager for the coming of skilled demagogues. It may be only temporary good fortune that the nation seems so far to have nobody of the talents of a Huey Long, ready to take advantage of the public's frustrations and pervert its ideals and government into a glossy American form of neofascism.

Having chosen 200 years ago to pursue the road of individual initiative and freedom of choice; having invested great faith that these, coupled with hard work, would result in an ever more comfortable and rewarding life; and having come a long way along this road, the nation is now culturally unable to adapt to or adopt a Marxist or

Maoist unifying vision. Satisfying as it may be to the Chinese, the Cubans, and others, it requires such an overwhelming subordination of individual to national ideals that it simply does not fit the requirements of the American psyche. Thus it would appear that Americans have no choice but to invent their own redeeming vision, or a group of such visions that will fit together and provide a unifying motif for a new civilization to replace the one that now seems to have run its course.

What Americans need is not a blueprint for survival, but a profound change in values and a compass that will take them in a new direction. It is not for this book to advise people, once they have seen the hazard of continuing the course we have been following, how they should reflect their new realization in their personal actions, or how they should go about changing the policies that currently dominate and direct our society. Once they have sorted out their values, Americans can be extraordinarily imaginative and resourceful and less inhibited than the people of any other nation in bringing their convictions to bear on both personal life-styles and public policy. "One person with a belief," said John Stuart Mill, "is equal to a force of ninety-nine who have only interests." Those "one in a hundred" people seem likely to steer us toward a very different future than most of us are yet prepared for.

Reference Notes

To list the sources of all the information contained in this book would require a great deal of detail to little purpose. The sources identified in the following notes, therefore, are confined to the principal references an interested reader might wish to pursue for further information. In general, statistics that are not otherwise identified here came from three standard sources: the *Statistical Abstract of the United States*; *Historical Statistics of the United States, Colonial Times to 1957*; and the annual budgets of the United States, all published in Washington, D.C., by the Government Printing Office.

INTRODUCTION

Donella H. Meadows, Dennis L. Meadows, Jørgen Randers, and William H. Behrens III, *The Limits to Growth* (A Potomac Associates Book), New York, Universe Books, 1972. See also Jay W. Forrester, "Counterintuitive Behavior of Social Systems," *Technology Review*, Jan. 1971.

CHAPTER I

John Maynard Keynes, *A Treatise on Money*, New York, Harcourt, Brace, 1930, Vol. 2, pp. 156-57.

Philip H. Abelson, "Troublesome Portents for Scientific Journals," *Science*, Nov. 22, 1974.

Gallup Poll, as reported in the *Washington Post*, Dec. 17, 1972.

Gordon Rattray Taylor, *The Doomsday Book* (a Crest Book), Greenwich, Conn., Fawcett, 1970.

Barry Commoner, *The Closing Circle*, New York, Knopf, 1971.

Roberto Vacca, *The Coming Dark Age*, Garden City, N.Y., Doubleday, 1973.

Peter Schrag, *The End of the American Future*, New York, Simon and Schuster, 1973.

Paul R. Ehrlich and Anne H. Ehrlich, *The End of Affluence*, New York, Ballantine, 1974.

Robert Heilbroner, *An Inquiry into the Human Prospect*, New York, Norton, 1974.

CHAPTER II

Walter Prescott Webb, *The Great Frontier*, Boston, Houghton Mifflin, 1952.

Elwood P. Cubberly, *A History of Education*, Boston, Houghton Mifflin, 1920, pp. 815-17.

August W. Steinhilber and Carl J. Sokolowski, "State Law on Compulsory School Attendance" (U.S. Office of Education, Circular No. 793), Washington, D.C., Government Printing Office, 1967.

CHAPTER III

Carl Kaysen, "The Computer That Printed Out Wolf," *Foreign Affairs*, July 1972.

Mineral Resources and the Environment, a report of the Committee on Mineral Resources and the Environment, the National Academy of Sciences, Washington, D.C., 1975.

Glenn T. Seaborg, "1994?", address at the Symposium on Major Features of the World in 1994, Annual Meeting of the American Association for the Advancement of Science, San Francisco, Calif., Feb. 27, 1974 (mimeographed). See also "The Prospective Change in Life Style Signaled by the Energy Crunch," *Public Administration Review*, July-Aug. 1975, p. 333.

Wassily Leontief, as quoted in *Newsweek*, September 30, 1974, p. 86.

Kenneth Boulding, as quoted by Leonard Silk in "Economics for the Perplexed," *New York Times Magazine*, March 2, 1975.

Herman Kahn and Anthony J. Wiener, *The Year 2000*, New York, Macmillan, 1967.

Peter C. Goldmark, "The Greening of the Pavement People," *New York Times*, Aug. 2, 1974, p. 27.

Agricultural Production Efficiency, a report of the Committee on Agricultural Production Efficiency, National Academy of Sciences, Washington, D.C., 1975.

CHAPTER IV

Laurence J. Peter and Raymond Hull, *The Peter Principle*, New York, Morrow, 1969.

John Kenneth Galbraith, *Economics and the Public Purpose*, Boston, Houghton Mifflin, 1973.

CHAPTER VI

Marion J. Levy, Jr., "Scientific Analysis, Subset of Comparative Analysis," in *Theoretical Sociology*, edited by John C. McKinney and Eduard Tiryakian, New York, Appleton-Century-Crofts, 1970.

Ivan Illich, *Energy and Equity* (Perennial Library), New York, Harper and Row, 1974.

Kenneth R. Schneider, *Autokind vs. Mankind*, New York, Norton, 1971.

Lewis Mumford, *Technics and Civilization*, New York, Harcourt Brace, 1934; *The Myth of the Machine: I. Technics and Human Development*, New York, Harcourt Brace, 1967; and *The Myth of the Machine: The Pentagon of Power*, New York, Harcourt Brace, 1970.

Garrett Hardin, "The Tragedy of the Commons," *Science*, Dec. 13, 1968; reprinted in *Notes for the Future: An Alternative History of the Past Decade*, edited by Robin Clarke, New York, Universe Books, 1976.

"Greece Striving to Protect Acropolis from Pollution and Tourists," *New York Times*, Feb. 19, 1975.

For a significant discussion of the subject of this chapter and the next two, see Lynton K. Caldwell, "Energy and the Structure of Social Institutions," delivered at the AAAS meeting, San Francisco, Calif., Feb. 25, 1974 (mimeographed); available from Professor Caldwell, Indiana University, Bloomington, Ind. 47401.

CHAPTER VII

For energy use per capita throughout the world, see *Energy, Economic Growth, and the Environment*, edited by Sam Schurr, published for Resources for the Future, Baltimore, Md., Johns Hopkins University Press, 1972; also *Exploring Energy Choices*, a preliminary report of the Energy Policy Project, Ford Foundation, 1974, p. 73.

For exponential curve of energy growth, see *Exploring Energy Growth (ibid.)*.

M. King Hubbert, "The Energy Resources of the Earth," in Energy and Power (A Scientific American Book), San Francisco, Calif., Freeman, 1971. For a much fuller statement, see *U.S. Energy Resources: A Review as of 1972*, a background paper prepared by M. King Hubbert at the request of Senator Henry M. Jackson, Chairman, Committee on Interior Affairs, U.S. Senate, Washington, D.C., Government Printing Office, 1974.

Stewart L. Udall, Charles Conconi, and David Osterhout, *The Energy Balloon*, New York, McGraw-Hill, 1974, Foreword, pp. 7-9.

The literature on energy has burgeoned since 1971. The following books about various aspects of energy have been especially helpful in writing this chapter and are recommended to those wishing to pursue the subject in greater depth: (1) *Energy and Power* (A Scientific American Book), San Francisco, Calif., Freeman, 1971; (2) Allen H. Hammond, William D. Metz, and Thomas H. Haugh II, *Energy and the Future*, Washington, D.C., American Association for the Advancement of Science, 1973; (3) *A Time to Choose: America's Energy Future*, report of the Energy Policy Project, Ford Foundation, 1974; (4) Wilson Clark, *Energy for Survival*, Garden City, N.Y., Anchor/Doubleday, 1975; and (5) *Energy and Human Welfare*, edited by Barry Commoner, Howard Boksenbaum, and Michael Corr, New York, Macmillan, 1975 (3 vols.).

CHAPTER VIII

Alvin M. Weinberg, "Social Institutions and Nuclear Energy," *Science*, July 7, 1972, pp. 33-34.

Mason Willrich and Theodore B. Taylor, *Nuclear Theft, Risks and Safeguards* (Energy Policy Project of the Ford Foundation), Cambridge, Mass., Ballinger, 1974.

Mihajlo Mesarovic and Eduard Pestel, *Mankind at the Turning Point: The Second Report to the Club of Rome*, New York, Dutton/Reader's Digest Press, 1974.

J. Ward Harris, in *A Time to Choose (op. cit.)*, pp. 409-10.

Alvin M. Weinberg, "Prudence and Technology: A Technologist's Response to Predictions of Catastrophe," *BioScience*, Apr. 1, 1971.

"A Zero Energy Growth Scenario," in *A Time to Choose (op. cit.)*, Chapter 4, pp. 81ff.

"The National Council of Churches and the Issue of Plutonium," news release, New York, National Council of the Churches of Christ, Division of Church and Society, Oct. 20, 1975. See also *New York Times*, Oct. 11, 1975, p. 62.

CHAPTER IX

Ansley J. Coale, "The History of Human Population," *Scientific American*, Sept. 1974, p. 51.

U.S. fertility statistics are drawn from Ansley J. Coale and Melvin Zelnik, *New Estimates of Fertility and Population in the United States*, Princeton, N.J., Princeton University Press, 1963 (figures from 1800 to 1960), and U.S. Bureau of the Census, *Population Estimates and Projections* (Series P-25, No. 545), Apr. 1975.

Demographic statistics on India come from the International Division, U.S. Bureau of the Census, and from the Population Reference Bureau, 1754 N St., N.W., Washington, D.C. 20036. See especially "India: Ready or Not, Here They Come," *Population Bulletin*, Nov. 1970.

Cecil Woodham-Smith, *The Great Hunger: Ireland, 1845-9*, London, Hamilton, 1962.

Robert E. Kennedy, *The Irish*, Berkeley, Calif., University of California Press, 1973.

Georg Borgstrom, *The Food and People Dilemma*, North Scituate, Mass., Duxbury Press, 1973.

Charles Westoff, "The Population of Developed Countries," *Scientific American*, Sept. 1974, p. 113.

John and Carol Steinhart, "Energy in the United States Food System," *Science*, Apr. 19, 1974, pp. 307-16.

E. F. Schumacher, *Small is Beautiful: Economics as if People Mattered* (Harper Torchbook), New York, Harper and Row, 1973.

"TV Satellite to Serve Schools in India After Shift East," *New York Times*, May 18, 1975. It may also be worthy of a footnote that the author participated in a panel at the annual conference of the American Society for Public Administration in San Francisco, on March 31, 1967, on the subject of "Population and Public Policy," in which he recommended, in his prepared paper, that the United States donate a communications satellite in orbit to India, permitting India to broadcast from a single ground station to all its half-million villages, using multiple language soundtracks so as to reach all in their native tongues.

A prediction that the American birth rate will rise in coming years is contained in June Sklar and Beth Berkov, "The American Birth Rate: Evidences of a Coming Rise," *Science*, Aug. 29, 1975, p. 693.

CHAPTER X

Georg Borgstrom, *op. cit.*, p. 57.

Lester R. Brown, *In the Human Interest*, New York, Norton, 1974.

For a report on the Population Tribune in Bucharest, see Judith Miller, "The Politics of Population," *The Progressive*, January 1975.

Dudley Kirk, "A New Demographic Transition?", in *Rapid Population Growth: Consequences and Policy Implications*, prepared by a study committee of the Office of the Foreign Secretary, National Academy of Sciences, Baltimore, Md., Johns Hopkins University Press, 1971, pp. 123-47.

Data on Sri Lanka (Ceylon) come from reports of the Population Council, 245 Park Avenue, New York, N.Y. 10017, and the Population Reference Bureau, 1754 N St. N.W., Washington, D.C. 20036.

Josue De Castro, *The Geography of Hunger*, Boston, Little, Brown, 1952.

Karl Sax, *Standing Room Only: The World's Exploding Population*, Boston, Beacon Press, 1960, Preface to the New Edition.

William and Paul Paddock, *Famine, 1975! America's Decision: Who Will Survive?* Boston, Little, Brown, 1967.

Garrett Hardin, "Lifeboat Ethics: The Case Against Helping the Poor," *Psychology Today*, Sept. 1974.

Lester R. Brown and Erik P. Eckholm, *By Bread Alone*, New York, Praeger, 1974.

Lester R. Brown, "The Global Politics of Food: Role and Responsibility of North America," Marfleet-Falconer Lecture, University of Toronto, Sept. 24, 1975 (mimeographed); available from the Worldwatch Institute, 1776 Massachusetts Ave., N.W., Washington, D.C. 20036 (figures on expected grain shipments of the United States and Canada in 1976 and a discussion of the U.S. role).

Francis Moore Lappé, "Fantasies of Famine," *Harper's*, Feb. 1975.

Nuclear blackmail is discussed in Richard Falk, *This Endangered Planet*, New York, Random House, 1971, p. 420, and in Robert L. Heilbroner, *An Inquiry into the Human Prospect*, New York, Norton, 1974, pp. 43-46.

CHAPTER XI

John Kenneth Galbraith, *Economics and the Public Purpose*, Boston, Houghton Mifflin, 1973, pp. 313-16; see also *Money*, Boston, Houghton Mifflin, 1975.

Roberto Vacca, *The Coming Dark Age*, Garden City, N.Y., Doubleday, 1973.

For a report on the magnitude of the FBI's checking operation in their search for Patty Hearst, see *Newsweek*, Sept. 29, 1975, p. 21.

Figures on the growth of the administrative budgets of the U.N. agencies are taken principally from *U.N. Yearbooks*, 1947 and 1972.

Report of the action by Canada in respect to its oil appeared in the *New York Times*, July 13 and 26, 1975.

CHAPTER XII

McGeorge Bundy, "After the Deluge, The Covenant," *Saturday Review/World*, Aug. 24, 1974, pp. 18ff.

Richard A. Falk, *This Endangered Planet (op. cit.)*, pp. 362-65.

Reports on hazards of ozone depletion appeared in *Science*, Oct. 25, 1974, p. 335, and Mar. 28, 1975, pp. 1142, 1181. See also *New York Times*, Feb. 28, 1975, p. 20.

For possible use of ozone destruction as a military weapon, see the *New York Times*, Feb. 28, 1975, p. 20. The quote from Dr. Michael B. McElroy appears there also.

Barry Commoner, *The Closing Circle*, New York, Knopf, 1971, especially Chapter 9, "The Technological Flaw."

William Murdoch and Josephy Connell, "All About Ecology," *The Center Magazine*, a publication of the Center for the Study of Democratic Institutions, Santa Barbara, Calif., Jan. 1970.

Roy A. Rappaport, "The Flow of Energy in an Agricultural Society," in *Energy and Power*, San Francisco, Calif., Freeman, 1971.

Barry Commoner's "First Law of Ecology" ("Everything is connected to everything else") comes from *The Closing Circle*, p. 33.

CHAPTER XIII

George M. Woodwell, "Short-Circuiting the Cheap Power Fantasy," *Natural History*, Oct. 1974, p. 16.

Lynn White, Jr., "The Historical Roots of Our Ecological Crisis," *Science*, Mar. 10, 1967; reprinted in *Notes for the Future: An Alternative History of the Past Decade*, edited by Robin Clarke, New York, Universe Books, 1976.

Humanist Manifestos I & II (A Prometheus Book), Buffalo, N.Y., The Humanist, 1973, p. 21.

The quotation from Michael Oakeshott, according to Daniel Patrick Moynihan in "The Crises in Welfare," *The Public Interest*, Winter 1968, was taken from Oakeshott's inaugural address when he succeeded to Harold Laski's chair in the London School of Economics and Political Science.

For an integrated consideration of the clash between the ecological imperatives that now confront us and the traditional ideologies of liberalism and Marxism, see especially Lynton K. Caldwell, "1992: Threshold of the Post Modern World," Franklin Lectures in Science and Humanities, Auburn University, revised, Mar. 23, 1973 (mimeographed); available from Professor Caldwell, Indiana University, Bloomington, Ind., 47401.

CHAPTER XIV

Energy figures are taken from Earl Cook, "The Flow of Energy in an Industrial Society," in *Energy and Power (op. cit.)*

Lewis Mumford, *The Myth of the Machine: The Pentagon of Power*, New York, Harcourt Brace Jovanovich, 1970, p. 403.

Robert L. Heilbroner, "Second Thoughts on the Human Prospect," *Challenge*, May-June 1975, p. 26.

The holistic perspective of René Dubos is evident in all his writings, especially *So Human an Animal* (Scribner's, 1968), *A God Within* (Scribner's, 1972), and his regular philosophical essays in *The American Scholar*, under the title, "The Despairing Optimist."

INDEX

Accelerative thrust, 13
Advertising, 39
Aeschylus, 192
Agricultural technology, 33
Alfven, Hannes, 124
American Institute of Architects, 117
Apollo program, 40
Appleby, Paul, 71
Atomic Energy Commission, 198
Atomic Industrial Forum, 125
Automobile culture, 35, 95-99

Bangladesh, 143-45, 161-63, 166
Behrens, William W. III, 1
Bicycles, 95-96, 102
Borgstrom, Georg, 152
Borlaug, Norman, 143
Boulding, Kenneth, 11, 49
British coal miners' strike, 62
Brown, Lester R., 153, 161, 164
Bundy, McGeorge, 192-93

Caldwell, Lynton K., 239, 243
Canada, 190
Capital shortage, 56
CARE, 164, 165
Castro, Josue De, 159
China, 151
Christianity, 25, 127, 211-12
Civil Aeronautics Board, 178
Cleveland, Harlan, 133
Club of Rome, 1
Coal, 111-13
Coale, Ansley, 136
College enrollment, 52
Commoner, Barry, 19, 201, 205, 206
Concorde, 14
Connell, Joseph, 203-4
Credit system, 39

Crowdedness, kinetic, 24

Darwin, Charles, 172
Davis, Kingsley, 149
Dontas, George, 100
Dubos, René, 124, 234

Ecologists, 201-5
Economists, self-criticism, 11, 49
Ecosystems, degree of
    interdependence, 206
Energy, 16, 17, 21, 22, 45-48, Chapters
    VI, VII, VIII, XII, and XIV
Energy Policy Project, 48, 123-26
Entropy, 205
Ehrlich, Paul and Anne, 19
Expectations, 79-84

Falk, Richard, 167, 199
Famine, 142-59 passim
Federal Aviation Administration, 178
Fertility rate, American women,
    137-40
Food bank, 166
Ford, Gerald R., 52, 185, 187
Ford Foundation, 48
Forrester, Jay, 237
Fossil fuels, 29, 30, 104-20 passim
Frejka, Tomas, 148

Galbraith, John Kenneth, 71, 174
Gas, natural, 111

Hardin, Garrett, 99, 161
Heilbroner, Robert, 19, 167, 232
Heller, Walter, 45
Hocevar, Carl J., 116
Hubbert, M. King, 105-6, 115
Humanist Manifesto, 217

244

Illich, Ivan, 95
Immigration, 28
Independence, Project 107-9
India, 143-45, 149-51, 161-63, 166
Industrial Revolution, 27
Inglis, David, 124
Interdependence, 170-207 passim

Japan, 24, 27, 129, 163
Johnson, Lyndon, 18
Jones, Jesse, 48

Kahn, Herman, 50
Kaysen, Carl, 46
Kendall, Henry W., 117
Keynes, John Maynard, 9, 45, 226
Kirk, Dudley, 157
Kissinger, Henry A., 16, 107, 187
Kneese, Allen, 123-24

Lappé, Frances Moore, 161
Law of the Sea Conference, 197
Leontief, Wassily, 49
Levy, Marion J., Jr., 90-91
Limits to Growth, 1, 2, 3, 45-46, 75
Local government, 52, 184-85
Lippmann, Walter, 7
Lifeboat ethic, 161

Malthus, Thomas, 154, 155, 217
Mankind at the Turning Point, 124
Marx, Karl, 154, 155, 172, 173, 181,
  219, 221, 227
Mass market, 36
McElroy, Michael, 200-1
Mead, Margaret, 124
Meadows, Dennis and Donella, 1
Mill, John Stuart, 236
Mineral Resources Committee, 48
Miniaturization, 51
Mishan, Ezra, 97
Mumford, Lewis, 95, 231, 233
Murdoch, William, 203-4

Nader, Ralph, 114, 133
National Council of Churches, 124-25
Net energy, 47
New York City, 63, 184-85
Nixon, Richard M., 18
Non-compliance, 63
Nuclear energy, 104-35 passim, 226-36
  passim

Nuclear Regulatory Commission, 198

Oceans, 196-200
OPEC, 106-8, 163, 186, 190
Ozone layer, 200-1

Paddock, William and Paul, 160-61
Palestine Liberation Organization,
  181, 187
Peter, Laurence J., 70
Population, 136-69 passim
Productivity, 53-55

Randers, Jørgen, 1
Rappaport, Roy A., 204
Responsibilities, 76-88
Rights, 76-88
Rockefeller, John D., III, 156
Rome, 176
Roosevelt, Franklin D., 7, 80
Rowland, F. S., 200

Sabotage, 64
Sax, Karl, 159
Scali, John, 187
Schneider, Kenneth R., 96-97, 98
Schrag, Peter, 19
Schumacher, E. F., 150
Seaborg, Glenn, 47-48
Service sector, 51
Sierra Club, 199
Slavery, 26
Smith, Adam, 26, 172
Social Security, 82
Solar energy, 104-35 passim, 226-36
  passim
Sri Lanka, 157-58
State government, 52
Steinhart, John and Carol, 149
Supersaturation, demographic, 143
Symbionese Liberation Army, 182

Taylor, Gordon Rattray, 19
Taylor, Theodore B., 123
Teller, Edward, 113
Thomas, Lewis, 199
Toffler, Alvin, 14-15
Transportation system, 37
Triage, 160

Udall, Stewart, 106
Unemployment, 58-61

Vacca, Roberto, 19, 179
Vietnam War, 17, 228-29

Wald, George, 124
Ward, J. Harris, 126
Watergate, 18
Watson, James D., 124
Webb, Walter Prescott, 21
Weinberg, Alvin M., 122-23,
Welfare, 73
Westoff, Charles F., 145

White, Lynn, Jr., 211
Wiener, Anthony, 50
Willrich, Mason, 123
Women, employment of, 40
Woodwell, George M., 209

e, 147